BOXES OF SECRETS

A gripping true account of overcoming sexual abuse in a "perfect" Christian home

my real-life story
veronica k wright

If you would like additional copies of this book or would like
to contact us, you may visit
<u>veronicakwright.com</u>
or write to:
Veronica K Wright
28562 Oso Parkway, #D438
Rancho Santa Margarita, CA 92688
USA

Scripture quotations marked "The Message" are taken from The
Message Bible, by Eugene H. Peterson - NavPress Copyright © date
2005. Used by Permission of NavPress, All Rights Reserved.
www.navpress.com (1-800-366-7788).

First printing 2010. Printed in the United States of America
ISBN 978-1-4507-0127-3

Acknowledgements

This book would have never been written without the love and support from my wonderful husband Jerry. I could have never asked for a better partner to accompany me on my incredible journey!

A heartfelt "Thank you" to Dr. Kim Paul Storm. He went above and beyond the call of duty, and as promised, he never gave up on me. A trusted counselor and friend, his morsels of wisdom continue to guide me to this day.

I would also like to thank my beautiful friend Michele McMinn. She never grew weary of offering her strength and encouragement in helping me to document my story. I will forever be in her debt for the countless hours she gave to proof reading the book and the often grueling editing process.

In addition, a special "Thank you" is given to Rob Nelms, an attorney and consultant for the book. He gave me the inspiration and courage to write details that made my story come alive. "Boxes of Secrets" is a better work because of his relentless pursuit of truth and excellence.

TABLE OF CONTENTS

Prelude

Looking back, I can see now that it all started with a prayer. I had been studying the Book of Daniel and saw how God actually conspired with a man to change the world around him. I had always been fascinated with the stories in the bible of Noah, Abraham, Moses and Esther. It was remarkable to me that they could be in such an intimate relationship with God that He would actually collaborate with them to do things they could have never done on their own. This inspired me to pray a prayer that would change my life.

"God, I want to see Your hand in my life like Daniel saw it. I want to partner with You for the miraculous!"

Little did I know that God would take me seriously. He did answer my prayer; however, the answer didn't look like I thought it would. In reality, I was standing on the edge of an incredible adventure. I had no clue that I was still a slave to the dark secrets of my past, in bondage to a religious code of silence. I was on the brink of a disaster, and God was going to show up and show off in my life as only He can do. When I prayed that prayer, I expected to see the miraculous take place in the world around me. God saw it differently. He was going to do the miraculous all right, He was going to do it in me; He was ready to set me free.

1

Elie Wiesel once said, "God made human beings because He loves a good story." Frederick Buechner once said, "My assumption is that the story of any one of us is in some measure the story of us all." May God—through His love, mercy and grace—miraculously take the story of each of us and re-write it into His story of redemption and freedom for us. May the truth set us free. May the darkness be brought into the light. May we be healed by Him and then used by Him as healers in this fragmented world.

Veronica Wright, 2010

CHAPTER ONE

The Call

"Are you kidding me? He was convicted on twenty one counts of sexual assault?" I couldn't believe what I was hearing. My sister called to fill me in on the latest family gossip. She was my only true link to my family. My mother served as the information hub for all family dealings, but that link had been severed months and months before; my mom and I hadn't spoken in nearly two years. When my sister called, I was appalled to hear what she had to say.

Apparently, months earlier, when our cousin left her husband to file for divorce, her daughter wanted to stay with the step-dad. Even after she was allowed to stay with him for a week or two, she still refused to leave and come live with her mother. Suspicious, my cousin began a little investigation of her own and found out that her now 13-year-old daughter thought she had a "special" relationship with her step-dad— he loved her in his "special" way. Attorneys were contacted, and the police were notified. After some interviews with her, the truth came into the light: the step-father had been molesting her for at least a decade ... since she was two or three.

My sister and I shared our mutual disgust and disdain

with each other over the phone, the details of the abuse causing our skin to crawl. Aghast, my sister was completely appalled by the fact the daughter wanted to stay with the step-dad after such treatment. "How tragic that she didn't even know it was wrong. Why would she have stayed?" she wondered.

The answer came to me immediately. "I know why she wanted to stay," I said. "She thought she was special. He hand-picked her. It must not have been violent, and, obviously, there was no physical pain involved. Of course she would want to stay...."

We continued to talk a-mile-a-minute but I was baffled by my sister's confusion about my cousin's daughter's decision. A little unnerved at how I could so easily understand, I quickly dismissed such thoughts and continued the conversation.

"Now what? Is she going to get her daughter help?" I asked.

"I'm pretty sure she is already in counseling, but our cousin is already in another relationship and is living with the man," my sister reported.

I was genuinely disgusted. "Our family is so screwed up I can hardly stand it. I swear, how can so many bad things happen in one family? I mean, when are they going to learn?"

The conversation went on for at least a half hour; all the while, my sister and I gushed at how lucky we were to have escaped the darkness and destruction that seemed to saturate our extended family.

With the dinner hour approaching, I told my sister I had

to go and get on with my evening chores. Before hanging up, my sister reiterated again, "We are so blessed that we were raised by Christian parents and were able to escape this stuff."

"I know," I said. "It would be awful to have been a part of that...."

****

I began the familiar routine of preparing dinner, washing and cutting the vegetables while the conversation with my sister echoed in my mind. Moving quickly, I scrubbed and chopped, but the activity was not enough to keep me distracted from some of the things that we had talked about. Certain words and certain phrases kept repeating themselves—and they just didn't line up. I tried to leave them alone; I tried to stay focused in the present, but my mind kept drawing me back ... back to a hidden and private corner of my mind: my secret closet of memories. It is a place in my mind that I had created long ago to house all of my childhood and adult memories. Its shelves are stacked high with boxes containing the images, sounds and smells from my past.

Reluctantly, I unlocked the door and stepped in. Before me, I saw all of my memories in neatly packaged boxes of my own design—an inventory consisting of lovely wrapped boxes—some with ribbons, others without—all safely placed on their shelves. I scanned the boxes stacked in front of me. Picking carefully, I pulled from the shelf a package that held an important memory. Carefully, I opened the box and looked inside at the contents, seeing things I hadn't looked at in years:

> *We are walking together, and he is laughing with me again, telling me he likes my hair. His words are like cool water to my dry and thirsty soul—an oasis of affirmation in an emotional desert of relationships. Here, with him, I exist. I am someone.*
>
> *We are talking and I am smiling as he is, because I am ... special. Yes, he makes me feel special.*
>
> *He is water in my desert, my refuge from the winds, sheltering me with his attention, guarding me with his compliments. In the midst of a hurricane that rages around me, he is a safe place, my friend and my confidant. He is watching out for me. He is protecting me.*
> *And I am ... safe. Yes; he makes me feel safe. Safe and special.*

"Why wouldn't she want to stay? He was probably nice to her," I almost said out loud. The twisted rationale startled me; a feeling of disgust with my thought process and reasoning jolted me. I quickly replaced the lid on the box, returned it to its rightful place on the shelf in the storage room, and shut and locked the door.

Over the following days, however, the conversation plagued me. I tried to ignore it, refusing to give mental voice to it. Besides, there were tasks at hand, one of which was preparing a lesson that I would be teaching at an upcoming women's group. I would be teaching the same message to two different crowds two mornings in a row: "How to Celebrate Who You Are." I loved that topic—it's one of my favorite messages to give and one that women are always so grateful to receive. As I started to get my outline prepared, however, a new thought came to me, *'Instead of teaching to these moms as you always do, why don't you share where you have come from? How will they know His glory if you are unwilling to share your story?'* I had no idea where that thought came from. I never had—and I vowed that I never would—share my family history. This was an agreement that I had made long ago with the Lord. I would study and teach my little heart out on whatever topic was thrown my way, but I had long ago promised that I would never tell anyone about my past. *Absolutely not!*

I was an accomplished speaker and teacher. In my messages, I would sometimes briefly share that I didn't come from the "best of backgrounds." I sometimes alluded to the fact that my relationship with my mom was strained and then quickly emphasize that, by God's grace, I had been able to have a great family of my own. I often expounded on the fact that I totally gave my life over to the Lord in my early twenties when I was on the verge of a nervous breakdown. I shared how I spent the better part of two years researching the Scriptures to find out how God's mercy could help me overcome the pain of my past—but I never went into the details; that hardly seemed necessary. The past was the past, after all, and I had it all packed safely away in the boxes in my closet. Now it seemed God was telling me to share some of the darker contents of those boxes with others. Refusing to entertain such a thought, I continued with my teaching preparations. But I couldn't shake the feeling that I was supposed to share with these women about my childhood and my family....

Maybe Sandra can get me out of this, I thought. Sandra was the group leader. She was a close friend and a great organizer and coordinator. *Certainly she won't want me to deviate from the already agreed-upon plan,* I hoped. Knowing that she would never go for it, I made another deal with God. "OK, I'll share my background and give my testimony if Sandra lets me do it. If she says 'no' then I will teach from my notes. Do we have a deal?"

When Sandra called to pray with me the night before the speaking engagement, I casually asked her about sharing my story. "Veronica, that would be wonderful! I think that is a great idea," she exclaimed. "You have been teaching these ladies for years, but no one really knows anything about you. Being vulnerable and letting them into your life is exactly what the group needs."

I tried to protest, but she was emphatic. "No, I know for a fact that it would be great. I would like to hear more about you too. You are always so vague. I know there is a story just waiting to be told. I'm proud of you, that you would be willing to do what is on your heart. Can I pray for you?"

"Yeah, I think prayer is pretty necessary right now," I said.

I spent the night moving in and out of my mental storage closet, picking and choosing which boxes to retrieve and which ones to leave unopened. Remembering the information I was just given regarding my cousin, her daughter, and the stepfather, I decided that should be included on the list. Very carefully, I chose only the boxes that contained the memories of my extended family, not those of my immediate family. *Those boxes are never, never, ever to be opened in public*, I reminded myself. I carefully opened the selected boxes and cautiously pulled out selected contents.

> *Two little white coffins, one with pink flowers on top, the other with blue...*
> *The gavel of a judge slamming down, pronouncing guilt and condemnation....*
> *The words of a mom, so bitter and so powerful...*
> *The silence of a dad, present but so emasculated...*
> *A little girl searching desperately for the means to end the pain once and for all...*

After several hours of sifting through boxes, my work was complete. I gingerly replaced all the figurines back into their rightful containers and returned them to the storage closet of my mind. While there, I stepped back and looked at all the containers. *Too many, too many, really.* Not wanting to return anytime soon, I locked the door and returned to my notes for the next day, rehearsing over and over what to say and how to say it. Falling into bed, I simply wanted to sleep this whole nightmare away.

****

The alarm clock went off, and immediately my stomach was in knots notifying me of the day's schedule—I would be sharing my background to a large group of women. As I made final preparations and then finally walked into the room of familiar, smiling, and expectant faces, I kept thinking there must be some way out. There wasn't. A couple of songs and a few announcements later, I was introduced. I walked to the stage, opened my mouth, and words started to come out, then more words, then more. I started to go off my rehearsed talked and shared some things I never intended to, actually surprising myself with my forthrightness. I scanned the audience expecting to see the usual nods of understanding and smiles of approval. A roomful of shocked and sad eyes looked back at me. I tried to figure out why my carefully chosen stories were so upsetting to them. I had intentionally kept the bad packages safely untouched.

I left the platform and stepped into a sea of visibly upset souls. With tears in their eyes, the moms thanked me for having the courage to share such a story of hope and survival. I was terribly confused. I didn't consider anything I had shared to be that big of a deal. Some longtime friends came up to hug me and told me they had no idea I had overcome so much. I just smiled and thanked them, but I truly had no clue what they were talking about.

Driving in the car back home, I made another deal with God, one that I hoped He would respect. "OK, I shared this one time, but I won't do it again after tomorrow. We had a deal, remember? You help me to never have to look at my past, and I live my life teaching the Bible and raising my kids to know You. I have kept my end of the pact; You need to keep Yours."

The next day, I shared my story again and received a similar reaction. The response was affirming but unnerving. But, hey, I did it and now I was done with it. With the whole "testimony" thing out of the way, I could now get on with my life and my ministry as usual—with all my boxes safely sorted and stored back on their shelves in my mental storage closet.

A few weeks later, I was scheduled to speak at a women's Bible study at our church. I'd stepped back into my normal routine, and, other than being followed by the unsettling memories that were resurrected in my mind of when I gave my message to the moms, I thought I was back on track. They asked me to speak on "the Goodness of the Lord" (another favorite and familiar topic). Taking the day to fast and pray, I went to my teaching archives and gathered notes from prior lessons I had taught on the topic. At lunchtime, instead of eating, I retreated to my bedroom for a time of prayer in preparation for the Bible study that night. Mentally going over the lesson in my head, my plans were interrupted with a thought: *I am not to teach tonight; I am to share my story.* I tried to dismiss the idea on practical grounds. *I have pages upon pages of notes that I can choose from to compile my teaching. I love teaching about God's goodness. This is a message that women so desperately need to hear.*

Successfully disregarding the thought, I continued with my teaching notes. Not allowing me to go any further with my plan, the Lord interrupted, His command resonating from within my spirit. *"Share your story tonight, Veronica.*

Some of them need to know how good I AM."

Are You kidding me? I have no intention on giving my testimony again. We had a deal, remember? I already did that, and I'm still trying to get over it. I didn't want to share it then, and I don't want to share it tonight."

The thoughts continue to flood my mind, *"You are teaching about My goodness; do you remember how good I AM?"*

"Of course I do. I remember how good You are!"

"Veronica, do you remember? Do you remember what I have delivered you from? Do you really remember how good I AM?"

Weeping with my face buried in a pillow, thoughts and recollections came flashing back in an unwelcome vision across my mind's eye. Crying from both fear and the thought that God didn't think I valued Him, I replied, "Yes, I remember Lord; I remember how good You are. I am so sorry I haven't thanked You enough lately and that I have purposed not to remember, but I do. I really do remember! You have done so much for me and I know I have taken it for granted. Please accept my apology, I remember and I'm thankful, I truly am!"

"Then tell them how good I AM Veronica, tell them where I have delivered you from. How will they know My glory, if you are unwilling to tell your story? Some of them don't know I can heal and deliver; you need to let them know how good I AM."

****

I walked into the room that night scared half out of my mind. After being introduced, I walked up to the platform to address a room full of familiar, eager listeners who were waiting for my normal repertoire of inspirational stories and energetic Bible teachings. For years, I had only shown a thin veneer of who I was and where I had come from. Had I lied? No, just not told the complete truth. Feeling as though I needed to offer them an apology, I looked into their happy faces as they waited for my usual humorous and energetic presentation. But that night I would be neither light nor funny. I would be authentic. I would be real—at least partially. With so many boxes still locked away in the darkness, I had cracked the lid on just a few, recalling the contents that still seemed so familiar and so … so normal.

> *A young girl hiding from the anger of the matri-*
> *arch who is supposed to be her caretaker…*
> *Daddy's girl drifting in the absence of a father,*
> *the "protector" turning a deaf ear to the on-*
> *slaught unleashed again on his daughter…*
> *The little white caskets adorned with flowers…*
> *The step-dad, the daughter of my cousin, twenty-*
> *one counts of sexu…*

Story by story, the carefully articulated accounts from my extended family moved smoothly from my lips, almost without effort. All the while, my mind tried to make sense of what was happening again in front of me. Seat by seat, table by table, I looked into tearful wide-eyed looks of compassion. The same confusion flooded my mind. Once again, I couldn't figure out why they thought my stories were so awful. I didn't cry over them, why should they? I was being

13

so careful on the platform, sharing only carefully selected memories from the closet, and they were shaking their heads in disbelief.

Then it happened. My thoughts were briefly interrupted by my own words. "I don't know of any female in my family line who hasn't been sexually violated—usually by another member of the family...."

I paused briefly after the statement—less than a second of silence passed. I quickly thought of every adult female member of my family and then concluded that was an accurate statement. It had never really occurred to me before I spoke it that night. I quickly dismissed the thought and continued with my teaching.

I had given them 15 minutes of my personal struggle; now it was time for another 30 minutes of God's power and healing grace. With passion, the Truth poured forth regarding His willingness to take us, love us, and redeem us for the future that He has called us to live. With authority, I proclaimed that it was by the grace of God that I stood there that day. With passion, I convincingly expounded on the healing mercy of God.

As if waving a magic wand over the crowd, I closed with the promises of God and capped it off with a prayer of praise and thanksgiving. I stepped down from the platform to thunderous applause.

Just one problem. The magic wand seemed to work for them, but it wasn't working for me; not anymore. I was spent, weak-kneed and dizzy—as though I had run a marathon. In the spotlight, I maintained poise and spoke articulately. On the floor, a surge of thought and emotion crashed over me, and I began to feel physically ill. I made a dash for the door, but the group leader intercepted me with tears in her eyes. "Please stay and join that table over there for the discussion time. I know those women, and they all are in a tough time right now. Your story brings such hope; I know they would value your input during discussion."

I forced a smile and said, "I ....I, I'm sorry, I can't stay, I have somewhere I need to be. I would love to help but I can't."

She pleaded, but I knew I had to leave; I was emotionally hanging on by a thread.

I rushed to my car with tears already streaming down my cheeks. Scrambling for my keys, I opened the door and slid into the driver's seat. Tears were flowing steadily now, but they could do nothing to cool my boiling rage. God had not honored His part of our deal. In total terror of what was unfolding before me, I recoiled with horror as the memories I suppressed on stage came back in with a vengeance. With my fist clinched, I banged with all of my might on the dashboard and I screamed at my Maker. "Why are you doing this to me? For decades, I have gone without having to share about my past or even look back! Why now? Leave me alone! Do You hear me? BACK OFF!"

I slammed my fist down again and again on the dashboard and planted my face on the steering wheel. In a dark church parking lot, the woman who seemed to have it all together unraveled; the one who had showed so many how to be saved cried the cry of the lost.

"If this is what You want me to do, I want out! I will never go back up on a platform to speak again. Do you hear me? I will never tell my story again. It's too hard and too painful. Please, I beg of You: leave me alone!"

With my vow in place, I turned the key in the ignition and raced out of the parking lot. I wanted off the church property; I wanted out of my life. *Why are You doing this to me now, what have I done to upset You?*

****

In the driveway of my house, I pulled myself together. With one big breath, I left it all behind and stepped into a different mental world where I was a mother and a wife. Unfortunately, this world had troubles of its own. In spite of everything that had taken place over the past several weeks, I had not spoken about any of it with my husband, Jerry. Financially, we had taken a hit due to layoffs at Jerry's work a year earlier. Nine months without income would place us in financial turmoil. I once heard it said that people are like tea bags: You don't know what's in them until you get them in hot water. What was seeping out of our tea bags was not a pretty sight.

Exhausted and unwilling to tolerate one more fight, I walked through the door that night determined to avoid conflict. That proved to be an exercise in futility. Within no time at all, Jerry and I were at complete verbal blows with each other, screaming over reoccurring issues that never found resolution and now seemed too much for us to bear. Once each other's strongest allies, we were now enemies with clearly drawn battle lines.

For the next several weeks, we lived in the tension of a

fragile cease-fire. Then one afternoon I came home from the beach with my children and greeted Jerry. We gave each other the obligatory hug and smiles. I just kept thinking, *Remain silent and go with the flow.* Under the surface, however, our marriage was like a minefield. He was a man on the verge, and I was a woman on the edge. That would prove to be a disastrous combination. No matter how carefully each of us would walk, we would inevitably step on an issue that would trigger a violent vocal explosion. That night, our explosive dialogue rose to a whole new level. Reason was totally left behind and emotion, confusion and pain ignited within us and between us.

Unable to handle it any longer, I ran upstairs to pack my suitcase. Nothing made sense any longer. I desperately needed some space, some relief ... some distance. Jerry panicked and tried to convince me that we could work it out. I gave assurances that I was leaving only for the night—but I was adamant that real change needed to take place.

Driving with nowhere to go, the headlights of my car illuminated only the night. Life was totally spiraling out of control. *What in the world is going on? What am I doing?* I tried to calculate my next move. *Who can I talk to? I don't want my marriage to end, but it can't continue with the same madness we have grown so accustomed to.*

A few hours later, I returned home where Jerry and I tried once again to put the puzzle of life back together ourselves. But, as usual, none of the pieces fit. We each slept on our own side of the bed, carefully making sure the imaginary middle line on the mattress was not crossed. Jerry left the next morning for a weeklong business trip; we both agreed to not call, text, or email. I would be alone with my thoughts and have a chance to take an honest look at where I was. What I saw was not good.

My marriage was crumbling, its carefully crafted façade ready to collapse. My ministry was being invaded by my past, destroying the pleasure and affirmation of church life. And worst of all, my secret storage closet was in danger of being exposed. All the beautifully wrapped packages on the shelf of my mind were beginning to tremble. They were demanding my attention, but I refused to deal with the contents of my boxes that were starting to plague me.

Out of control, it felt like all hell was beginning to break loose. *Maybe I can't control my past, but I can control my present and future,* I thought. Doing what only months before would have seemed unthinkable—and also completely inappropriate—I picked up the phone and began to punch in the number of a person I never thought I would call....

CHAPTER TWO

Calm Before the Storm

With the phone pressed up to my ear, I waited with great expectation. Finally, he answered. I introduced myself, trying not to sound as desperate as I felt. He introduced himself as Dr. Storm and asked me how he could help. *What a loaded question* I thought. I had never talked to a therapist before. Was he being polite or had the counseling session begun? Would I be billed for this call? I hardly knew where to start.

Our conversation went on for roughly twenty minutes. He sounded nice enough, but, boy, did he get an earful. I lamented about the state of my marriage and how we were in dire need of counseling.

We made an appointment for Thursday, which came quite quickly. Believe it or not, my first concern was what I should wear to a psychologist's office. Wardrobe is a chief concern for me. If I came dressed as I felt, I would have worn sloppy old sweats and my hair up in an unkempt ponytail. However, I didn't want to look like a frazzled housewife because then he might not take me seriously. I also knew that I shouldn't be overdressed because then it would look like I was trying too hard. I finally decided that navy blue capris, red-and-white striped tank top, and a classy red sweater would be just the right attire for such an occasion. As you can tell, the distance between me and crazy was a ridiculously short commute.

I sucked it up and drove down to his office in beautiful Newport Beach. By then, I was almost in a daze. I just kept thinking, *I can't do this one more day, not one more day.* Those words rolled around and around inside my head as I entered into his office. I sat in the waiting room. I couldn't believe that I, of all people, would end up in a shrink's office. The whole idea of me sitting on a therapist's couch whining and crying my eyes out was way beneath me. I had never been one to complain about my past or my present. I was the fixer, always in control, the *never let them see you sweat* kind of gal.

However, I had found myself coming completely unglued and in serious need of a lifeline.

I walked into the small waiting room of his office. As soon as I opened the door, I heard the sounds of classical music filling the air. The colors were warm, helping to create an atmosphere of tranquility. There wasn't a reception desk, so I was unclear as to how the doctor would know that I had arrived. I sat down on the sofa and picked up a magazine to help distract my mind from my churning stomach. I heard a door open from around the corner and waited to see who would appear from the hallway. A man approached, smiled, and introduced himself as Dr. Storm. He was so much taller than I expected. I didn't know why that mattered: I just thought shrinks would live up to their name and be small, I guess.

He stood about 6'4" tall, with a thick mustache over his top lip. Much like Jerry's goatee, I would guess that for years his mustache had been as permanent on his face as his eyes and nose were. My first impression from having talked to him on the phone and then seeing him in person, was that he was a gentle giant. He was wearing a plaid short-sleeved—cotton—buttoned-down shirt with grey slacks. Much more casual than I expected. I supposed it was to give the feeling of ease, unlike what a suit and tie would have suggested. If that was his strategy, it didn't work. I was still as tightly wound as a top. I half-feared him pulling my emotional string, which might have spun me wildly out of control.

He escorted me down a short hallway, back to his office. It was a comfortably sized room–not too big, not too small. On one side of the room was a large leather executive chair and on the opposite side was a large leather couch with only one decorative pillow. The first thought that sprang to my mind was, *Why on earth would there only be one throw pillow for a sofa of this size?* My world was falling apart and I actually had the inclination to care about the decor. Yep, the doctor clearly had his work cut out with me.

For the 1½-hour session, I told Dr. Storm about the mess of our marriage. I conveyed how I thought Jerry was serving me up a little slice of crazy everyday. The problem was I already had my own crazy, so his crazy with my crazy was a volatile mix. At one point, Dr. Storm mentioned that I said that we went to church. I have to confess I didn't remember saying anything related to church. Then he asked me what church we went to. What was I supposed to do? I was a teacher, leader, and extremely active in my church. The last thing I wanted to do was let him know which one I went to. I was embarrassed for my church and wanted to tell him that normally they do a much better job with people. I threw caution to the wind, and I told him the name. He said he was familiar with it and said he was thrilled we were all Christians.

He continued. "Now, I know that we are all on the same page and that divorce is not an option here. Not all of my patients are Christians so they don't use the Bible as their standard for marriage. Because we are all Christians, I can take a different approach in the counseling. You and Jerry took an oath before God and man and swore 'Till death do you part.'

I have to admit all I could think of was *I am a woman on the edge ... you seriously don't want to use the words death and husband in the same sentence right now!*

I wasn't too thrilled to have our counselor be a Christian. I would have never gone to him if he weren't so highly recommended by my friend Michele. Some of the men I have found in the Christian faith seem to be bullies, using the Bible and God as a tool to control the opposite sex. If he began quoting scriptures about wives needing to submit to their husbands in every circumstance, we were going to have a problem. To my surprise, he did the opposite. He said the marriage relationship is a partnership, not a dictatorship. Wives can only feel safe enough to submit if the husband is following God's plan by loving her like Christ loved the church.

By that time, I could have really cared less. My life was

spiraling out of control. I was trying to keep my emotions in check that visit. Not being very successful on that endeavor, tears were streaming uncontrollably down my cheeks as I continued to tell him our situation. I asked Dr. Storm how I was to handle it when Jerry got home Friday night.

Dr. Storm said enthusiastically, "Maybe the two of you could spend sometime alone together; maybe go for a walk along the beach. You should just enjoy each other's company and agree not to talk about anything that would cause a fight."

I had never wanted to physically hurt a man so much in my life. I knew he might be much larger than I was, but I truly thought I could take him! What I lacked in size I more than made up for in rage. I crossed my arms, and scowled, "Absolutely not!"

Dr. Storm was noticeably surprised by my reaction, and I continued, "I won't do it! Don't you see that's how I ended up here? I refuse to act controlled and as if nothing is wrong. That's all I've been doing for months. That's how I landed in your office for heaven's sake!"

Well, I guess that came through loud and clear. Completely changing tactics, he asked me if I was willing to talk to Jerry on the phone and tell him that I saw a marriage counselor today. "Just tell Jerry I recommended that you not have any communication with each other until you are both in my office."

I agreed to that.

Trying to regain some ground, Dr. Storm looked at me with total sympathy. "Veronica, I know you're hurt and scared. You think you have tried everything, but you haven't tried me, you haven't tried counseling. Trust me, we will work together to make this turn around, but you have to at least try."

Looking down with my head shaking, I said, "I don't know if I can. I'm just so tired Dr. Storm; I really don't care anymore."

"Now, wait a minute. I'm never concerned when a man says he doesn't care anymore, that can be a typical response from a man. When the wife says it, it's serious. Veronica, you need to care—you need to hang in there. If I don't have the involvement of the wife, there's nothing I can do to help. Please promise me you will give this a chance."

I felt like all the energy I had left in my body was spent on the session. I wanted him to just make it all better, make *me* all better. If I could lie down and take a nap that would last for at least ten years that would have been wonderful. I thought to myself, *No one has ever known how hard it is to be me. Everyday it is a purposeful decision to get out of bed and survive one more day. I'm dying and no one even knows it.*

We were at the end of our session, and I was completely exhausted. I asked him when Jerry and I could come in for our first visit together. "Why don't the two of you plan on coming in on Saturday?"

Surprised I asked, "Oh, do you work Saturdays?"

"No, not normally. But I'm willing to make an exception for you. I can see this is somewhat of an emergency."

I don't know why, but when he said that, it kind of tickled me. My whole countenance must have been screaming 911. Oh well, at least now I know that when Jerry comes

24

home Friday night, I will only have to wait until the next day to have some mediation.

On the drive home, thoughts of the session and complete despair threatened to overwhelm me. I had lost my love for life and my ability to cope. While still driving, my friend Michele called to see how the session went.

"I don't know Michele, this might not work. I'm just so sad and overwhelmed—what in the world is wrong with me? I don't know if Jerry and I are going to make it."

"Of course you guys are going to make it. Veronica, the process has only just begun, give it a chance."

"It's just so dark Michele. I can't see the light at the end of the tunnel."

"You don't have to; I can see the light for you. I see the end and trust me—you make it."

The Lord would use her and my other friends to keep me going. It was an amazing thing for me to experience. I had never allowed anyone into the dark places of my life and now the door was flung wide open for all to enter.

Jerry called later on that evening. I did exactly as Dr. Storm recommended. I told him we shouldn't talk until we were in his office on Saturday. Jerry was terrified at how bad our marriage had become. He readily agreed to the conditions, not knowing what else to do. When Jerry got home on Friday night, I met him at the door and gave him a quick peck on the lips. He looked utterly drained and said he was glad to see me. We both stood there silent not knowing what to do. We went into separate rooms for the remainder of the evening.

The next morning I woke up relieved that we were going to Dr. Storm's office. The entire morning Jerry and I avoided each other all together. If I was upstairs, he was downstairs and vice versa. We even drove in two separate cars to our appointment. We didn't want to suffer the silence on the thirty-five minute car ride down to Newport Beach. Arriving at his office, we walked together in silence, two wounded individuals lost and unable to find their way. Dr Storm introduced himself to Jerry and expressed how grateful he was that Jerry had agreed to counseling. With my permission, he told him about the session with me a few days earlier. The session was an orientation of sorts describing what the counseling would look like and what we were to expect.

Our counselor gave us some papers with words on them, but I really couldn't bring myself to follow along. I wanted him to wave a magic wand and make everything OK. I honestly felt like I was circling the drain for the last time.

Dr. Storm must have noticed that I wasn't too engaged in the process because he stopped and looked at both of us. With a firm tone, he implored, "Look, you two. One day I will be standing before God and He is going to ask me if I did everything possible to save the marriage of Jerry and Veronica Wright. I am going to tell Him that I did all I knew how to do to save your family. But, make no mistake, you also will be standing before God and He will ask you the same question, what will your answer be?"

Wow, who put the burr under his saddle? He actually seemed visibly upset. I knew it was supposed to be a wake-up call and most reasonable people would have responded accordingly. My brain was busy compiling a whole host of possible reactions and answers I should give. Do I remain calm to give him the impression that I'm a Godly woman so he would like me? Put on a fake persona and say, "But, of course, I am going to do everything in my power to make this work, that's why I'm here"?

Or am I allowed to scream bloody murder and say, "Back off! If I wanted a sermon, I would have gone to a freaking church! For the love of all that is holy, I know all the scriptures! I could quote them to you for gosh sakes! It's not working—can't you understand that? So listen up doctor, I want only two things from you: psycho babble and, with any luck, a prescription!" For the life of me, I seriously didn't know why I wasn't heavily medicated by that time.

But, of course, as always, I went with the good girl response. I would never actually have the nerve to speak my mind. I nodded my head and said I was willing to try to work this out. So far, things didn't appear to be going my way. As crazy as this sounds, while leaving, I actually thought, *Even though it didn't go well, on the upside, I think I chose the right outfit for the session.* I, of course, was worried about such things.

Before leaving his office, we scheduled another appointment for Tuesday. That would make three sessions in less than a week. This was going fast. I couldn't have been more thrilled. No one on the planet needed more help than we did, and the faster we could plow through the muddy mess the better!

Tuesday arrived before I knew it. Was this really going to work? Had we gone too far to save this train wreck of a marriage? I promised to give counseling a try, so I would. I wasn't expecting much. I really couldn't see how this marriage could be salvaged.

Dr. Storm began with an electrified topic, our finances. It didn't take too long before we came to verbal blows. Angry, I interrupted Jerry mid-sentence. Apparently that isn't something you want to do in front of a marriage counselor. Dr. Storm was quick to referee.

"Veronica, you need to allow him to speak."

Shocked, I stopped, looked across the room at the man giving me instruction. Jerry and I had both been interrupting each other; why was he only stopping me? Dr. Storm continued his counsel. "Veronica, look at Jerry and tell him you hear him and thank him for telling you his side."

Stunned, I sat there and glared at Dr. Storm. He repeated himself and told me once more to say it. I felt all the blood drain from my face. Out numbered by the men, I despised myself for what I would do next. I stopped, looked at Jerry, and obeyed the doctor. As far as I was concerned, my marriage was officially over. My husband and therapist could not be trusted. I determined never to return to that office.

Then Dr. Storm did something that was either brilliant or divinely inspired. As I came to know him, I decided it was probably both. He asked us to share our childhoods and family dynamics. He instructed, "Although I want to know about your backgrounds, I don't want to hear it coming from you. Veronica, you tell me about Jerry's childhood and family, and how you see the family dynamic today. Then Jerry, you tell me about Veronica's background. That will help me know why you react to each other the way you do."

Still upset from the earlier correction, it was hard to engage in what I considered a mockery of a counseling session. Wanting to get it over with, I took the lead. I gave details to Dr. Storm about Jerry's childhood, his parents and his two brothers. I actually knew quite a bit of Jerry's history. Remarkably, while sharing about Jerry's childhood, my heart began to soften. Jerry really was a pretty good husband. I was proud of where he came from. When I was finished, Dr. Storm thanked me. It was Jerry's turn.

With great conviction he began, "First off, Dr. Storm you must understand that Veronica's mother is evil. I know people use that word all the time, but I'm not one of them. I don't take that word lightly and have never used it to describe any other person in my life. She is cruel and abusive to Veronica, and it has cost my wife dearly. For whatever reason, she decided to target Veronica years ago as the recipient of her cruelty and the deeds continue to this day. Her mom was inequitable in her treatment of the children both for good and bad. Her brother and sister were able to escape the undeserved cruelty; Veronica never did. While she would shelter and coddle Veronica's older sister, Veronica would be on the receiving end of her mother's deeds."

Jerry went on, systematically outlining the many offenses he had observed in our twenty-five years of knowing each other. He pretty much began when I was seventeen and went to present day. He said it was hard to have had to remain silent all these years. He couldn't stand the way my family treated me, but he agreed to my terms of staying out of it years ago.

I was struck by the pain and compassion with which Jerry shared these stories. It never occurred to me that he had a clue to how painful it all was to me. However, it also surprised me that he started my childhood at age seventeen. Did he not know what went on in that house from infancy to age seventeen? Is it possible I'm a stranger to my husband of twenty-three years?

Jerry wrapped up the stories of my childhood. Dr. Storm looked at me and said he was sorry it was so difficult for me. Now this was all too confusing. Why would he think what Jerry said was so difficult for me, and better yet, why did Jerry think those were the painful experiences? What he listed was nothing compared to the horrifying things that took place under the roof of my childhood home.

Then Dr. Storm asked the question that would change my life forever. "Was anyone in your family safe, Veronica? Did you have anyone you could trust?"

I smiled and glowed. "Yes, my brother was safe. He sometimes would be the only one who ever even asked me how my day was or seemed to care." I told him we were very close both now and back then.

Dr. Storm smiled and said seven simple words that rocked my world. "Good, I'm glad your brother was safe."

Shocked, I looked at Dr. Storm wondering why he would say such a thing. It didn't sound right when he said it. I mean, when I said my brother was safe, I knew what *I* meant. He was safe except when he *wasn't* safe. Why would a counselor say that my older brother was safe when he knew what all older brothers do to their younger sisters? I could use the word "safe" and keep it in the proper context of my own mind; when Dr. Storm said it, he might be taking it at the literal meaning.

Was I the only one in this room who knew what goes on in every home by the older brothers?

That officially ended our session. I had thought earlier in the session, when Dr. Storm corrected me, I would never return. By the time we were leaving, I was so confused I didn't think I even knew my own name anymore. We made the appointment for the following week. I was still unsure if I would show up.

The next day, I met my friends from bible study for breakfast, I decided that I would tell them about my troubled marriage. I had let them know months earlier that Jerry and I were in financial trouble, but I had never been so transparent before. As far as I was concerned, everyone was on a need-to-know basis only. Appearing to have it all together took effort, but it was what I had been doing since childhood. Letting anyone ever see lack of faith or failure on my part, simply went against how I was raised. For some reason that time, it was different. I couldn't play the game anymore. I had lost my will to hide.

Much to my surprise, they were safe with the information. Even more surprising, it even seemed to be drawing us closer. They were compassionate and understanding. It also seemed to give them license to open up about their own troubles and issues. Not in a "misery enjoys company" kind of way. More like, we all began to feel safe knowing that we were in the company of women who could truly understand.

While driving back home from breakfast with my friends, my mind was obsessing over the session with Dr. Storm the day before. *Good, I'm glad your brother was safe.* Why was that so upsetting to me? I was the first one to say it. He was simply repeating me. I began to get incredibly anxious. My heart started racing at record speed. I had enough butterflies fluttering around in me to start a colony.

I arrived home. Jerry was working from the house that day. Not one of his better decisions, to be sure! When he walked into the kitchen, we got into another explosive argument. The heated exchange was over something totally insignificant. "Majoring on minors" had become our standard method of operation. While fighting, I told him I didn't even want to go back to Dr. Storm's office again. It was all a waste of time. Enraged with tears, I bellowed, "How could you just sit there and let him treat me that way! He made me say something against my will that was totally absurd. Why should I be the one to apologize when you were interrupting me too? I don't like Dr. Storm, I don't want to go back. I hate Neanderthal Christian men who tell women what to do!"

Jerry replied, "I know you do; you were the one who chose the doctor. We can change therapists and try a female one; it really doesn't matter to me."

I lost my need to fight. Completely frustrated I conceded. "I don't know of any other marriage counselor to call. I don't know whom I would trust anyway. I guess we could go back to Dr. Storm's office again; it really doesn't matter anymore."

Trying to go on with my day was futile. Those stupid words would continue to press their way into my thoughts. *Good, I'm glad your brother was safe.* I couldn't sit still for more than a few minutes. I was walking around the house trying not to come completely unglued. Why would Dr. Storm say my brother was safe? I sat on my couch contemplating all the possible answers. I knew Dr. Storm was a seasoned counselor so he had to be aware of what older brothers did to their younger sisters. Everyone knows that. So if he knew that my brother wasn't safe, then why did he say it? My heart was actually in pain with all the adrenaline pumping through it. Dots were beginning to be connected in my mind. If Dr. Storm didn't know this piece of information, then why didn't he? Is it possible it doesn't happen in every family?

My head was spinning as I was trying on my own to assimilate the information. *Think Veronica, think*, I was telling myself. My heart was pounding, and those awful stupid butterflies were continuing to torment me. I nervously got up off the couch and began frantically pacing the room like a caged animal. *Think Veronica, if Dr. Storm didn't know about what your brother did to you, why didn't he*? He should have known; he has been counseling for years, *unless*....

"OH NO!" The revelation hit me like a thunderous blow. "OH NO", I exclaimed although no one was in the room but me. I began chanting, "Oh no, it's not normal! It's not normal! It's not normal! It's not normal! Why didn't I know that? My brother was safe? What a joke!" I continued pacing back and forth sobbing uncontrollably. I finally faced the reality I had hidden from myself all these years.

I was the victim of incest.

Ugh, I hated that word, *incest*. It's such an ugly word, and it should never have to be attached to any self-respecting individual. How could I have possibly placed my brother's actions under the category of normal all of these years?

I flopped on the sofa, placing my hands over my face, and began rocking back and forth. It felt like a thousand volts of energy were pulsating through my muscular system. For the first time in my life, my mind and body were no longer under my control. Is this what a nervous breakdown felt like? Every once in a while, I would get back up and continue to pace back and forth across the room. I tried desperately to convince myself that I wasn't losing my mind. After several hours of unfruitful attempts to calm myself, I thought perhaps going to bed would send the message to my nerves that it was time for rest.

I went upstairs to the bedroom, sneaking in as not to wake Jerry from his sound sleep. I tried to turn off my brain from its endless dialogue. I tossed and turned for hours. Sleep would not find me that night. I would be too busy dying a thousand deaths.

The next day I was barely able to function. I drove the kids to school and went back home to an empty house. Once again, I found myself on the couch trying to connect more dots. Why wasn't I angry with my brother? How could I have been in a relationship with him and not have gotten completely sick to my stomach? I began to shake uncontrollably. Tormented, I needed to talk to someone. Should I call Dr. Storm and try to make an appointment? I didn't even know if he would see me without Jerry being there.

I was absolutely not going to tell Jerry this little newsflash. Good gosh, how would I explain it to him? *I know we hang out with my brother and his family sometimes. Oh by the way, did I ever tell you he used to molest me*? No freaking way was that 411 going to make it to Jerry. I got the courage to call Dr. Storm and ask him for an appointment. Shaking, I left a message asking to come in for an appointment today or tomorrow. I tried not to sound frantic, but it was hard to cover my desperation. My hands were trembling and I found myself rocking back and forth on the couch. *What will I do if I can't get an appointment*?

I needed to go back to my storage room. It was time to start pulling down some of my boxes. I didn't like what was inside them. I had spent my whole adult life never wanting to reveal their contents. Left with no choice, I found the box that would contain my answer. I chose the box carefully and, with much trepidation, opened it. As tears rolled down my face, I began to remove the contents and placed them on the table.

With my heart breaking, I begged, "Why now God, why won't You just leave me alone?"

CHAPTER THREE:

The Awakening

So many boxes. Too many boxes, really, for only one girl to own. On the outside, they looked so clean and pretty but on the inside could be found the darkest of tales that could make the strongest individuals crack. They contained tales of sexual deviance, criminal acts, and cruelty. No one was to know about those boxes. That soon was going to change.

Unpacking the first box, I began the methodical process of sifting through its contents. I had chosen the box well—it contained my answer. Now I would carefully place all the contents back into the box and place it back on the shelf.

Trembling with my answer, I inquired of God, "Why now? I thought we had a deal! I served You and memorized enough scriptures to make a monk jealous and You were supposed to help me forget the pain of my past. What have I done to anger You? Why are You recanting on our deal?"

Several hours later, the phone rang. Being antsy, I about fell off the couch at the sound of it. It was Dr. Storm telling me he had an opening at 3:30. That was enough to calm me down a bit. I began mentally preparing for the session. With a pen and notebook, I carefully started to write down all the things I wanted to tell him. I had no intention of showing this man my entire hand. Being completely terrified, I was concerned that I might chicken out. The contents of the box I was going to discuss had been a safely guarded secret for over thirty years. After reviewing the contents, I understood why I answered Dr. Storm's question by telling him my brother was the safe one. I felt it was still the reasonable, normal reply. But, wait, another question began swirling around inside my head.

Why would my brother do it? He was always so nice to me; he, as mentioned earlier, was the safe one. Why, why, why? I needed another box. That box was the easiest for me to locate. It had always been one of the largest boxes on my shelves. With some hesitancy, I pulled it off the shelf. Do I dare? Should I open another box? Shaking and with tears streaming, I conjured up the courage to open it. Just untie the bow, place the ribbon on the table, and remove the lid. With my heart racing, I began to peek into the dark gruesome contents. I would assure myself that this too was normal. All families have had something like this happen to them. With those false assurances I examined its contents. Yes, once again, I had chosen well.

Methodically, item by item, I began carefully placing the items on the table as though I was removing some precious, delicate figurines. Although I was taking much care, these were not lovely artifacts. They were ugly grotesque articles that no one should have the burden of storing. As I examined each article, I was continuing to tell myself *Normal, it's all perfectly normal and accounted for. Your brother survived, you survived and your sister survived, really no big deal at all.*

I continued to write down all the contents that were lying on the table before me. One by one, as though I was a chief accountant for a large company, I would itemize all items on the table. *Normal, it's all normal* would be my mantra to get me through the documentation process. Ugh, those annoying butterflies would continue to torment me. If I could have swallowed a gallon of pesticide to kill off those buggers I would have. Regrettably, I thought I would be the only casualty in that plan, so I passed on the idea.

It seemed to take a lifetime for 3:30 to arrive. For the first time, I was totally unconcerned with my wardrobe choice. Now I found myself driving down to the appointment not even remembering if I had bothered putting a brush through my hair that morning. I just needed Dr. Storm to tell me it was normal. I needed him to assure me that he knew all along. If he didn't, I was pretty sure that would land me right into the crazy category. I couldn't be that crazy, could I?

Driving down to his office, you can see the ocean. I just love the ocean, so big and vast, powerful and majestic. It screams of something so much grander than I. It was another beautiful day on the outside and such a tormenting day in the inner parts of my soul. I just needed this to be over. I thought, *I can't wait for it to be over*.

I sat in the waiting room of his office feeling like I might just throw up. I couldn't get those perverse images out of my mind, and my heart was still fluttering with butterflies. Dr. Storm came out to greet me.

"Veronica, I'm glad you were able to make it."

As I forced a smile, we walked back to his office. Trembling, I sat on the couch, grabbing for the decorative pillow, holding onto it as if my very life depended on it.

I began the session by telling him about the argument Jerry and I got into after leaving his office.

"I was so angry that you made me tell Jerry I was glad

he shared and thank him. I didn't think I would ever come back. More importantly, I was mortified with myself. I am a grown woman; I don't know why I thought I was powerless to not just tell you no."

Dr. Storm's facial expression changed dramatically. "Oh, Veronica. I am so sorry I upset you like that. I could tell I had done something terribly wrong, but I didn't know what it was. Your face looked like I had just punched you in the stomach. I'm sorry, I won't correct you like that again. I was really only trying to teach you both some communication skills. But I shouldn't have singled you out."

To my amazement, he was totally serious.

Can a man in authority actually be sincerely apologetic? It caught me completely off guard. I decided at that moment that he was no longer on my list of people I couldn't trust. Of course, that didn't immediately qualify him to be added to the list of people I did trust; that would take some time. So much score keeping; it is exhausting being me. Much to my dismay, I would find out later that wasn't normal either.

A little distracted by Dr. Storm's response, I had to catch my balance. I thanked him for his apology and then told him that wasn't the reason I came in. I elaborated on the argument between Jerry and me. I told him the comment I made about Neanderthal Christian men in authority. This seemed of special interest to him. I had no idea why.

Now came the scary part, I had to recall the contents of the first box. Visualizing the memory made me physically shudder. I sat there trying to keep myself still and not have my body betray me with its trembling. I had to let go and let my body do what my mind had never allowed it to do: feel the pain that I had tried to mask all these years.

With incredible fear, I continued. "You asked me if there was anyone in my family that I thought was safe when I was younger and I said yes. Well, the thing is, I got to thinking about that and maybe that wasn't totally correct. I mean, my brother was safe except for when he wasn't safe. I never considered it a big deal. I'm pretty sure all older brothers do that to their younger sisters."

I looked across at the doctor to see if he was tracking with me. I was sitting as far over on the couch as I could go. My body was pressed up against the armrest, which was holding me fast in place. My legs were crossed, with my foot wrapped around my ankle. My hands were tightly clasped, with my thumbs switching back and forth positioning for their place on top. My mind was racing with the questions *Do you understand? Are you catching what I'm throwing your way?*

He looked serious but remained silent. I took that as my cue to continue.

"You see, my brother was the nice one; he really did treat me the best out of all the family members. He would come and sit on my bed when he got home late from work and he would see if I was still awake so we could talk. He would ask me how my day was and how everything else was going. I looked forward to our nightly visits."

"You have to understand, I don't think my mom was very nice to me. As a matter of fact, it was all perfectly horrible for me at home. So, this is why I said he was the safe one. It always seemed to me that my mom got pleasure from my pain. She would do things that would hurt me so deeply but I would try to resist the urge to break. She wouldn't let up until I finally would show the true pain she had inflicted. Then she would seem to me to be satisfied, even gratified with the effects of her efforts. I hated to look into her eyes and see the satisfaction of the emotional blow she had so perfectly inflicted."

"My brother, on the other hand, would never do anything like that to me. He would never get pleasure from my pain. When he did, what he did, he was merely trying to gain his own pleasure, not try to cause my pain. This puts him in an entirely different league than my mom, don't you see? His pleasure, of course, was at my expense, but I always considered that a lot less brutal than what I had to face from my mom."

There, I said it! I hoped I had worded it correctly. My mind was swirling with various questions. Does he agree with me that my brother for all intents and purposes was the safe one? Was what happened between us normal? Does this go on in most homes?

With eyes that screamed of inquisition, Dr. Storm leaned forward in his chair and said, "Veronica, are telling me what I think you are telling me?"

Hesitantly, I looked at him and nodded. "I think so."

"Are you telling me your brother molested you?"

That word, that awful word. How could I possibly link it to my brother, how could I possibly link it to me? I almost choked on my answer. "I never thought of it that way. But, yes, I guess my brother molested me."

Dr. Storm asked some dreadful yet therapeutic questions. "How old were you when it first happened?"

Bewildered and in a hushed tone, I replied. "I was around age eleven."

"How old was your brother?"

"Almost fourteen."

"How often did it occur?"

"A lot at first. It was the summer. My sister and both my parents were at work, so we were home alone in the day. It would happen for days at a time, hours at a time."

He wrote some notes in my file then continued with his line of questioning. "How long did this continue?"

"I'm not too sure really. It did go on for some time though. For some reason it stopped, but, for the life of me, I can't remember why. Then it would happen again some years later."

"When did it happen again Veronica?"

"Years later, he started coming into my room when he thought I was asleep. I learned to sleep very shallow so I could wake up if he entered. If he thought he had awakened me, he would quickly leave my room and I would be safe. One night I didn't wake up in time, it was too late. When I woke up, I was so startled. I told him to get out but he refused to go. I told him again to leave and he begged me to stay. I told him I would scream if he didn't leave immediately and he believed me. He apologized as he was leaving and begged me not to tell."

Dr. Storm continued with the questioning. "How old were you when he came into your room for the last time?"

I had to stop and think about this one. I recalled the contents of the first box and said, "I was around seventeen to eighteen years old."

This seemed to shock him. He said, "Wait. That would make your brother at the time around twenty to twenty-one years old, right?"

"Yeah, that sounds about right."

Why was this so alarming to him? I was missing something but I was unable to figure out what it was. I could tell this was a critical point, but it was totally lost on me. I then told him there were other instances in between age eleven and the last time when I was around eighteen, but I didn't really want to talk about those. He respected my unwillingness to discuss it further.

After I was done with the long, gory details, I felt so disgusting and completely exposed. However, I also had the feeling of freedom all at the same time. I didn't want to make eye contact, as a matter of fact, I wanted to crawl under the couch and be left for dead. Dr. Storm looked so compassionate and told me he was so sorry.

"He had no right to do that to you, Veronica."

I was certain those words would be etched on my heart forever. My body was still in the same twisted posture it was when we began the session. Every extremity was either embracing or being embraced by another. I was crying and shaking as the secrets were being told.

I knew I wasn't done with the unveiling yet. There still was the matter of the other box. It was time to begin to reveal its contents, but would I be believed? That brutal incident was almost beyond description.

"Believe it or not, Dr. Storm, I know why my brother did that to me. It's all totally understandable, if you knew what happened to him."

I had felt so powerless to protect my brother decades earlier when the contents of that box were created. I have to defend him now. The rush of guilt from not having helped him those many years ago would plague me. I would not allow that to happen again. I needed to explain my brother's actions to Dr. Storm and make a strong case for him. I was so young, so very young to have witnessed such a crime. I was only seven years old when the articles were placed in that box for the first time.

****

I was trying to decide how to disclose the contents of the second box. I carefully watched Dr. Storm's expression to see if I was believed. The items in that box needed to be handled with much care so as not to upset the delicate balance of the shelf. If he showed me any sign of doubt, I would simply stop the unpacking process. I was the master of half-told stories. I let people know what I wanted them to know, when I wanted them to know it. That time would be no different.

"My brother, you see, had a very good reason for acting out like he did. You mustn't think ill of him. He was simply trying to survive, I suppose. That's the best any of us can do really; I mean, after what that horrible babysitter did to him."

"What babysitter?"

"Well, there was this babysitter that my parents hired to come watch us. They didn't know her. She simply went door to door in the neighborhood leaving a flyer on each door saying she was available for babysitting jobs. So they hired her to watch the three of us one night. She was a horrible person. I didn't know a girl, who was in her late teens, was capable of such acts."

As I studied Dr. Storm's expression to see if doubt or belief existed, I saw interest. So I cautiously continued.

"The babysitter took my brother into his bedroom and closed the door. My sister and I were standing on the outside with our ears to the door listening to what was happening."

Then with my head down and eyes locked on my lap, I described in grave detail how I heard the violent sexual

44

assault of my brother at the hands of the babysitter.

Looking back up, I saw Dr. Storm's face go from interest to shock. My mind began swirling. *Oh no, it's happening again. Not normal, Veronica, not normal.* I mean Dr. Storm would only act shocked if it was something out of the ordinary. How could that be? It wasn't handled as extraordinary when it happened. In fact, my parents would never speak of it after they found out. That placed it in the "no big deal" category. If it was such a horrifying and outrageous incident, like Dr. Storm's face suggested, then they would have talked about it, right?

Dr. Storm began his inquisition. "The babysitter sexually assaulted your brother?"

I nodded my head.

"How old was he when this happened?"

"I can't really remember exactly but, I think he was around age nine."

"What did you and your sister do after it happened?"

"Well, when she came out of the room, she saw us. She was shocked to see us standing there. She insisted that we were never to tell anyone. Then she threatened us and said she would come back and kill us if we did tell. That was enough to keep us quiet. So my parents hired her a few more times and the babysitter did it again and again."

"Wow, Veronica, then what did you do?"

"Finally, my sister got enough courage to tell my mom about what happened. I was sitting next to her when she was telling my mom, but I was too afraid to speak."

"What did your mom do?"

"She said she would handle it. I'm not too sure what that meant. She left immediately and went to the babysitter's house. When she got back, we ran to the door to see what happened. I was terrified because the babysitter said if we told, she would kill us. As far as I was concerned, my very life depended on it. My mom said she took care of it. My sister and I asked her for details but she made it clear it was a closed subject. We never spoke of it after that."

Dr. Storm looked even more concerned. "Did your dad know? Did he talk to your brother?"

"I'm pretty certain he knew, but I don't think he ever mentioned it to my brother. Like I said, Dr. Storm, we never talked about it after that."

I began to reconsider the contents of the box I had just spilled all over his office. They looked dark, ugly and terrifying. Before I shared the contents, they had simply looked normal to me.

Once again, Dr. Storm expressed his deep regrets for me to have gone through something so awful in my life. Why did I not see them as awful? I was terribly confused as I continued to survey the wreckage of the boxes. I didn't know how to get them back into what, I thought, should be their rightful place of normal.

"Veronica," he said, "Yes, that might explain why your brother acted out on you sexually. It doesn't excuse it, but it does explain it. No wonder you hate men in authority. Your older brother molested you, and your dad did nothing to protect you. He didn't even get you help after it happened."

OK, now Dr. Storm seemed to be the confused one. Clarification seemed to be in order.

"Like I said, I'm not mad at my brother and you have no right bringing my dad into this. I don't hate my dad. As a matter of fact, he was the only thing that kept me going sometimes." Ugh, this is one of the reasons I didn't like sharing the contents of my boxes. People simply didn't get them.

Dr. Storm asked if I have ever seen the *Prince of Tides* movie.

"Yes, I have."

"Did the story line seem familiar to you?"

"Actually, when Jerry and I saw the movie, I commented on how close that was to what happened with the babysitter. At the time, I didn't think the Nick Nolte character handled it as well as we did. I used to think we all got through it fine, totally unscathed. Now, I guess, I have to admit, it did affect us. At the very least, it seemed to have affected my brother. Oh, I don't know anymore; it's all too confusing!"

"Listening to your life, Veronica, is a bit like watching a horror movie. People pay good money to hear stories like these; except they only think it's entertaining because it's fiction. No one would enjoy it if it were based on a true-life experience. You're a survivor."

OK, so he just compared my life to a horror movie! I decided the articles needed to go back into their boxes. It was all a little too much to handle. I would explore the contents again when I was better able. Was he right? Was the story of my life read like a gruesome, fictitious tale?

"Does Jerry know about your brother?"

My mind screamed. No one knew the contents of the boxes. That was what the storage closet was good for, storing such safely guarded secrets. Dr. Storm mistakenly thought he had admission into my inventory. He wanted Jerry to have access to the boxes.

I firmly looked him in the eyes and said, "No! Jerry does

not know and I am going to keep it that way. He is to never know; you have to promise not to tell him."

"Of course, I won't tell him Veronica, but why won't you tell him?"

"If Jerry found out, it would crush him. We spend birthdays and holidays with my brother and his family. Jerry wouldn't know how to act. He might want to talk to my brother. I tell you that can never happen!"

I began to panic. This was all beginning to unravel. I had to protect my brother. I had been the guardian of this second box for over three decades. I had never even considered it my box. It was my brother's box for me to safely guard. He was nice to me when no one else in the house seemed to care. I owed him that much.

My heart was racing with the uncertainty of what had just taken place. "Do you think I should tell Jerry? Is it wrong to keep this information from him?"

Calmly, he assured, "Veronica, this is your story, and it is your life. You are the only one who should decide who knows. No one has the right to force you to tell the story or to keep it a secret. Your brother had absolutely no right to violate you and he had no right to ask you to keep his secret. You're free to do what you want to do."

That was revolutionary. It was as if the blinders fell off my eyes. I could see clearly for the first time in over thirty years. It didn't make the contents of the box any less horrifying, but I knew I was the rightful owner. I had never considered myself the owner of that box. I was merely the guardian. But, if it was my box, then I could unpack it as I saw fit. I decided all the delicate figurines must remain in their boxes. I would determine what to do with the contents later. A slight smiled crossed my face. It would be the first time I smiled in about three days. I actually saw a "small ray of light" coming out of the storage closet. Maybe there was hope. "Speaking of your brother," Dr. Storm continued, "You know you need to confront him, right?"

Well, that didn't last long. So much for the "small ray of light" from the storage closet.

"Are you freaking kidding me?" I bellowed. "There is absolutely no way I am going to confront my brother!"

"Why not?"

"Because he would be mortified, that's why. I'm sure my brother is sorry for what he did. I mean we never have talked about it, but I know he's sorry."

"OK. If your brother is sorry, then why don't you give him the opportunity to tell you himself?"

"I can't. It would be so embarrassing for him. I won't do that to him.

"Remember," I implored, "I don't think he ever meant to hurt me. He only meant to gain his own pleasure. Granted, it was the lesser of the evils, but if you lived in that house, you would know what I mean."

"Again, Veronica, it's entirely up to you."

The session was nearing an end; however, Dr. Storm seemed genuinely interested about something. Changing directions, he asked, "How did you survive all of this? Anyone with your background would normally be dead by life choices or suicide. If not, they would either be a prostitute, a drug addict, an alcoholic, on their fifth marriage or in a psychiatric ward. I cannot get over the fact that you have been married for twenty-three years, are the mother of four children, and still in your right mind. What have you done to survive this?"

I didn't have to think about my answer. "It's the grace of God."

Dr. Storm smiled. "Obviously, it's the grace of God, Veronica. Your life screams of His grace. But He measures out to all of us His grace. Not everyone taps into it. What did you do?"

"Well, first off, I did want to kill myself on several occasions actually. However, the last time I was suicidal, I was around twenty-four and had been married for four years. The inner rage and turmoil was just too much for me to live with. What made it particularly intolerable, I was already a Christian. I'm supposed to have the answer – right? But my relationship with Christ and my knowledge of the Bible didn't seem to quiet the inner demons. Now what was I supposed to do? I simply didn't think there was any other answer than death. I mean, I couldn't live with the torment any longer."

"So, Jerry came home from work one day, and I was on the bed in our room crying my eyes out. He asked me what was wrong and I told him, 'I couldn't take it anymore. You don't know what it's like to be me. You have no idea what my life was like. I don't know how to be happy, I am seriously depressed all of the time.' I never told Jerry all the details of my past. He doesn't have a clue who he's married to, Dr. Storm."

As soon as those words came out of my mouth, it occurred to me that my husband didn't even know me.

I quickly shook that last thought from my head and continued the story. "Anyway, I told Jerry that I didn't want to be like the other members of my family. I had studied my mom and all her behaviors and had purposefully done the

50

exact opposite. Nevertheless, I was still like her. I was depressed, raging, bitter and in a deep sense of despair. Jerry was so calm; he told me, 'Veronica, it's simple. You are studying the wrong thing. Don't focus on who you don't want to become, set your focus on who you do want to become. Keep your eyes off your family and focus on people who you admire. Jerry saved my life that day without ever knowing it."

"So you see, that's what I did to make it this far. After Jerry telling me 'Whatever you focus on the longest, becomes the strongest,' I went into seclusion for almost two years. I studied the Bible and took to memory all the scriptures I could find about being a new creation. I researched about being grafted into a new vine and what it meant to be a member of God's family. I got Godly women mentors in my life. I learned from them how to be a wife and a mother. I didn't want religious women, to be perfectly honest; I cannot stand them. I wanted women who loved God and were at peace. Practically the only music I would listen to was praise and worship. Most of the TV programs I watched were Christian teaching programs. It was life-changing for me. My life since that day has been far from perfect. But it was so much better than it was before. One of my key scriptures was, 'God's grace is sufficient,' and it always has been. For some reason, it's no longer working for me now. It has been a daily battle for me to be at peace. But, for the most part, it worked."

"Wow! That's extraordinary. It did work, Veronica. You are here; you're alive and now it is time for the next step. God wants to heal you from your past. God wants you to be free."

"Why now?"

"Only God knows the answer to that question. But His timing is perfect."

Those simple words were the beginning of a miraculous journey. It was the path to redemption. The Lord would use Dr. Storm as my trail guide while I was searching for my answers. I didn't know at the time that my answers could only be found in my mental storage room by examining the contents of each box. It was going to be a long, exhaustive, trip, but definitely one worth taking. There were still so many boxes, so many secrets to unpack. I would now cling to Dr Storm's powerful, life-giving words—"God wanted me free."

CHAPTER FOUR:

Religious Code of Silence

As I left Dr. Storm's office, I knew I had had a huge breakthrough. Now, would the Lord let it be, would He respect the storage shelf's delicate balance? On the drive back home, I couldn't help but to contemplate the power of the contents of the containers I had revealed. Not all the memories are mine; of course, I am merely the storage keeper. As a child, I appointed myself the storage keeper of the family secrets for the sake of my own sanity. Because the major events were never discussed, uncertainty would creep in and challenge my memory. Madness was imminent if the memory could not be located. To thwart this, the recalled incident needed to be maintained securely, even if only for my own sake

Being the collector of such articles had come with a great personal cost. I concluded, over the years, that my family never wanted me to accurately recall the events that unfolded in our home. We were known as the perfect church-going family, one that people aspired to be. Our reputation was of utmost concern in my family. Having a mom and dad as leaders in the church, our secrets needed to be watchfully guarded. Disobedience would not be tolerated; it might blemish the image of perfection we had worked so hard to achieve. Threats were used to ensure no child went astray. One such threat was that, before we were even teenagers, my sister and I were told that if ever we came home pregnant, our bags would be left on the front porch and we were never to return. This was effective in keeping us girls in line. Having a mom who was chronically depressed and raging in our teen years went against our family's perfect appearance. My father would deny that any anger or sorrow could exist in an ideal Christian family such as ours. Depression was not a valid disease when Christian excellence is the exterior for all to see. He did not see why his wife needed any earthly counselor if she had a personal relationship with Jesus, "The Counselor." Protecting our family name was our motto, and no one dared to question the creed.

Being the family's self-appointed memory keeper could be grueling. I tried to console myself that there was a positive aspect with the position. When you are the one who holds the key to the storage closet, then you are the one in power, you are in control. You collaborate with the subconscious in leveling the playing field of your mind. Being totally out of control, while the events took place, the subconscious, would demand to be the one in charge with the coping process. Only it could determine at what time the memories are to surface and how much exposure they are to receive.

My subconscious would summon the memories when a family member tried to rewrite a prior event. This would happen on a regular basis. When we reminisced about our family history, stories of a happy Christian home were the

only ones expressed. They would discuss—with true conviction—perfect parenting, unconditional love, Godly en-
vironment, and having raised well-behaved children.
Anyone within earshot of the recollections about our perfect
family were in awe that such a family existed. No one mentioned the criminal acts, sexual deviance, depression, or
abusive behaviors.

For example, our mom would continually tell us how
blessed we were that she was our mother, that, even though
she was abused, she never abused us. It was as if the depression that ultimately led to her hospitalization never existed. The outbursts, insults, and cruel manipulations were
entirely erased from the pages of our family history.

When I corrected their false reminiscences, I would be
shunned and made the offender. Emotional weapons
would be used to silence me. Withdrawing all outward affection and approval was one of the favorite weapons of
choice. Money also was used as a form of manipulation and
a unit of measurement for my worth and value. This man-
agement was used well into my adult years. There were
many instances that I could recall of such treatment. On one
such occasion, my mom was scheduled for an operation to
remove some cancerous growths.

My sister and I quickly volunteered to help my mom
with the recovery process. My parents purchased my sister
an airline ticket. She stayed for the first week of my mom's
return from the hospital. I was scheduled to fly up the following week and would need to purchase my own ticket,
arrange for my four children to be taken care of, and have
my husband take off work to help with the weekly duties.

While there, I would run various errands, cook, clean, and wake up in the middle of the night to administer medication to my mother. My mom's illness was taking a toll on my dad. He looked like the walking dead. He would go to work, come home, take care of the yard and animals and start it all over again the next day. He was glad to not have to take off time from work while my sister and I were there, so he could use his vacation time to help her after we left.

On the third night of my visit, it occurred to me that I needed to purchase my children's Halloween costumes. After cooking dinner and making sure I had properly cleaned the kitchen, folded the laundry and given my mom her medication, I asked my dad to borrow his car to run the errand.

Immediately, my mom yelled from her bedroom. "No, don't let her take the car, she will use our gas."

Knowing they had purchased my sister's airline ticket, and not mine, was a fact I would have to overlook. By her own admission, my sister had full access to their car taking shopping breaks to help ease the workload. Never clear on what my actual offense was, I would work tirelessly to regain their love and favor. Looking at my father I said, "OK, I'll put gas in the car before I return."

She spoke up once more and said, "It's not just gas, it is the use of the tires and overall wear and tear of the car."

No longer addressing my dad, I said to my mom, "I'll fill the tank with gas to make up the difference of the cost."

Appearing as though he didn't want to choose a side, my dad reluctantly gave me the keys to go purchase the costumes for my kids.

It was of grave importance to remind me of my role in the family. Never clear on my violations, the punishments were always read loud and clear. This time the message was: my sister is worth the price of an airline ticket and unlimited access to the car while in town. My mom is worth the price of my purchased airline ticket and a week's worth of labor. I, however, am not worth the price of a quarter tank of gas. It was a reprimand for an unknown infraction of the creed.

Therefore, when deceptive memoirs of perfection were presented at family gatherings, I would have to get the key, unlock the storage closet, and examine the appropriate containers. After careful inspection of the evidence, the truth could be determined. Of course, I wouldn't show the family member the truthful memory. It seemed that accurate record keeping was not tolerable in our family dynamic. Mentally documenting the events was my one anchor to reality. This way, no family member would be able to take away what was rightfully mine, the truth.

Now home, I felt as though I was in a daze and walking through a mental fog. I was in extreme pain and numb all at the same time. Although somewhat relieved to have shared my painful memories, I had the excruciating task of dealing with them. In Dr. Storm's office, a Pandora's box had been opened; there simply was no turning back.

I began to shake at the mere remembrance of the stories that were divulged. Rewinding the events of my life would be a continual process. It was of utmost importance to try to remember the dates and times of my childhood. Doubt was present and could only be conquered if the memory had a time stamp on it. If I was ever questioned, the memories must be able to stand up to the toughest of prosecutors and hold up under full scrutiny.

While playing the mental tapes continuously in my mind, I saw it again: the ominous box on the top shelf that always caused my heart to leap in fear. As always, I chose simply not think about that particular hideous event. There was enough to work through without that incident having to be in the mix.

It was hard to know how to pray for some reason. It appeared that God must be angry and punishing me. Why else did He take over the command post of my memory collection? For years, I had successfully discounted and ignored my painful past. But God was not letting it go. Timidly I asked, "Why God? Why now? What awful thing have I done that You need to punish me, by dealing with those memories? I thought the Bible was clear about not looking back and dwelling on the past. Now, for some unexplainable reason, You have taken Your grace from me. Was I complaining because, if I was, I'm sorry? Was I not thinking on the right things or quoting enough scriptures every day? I'll do better, I promise. Just please help me again. Your grace has always been enough until now. Is it possible that You too get pleasure from my pain?"

Finally, God spoke and what He said would be my compass for my journey. *Conceal, Reveal, Deal and Heal. Veronica, there is a four step process to a person's total healing.* He repeated the same four words, *Conceal, Reveal, Deal and Heal.' It is important that we return to the places of pain so I can heal you from all your past hurts. I want to make you whole.*

You have always wanted to go from "Conceal" to "Heal" but that will never bring you true healing. You're right, I have allowed you to get by all these years, but My love will not permit it any longer. I want you whole. I want to heal you. Veronica, I want you to be free."

The problem was that no one knew about my past. That was intentional. Not for the sake of deception, my past was too awful to disclose. What will they do when they find out? How am I supposed to live with the shame? Then, of course, there is the matter of my husband and children— what will I do about them? Not to mention my friends and fellow church leaders—they will think I have been hiding this from them all these years. They'll think I was lying and pretending I was someone I wasn't. I'll lose them; I'll lose everything!

For the life of me, I couldn't figure out what grace was for. My dialogue with God continued.

"What benefit was it for me to know the scriptures, claim the promises, if it doesn't work?" I thought grace was to relinquish the memories. Grace was promised to be sufficient. It seems absurd and even cruel to have me revisit the painful memories of my childhood. My doctrine of grace seemed to be incorrect, but I really didn't know what I was missing.

Conceal, Reveal, Deal and Heal that's all you need to know for now," He said again. *You will better understand it as we go along.*

I had no idea what the process would look like, but I

would hold onto those words as the compass for my journey.

****

The next night, Jerry and I were planning on going out to dinner. Should I tell him about the session with Dr. Storm? If I did, how would he take the information? To have held on to a secret for our twenty-three years of marriage might be like a slap in the face to him. Being Jerry's self-appointed protector from my past was not even known to him. I didn't want the revelation about my family to be something he would have to face.

While driving to make our dinner reservations, I swallowed hard and spoke. "You know I saw Dr. Storm yesterday, right?"

"Yes," he said.

"I know I asked you not to ask me questions about the session, but I'm ready to talk about it now."

Jerry looked at me deciding if he was supposed to say something and then figured he shouldn't. He smiled and nodded, as to not interrupt my train of thought.

I continued. "Well, at the time I thought it was personal but I have rethought that idea."

"OK, are you comfortable with telling me now?"

"Yeah, but I don't think you're going to understand, and I wouldn't blame you if you didn't."

Now the tension in the car was tangible. I began to recap the session with Dr. Storm from the day before. Trying to outline with clarity, for the first time, I told him the detailed disturbing facts about the babysitter. With great caution, I began telling him about my brother's violations towards me in my childhood home. Then doing what had always come natural, I remembered my role. I was my family's protector and guardian of secrets.

"Please don't be mad at him Jerry. You see why he did it; you can understand how it could happen, right? After what the babysitter did to him, he couldn't help but act out, I guess. I almost didn't tell you because I was afraid you wouldn't understand and that you might want to confront him. That can never happen, Honey, please tell me you won't do that!"

Jerry was considerably more calm and understanding than I would have thought him to be. "Your parents didn't call the police? They didn't get him help or help you and your sister?"

"No, it never occurred to me the police should have been called."

"Of course, it shouldn't have occurred to you, Veronica; you were only seven. They were the adults. What did they think would happen?"

Again, the ghastly images of the traumas were sprawled out on the table of my mind. "I don't know what my parents were thinking. I just know that it affected my brother, sister and I more than I ever gave it credit."

As though reading a horrifying movie script, I continued with my recollections. "My poor brother must have been so terrified and confused while it was happening to him." With a wealth of emotion, slowly and almost in an undertone I recounted, "I'll always remember my brother's face when the babysitter opened the door to leave his room. He was so frightened and his little face was red and soaked with tears. As I looked into his room, I could see him shaking, balled up in a corner crying. When he saw my sister and I standing there, in shame he turned away. He quickly struggled to get dressed but he was too disturbed to do it effectively. It was horrifying. I didn't know what to do, so I walked away. I never said a word to him that night. That is a decision that haunts me to this day."

Jerry listened in shocked silence as he heard the horrifying tales for the first time. I asked, "Are you going to be OK with my brother, now that you know what he did to me?"

He thought for a moment. "I think so, after all, he was a victim too. Are you going to be able to be around your brother now?"

A little disorientated, I murmured, "I think so. I really have no other choice."

Then I started to think about how gruesome his assault and my molestations were. It occurred to me that most would not have survived experiences like those. My heart began to be flooded with gratitude. God had incredibly spared me all these years from what should have been my rightful fate. I ought to have lost my mind. I had said it so flippantly the day before in Dr. Storm's office, but His grace was the only thing that spared my life. It was my sustainer all these years. I wonder why He took it away. I was now in for the fight of my life, *my sanity*.

****

Any soldier would testify that the battle for freedom is often a bloody one. Freedom is something that you must fight for, and there will always be casualties. You shouldn't go to war unless you have considered its fee. My emotional, mental, physical and spiritual well-being was on the line. The struggle was for my independence from the boxes that had held me captive for so many years.

After that night, I began experiencing the wonderful feeling of liberation. I was basking in the knowledge that I had faced one of my biggest fears, telling someone a portion of my past, and I actually survived. It would seem as if all my troubles were gone. The scriptures tell us that the truth will set us free. I felt for the first time in my life that I was truly free, and it was exhilarating!

My mind was still racing, compiling time lines and record keeping. *How, what, when* and *where* were all questions that must be answered for me to achieve complete inner peace. In my estimation, at that step, sleep was an unnecessary luxury. My mind would not allow me to stop for slumber until all past incidents had been carefully documented. When that was accomplished, they were logged on my inventory sheet and placed back up on their shelf.

One of the first things I needed to do was bring my friends in on my secrets. Determining to have people know the truth about my past was no small task. Everyone in my life already thought they knew all about me, so how could

I present the information? For some reason, I found I could no longer tolerate living the illusion I had masterfully created. I felt as though all my friends who didn't know the real me, couldn't rightfully qualify as friends. Only people who knew my past and knew me beyond my fake exterior, but loved me just the same, could be categorized as real friends.

My circle of influence at church was also coming under examination. Continuing to hide behind my masks and pretence was something I found impossible to do. I wanted genuine closeness with a passion. Not being concerned with what they thought about me wouldn't be simple, but it had to be done. I had to risk rejection in order to walk in the new freedom I had been given. I had to admit that living a life in secrecy, not being truly known, was a lonely life. Always feeling like there was something that couldn't be revealed about you is extremely isolating. I had lived with the assumption that if anyone knew the stories from my past, it would completely disqualify me from their friendship. Now, aware that I have never known true closeness was like a punch in the gut. Intimacy was something I started to crave, and I was willing to do what it took to achieve it.

With that objective in mind, I decided my best friend Michele would be the first to know. It was on her advice that I ended up in Dr. Storm's office. I set a lunch date with her and was a little nervous about what would transpire. It was the first time seeing her since my session with Dr. Storm. Knowing she would surely ask how things were going, I anxiously awaited the opportunity to fill her in. It was a funny thing to turn a corner in your mind so quickly:

one minute, I was living making sure my secrets wouldn't come out; the next minute, I yearned for them to be known.

Michele and I had been friends for over fifteen years. We met at a moms' group in church many years ago. Desperately seeking the friendship of other young mothers, I decided to try the newly formed group. Nervous because I didn't know anybody, I entered the large room where over two hundred moms were gathering.

After checking in, I was directed to a table of women where I would sit every week for the twelve-week session. I had been raised in church, so I understood getting to know churched women was no easy assignment. It seemed to me that there is some sort of handbook out there for churched women. One of the chapters clearly states that, when in the presence of other churched women, it is customary to be unreal and superficial. You must present yourself as a well-packaged person of perfection in order to be accepted by others.

Not that I am one to judge, of course. I was a girl who lived by that handbook. Heck, I think I might have authored some of the chapters myself. I followed it religiously, and I do mean religiously! It can take weeks to get to know the real woman. Given the fact that I had nothing but time on my hands it would be worth the endeavor.

Michele greeted us and introduced herself as the table leader for our group. She asked each of us to take turns and introduce ourselves. We were to share about our families and why we joined the group. It would appear as though each of us had referred to our handbook that morning. We had securely placed our insincere masks of perfection on before even leaving our houses. Each mom beamed as she gushed about her baby as though she had the corner on the market of happiness. No one mentioned the physical fatigue or emotional exhaustion that naturally comes with the motherhood package.

Not to be outdone, when it was my turn to share, I gave the brief description of what sounded like a perfect life: a husband whom I dearly loved and two daughters who were one and two years old. I loved my mask. It was everything I wanted to be when I actually grew up. All of us sat there satisfied with our sappy presentations; then it was Michele's turn. How was I to know that she didn't refer to the handbook before she left her home?

"Hi, like I said, I'm Michele and I'll be your table leader. To be perfectly honest, I don't even want to be here. My husband made me join this group. He said I don't get out of the house enough and that I read entirely too many books. Anyway, I knew the only way I would, in fact, show up is if I had to. So, I volunteered for leadership. After exploring the various positions, I chose table leader because it seemed the least of the grouping. Really, I don't care much for women, never have. I think they can be petty and catty, but I thought I would give this a shot."

I am not even kidding you; that's exactly what she said. You can't make stuff like this up! I could only think, *Holy crud, how did this happen?* I came here looking for friends, and I have a table leader who doesn't even want to be here or like women to boot! I wondered if it was too late to put in for a table transfer. Clearly being desperate for leaders, they would take anyone with a pulse.

After several weeks, Michele called to see if I wanted to have a play date with our kids. Lord knows I didn't have anything else on my calendar, so we agreed to meet, and the rest is history. When I arrived at the fast food place, she was sitting there with a book. I thought this might be two hours of my life that I'll never get back. Much to my delight she put down the book, and the conversation flowed with ease. Since that day, we have potty trained our kids together, weathered the first days of kindergarten, run the course of my two additional pregnancies and now are in the process of sending our kids off to college. We have held each other in the strictest of confidence about the deep secrets of our life, children and marriage. She is, as you would say "my sister from another mister."

Michele is truly one of the most genuinely authentic people I know. If ever given that stupid handbook for churchwomen, she would burn it! What you see is what you get and that would prove to be a breath of fresh air. She had always been so open about her childhood memories and experiences.

Choosing to tell her there were things she didn't know about me was a huge leap. Her always being open and vulnerable would make it look like I had been living a lie. Having her mistakenly think I kept quiet about my past because I didn't trust her was a great concern of mine. I would never want to wound such a valuable friendship.

We had decided to meet at one of our favorite sidewalk cafes in the community where I lived. It was another beautiful spring day. The sun was warm and inviting. The flowerbeds were absolutely radiant with vivid bright colors and fragrances. The petals splashed reds, oranges, yellows and pinks across the landscape. As usual, we picked a table outside so we could enjoy the warmth of the sun. The server delivered our fresh green salads that were garnished with sliced strawberries, candied walnuts, and a freckling of feta cheese. With a refill of iced tea, we were ready to catch up on the details of our lives. Wasting no time, Michele plunged in and asked how my counseling sessions were progressing.

Not wanting to leave out even the smallest of details, I slowly began to tell her what had transpired in counseling. I divulged secrets regarding my family history, the babysitter, and how my brother sexually violated me on and off for close to six years. I watched her intently to see the reaction I would receive.

She sat back in her chair and listened closely to each word as I spoke it. No longer bothering to eat, she became serious, looking deep into my eyes, giving the conversation her undivided attention. With an expression of compassion, she began to comfort me. "I'm so sorry that happened to you. I can't believe this, Veronica; why do you think it's coming out now?"

"For the life of me, Michele, I have no idea."

She began to probe and ask questions wanting to learn more about the newly revealed facts of her long-time friend. "What made you keep it a secret?"

"Well, as strange as this is going to sound, I thought it was normal, disgusting but normal. You only have sisters so it would not have occurred to me to bring up the subject knowing it was not something you ever had to deal with."

We continued talking and enjoying our lunch. After a while I said, "Ugh, I hate this."

"What do you hate?"

"I hate being included in that horrible club. I have spent my life not wanting to have that label placed on me, and now it's out for all to see."

"OK, you got me, what club are you referring to?"

" 'The incest survivors club.' It's totally revolting! No one was to know, I never wanted to talk about it. But, oh no, here I am a card-carrying member of that horrible, horrible club."

"Well, I have good news and bad news for you, Veronica. The good news is, you are not a card-carrying member of the incest survivors club."

"Thank you, Michele," I said with a huge smile.

"The bad news is, apparently you're the freaking CEO!"

Obviously, the smile had completely left my face. "Yeah, you know the 'thank you' I gave you? Well, I'm totally taking it back."

Michele said, laughing, "I know it sucks Veronica, but *it is what it is*. You did not choose your childhood or family, it was chosen for you. No one has the power to erase and rewrite the pages of their lives. Most of us have things or traumas that we wish were not there, but they remain just the same. It is our task to read those chapters in our book, examine them, learn from them, and go on. Running from those events or pretending they do not exist just perpetuates the madness. You will begin to see, facing the ugliness will prove to be the best thing that could have happened to you. It would be my guess that you will come out of this and be able to help others with what you learned. Just you wait and see—the Lord has some great things in store I just know it."

With those words, my smile returned. We continued our conversation, which was laced with both laughter and tears. We were both famished and began diving into our salads while taking turns talking. After we were finished and ready to go, she gave me a hug and told me she loved me. Leaving the restaurant, we were closer than before we entered.

CHAPTER FIVE

Dealing

Each day I had a whole new zest for living. Telling the women at my bible study group was the next item on the list for me to do. They had been faithfully praying, and I was thrilled to give them the praise report. Filling them in on the details of the past several days had them completely riveted. I expressed that as strange as it sounded, *I felt like I have met Veronica for the first time.*

Seeing the look of understanding on their faces would be my reward. The prize was well worth the claiming. My secrets didn't push them away; on the contrary, it drew them close. In the big jigsaw puzzle of my life, the pieces had begun to fall into place. Aspects of my personality started to clarify themselves with my newfound insight. I was eager to keep learning how to live free from having my past dominate who I was today. I craved knowing "why I do what I do."

Learning what was "normal" was also a continual quest of mine. I no longer trusted my ability to assimilate my experiences and family dealings, so I found myself telling some carefully chosen friends various recollections about my history and observe their responses. I then took their reaction as being the correct one, and then placed that memory in its proper grouping. The need to have outsiders accurately label my boxes could be a little disheartening.

Talking to God was no longer a problem. Sleeping for the first time in weeks was another great prize. It was a lot easier to face life challenges when I was rested and had the presence of mind to cope. I was enjoying everything. Life was sweet, relationships were intact and there appeared to be no disadvantage to the experience. I was aware that it was by the grace of God that I had survived as many years as I did. God's grace is real, and it can save you, even if you aren't aware that its power is active in your life.

Jerry and I were doing so much better as well. Of course, not all our problems were gone. We did, however, seem to approach them in an entirely different manner. He actually said, "I know we've been married for twenty-three years, but I feel like I'm meeting my wife for the first time." There was sadness mixed in with a statement like that. But his support would be one of the life rafts I would cling to when the sinking feelings returned.

I continued to be satisfied with my decision in not confronting my brother. Why upset an apple cart that is rickety at best? If I were to tackle this, there might be applesauce spewed everywhere! He was married with kids of his own. I simply didn't see the benefit in bringing such a nasty subject like that up. I did wonder, though, if he had thought about it as much as I had over the years. Only one of us should have to do time for the offense, and I would gladly serve it. In my assessment, he had already suffered his fair share of pain and dishonor.

Then something totally unexpected occurred. It was several weeks after the revealing session with Dr. Storm. After basking in the feeling of being free from my past, it happened. Suddenly, like an unwelcome nighttime intruder, I felt psychologically and emotionally ambushed. The feelings of elation were starting to cease. The joy and rest from my findings were being ripped from my very being. I was trying to hold on to the sense of peace as if my life depended on it. Freedom looked like a distant memory. It was as if it had become a carrot on a string held out to tease me. Was it ever in my possession at all? Just a few weeks earlier, I thought the truth had set me free. It appeared now that the truth might be the catalyst to my undoing.

****

It occurred to me that, while reading about the deliverance of the Israelites from the Egyptians, it's hard not to condemn. The constant doubting, whining, and overall annoying behaviors of God's children would have us think we are above such conduct. By golly, we put on our judge's robes, and, with our gavels firmly grasped in our hands, we cast down certain judgment. Reading of manna in the wilderness, quail for the asking, pillar of fire by night and a glorious cloud by day, we criticize their constant disbelief. Knowing if we were in their place, we most certainly would see God's continual provision and never allow such ingratitude to invade our heart.

They were traveling to the Promised Land and, because

it took some strenuous effort on their part, they wanted to quit. How quickly they forgot the pain of their enslavement, so they announced their desire to return to captivity. To have them constantly declare they wanted to return to the oppression of Egypt is more than we can comprehend.

As I dressed in my judicial garments to cast my verdict, I realized I was not one who could rightfully condemn. I also wanted to return to my place of captivity. It was all I had ever known. It appeared that there would be some grueling mental and emotional work ahead for me to make it to my "Promised Land." I began to doubt my decision to launch on such a journey. To set out on this new life of freedom, in the unknown territory of my mind, would be daunting at best. I had been conditioned over the span of my life to be comfortable in my discomfort. I distrusted my initial evaluation that I possessed the strength to take on the giants that kept me in bondage.

Now the path that led me to this place was the path where I wanted to return. What it would take to gain the victory in my battle for freedom started to overwhelm me. If I had known that all my boxes were going to have their contents carefully examined, I might not have begun this perilous voyage. The reality had begun to set in like a ten-ton weight. I didn't know breathing could actually become a chore. Although thrilled I was no longer the guardian of the secrets, now I had to face the ruthless reality of my life. Great mourning started to overtake me as I dealt with such truths.

Daytime proved to be the easiest part of the day. Getting out of bed, taking kids to school, continuing with my church leadership duties were all in a day's work. While performing these ordinary tasks, it felt at times like I was in a dream state, not being fully awake even though my eyes were wide open. I kept reassuring myself that God was in control, it was necessary for these artifacts to surface. No one should have to live with such memories and pretend they were not valid.

Realizing I couldn't be trusted about my past evaluations, I obsessed that I had mis-labeled other incidents as well. I would need to unpack more boxes. However, before I was able to get too far in the process, the first two exposures were beginning to plague me. Nighttime came to be something I dreaded the most. The flashbacks began to taunt me and did not let me sleep. I would shake at the hideous images from the traumas so many years ago. I tried not to replay the tape, but for some reason it was on constant rewind. Night frights were the worst of all. I would go to bed shaking and crying, as I was mentally reliving those terrible days. Finally crying myself to sleep, I would awaken in terror as though I was that frightened girl all over again.

Why did it have to hurt so badly and be unrelenting in its effort to ridicule my endeavor to sleep? To make matters worse, my body would betray me as well. I would feel the sensations as though they were happening in the present and not the past. How could physical feelings be so real when the perpetrator wasn't present? This seemed to be one of the cruelest jokes of all. My husband would reach over to comfort me, and I would jump at his touch. How unfair for him to receive the reaction that only the person to blame was rightfully due.

As if the mental images weren't bad enough, reflecting on my thought process at the time when I was eleven years old, would almost emotionally cripple me. I recalled waking up in the morning those summer months wondering what my brother had in mind for the day. Would my brother approach me? I remembered being told by my brother that he chose me because I was special, would invoke a childish desire in me to please him. Having him create special games to introduce the sex acts to me would haunt me as I remembered those horrifying days. Back then, such playful games made it all seem so innocent, so harmless. I couldn't shake his voice, his face and his instructions as the relentless perverse videos played out in my mind's eye.

I was repulsed that my brother would betray my love and loyalty and use it for his own wicked pleasure. His words would ring in my ears as I remembered him telling me how he had planned for months to be with me. He appeared so pleased that his choreographed plan had come together. His words spun a web of deceit that made me feel at the time that I must be special if he thought I was worth such an effort. I was so confused in those moments. It was not the violence I had witnessed four years earlier. This made it seem like less of an offense and I felt sincere gratitude that he was never physically violent. I knew he could have overpowered me, so in some sort of warped explanation, I felt a sense of obligation and appreciation for his approach.

I couldn't make sense of anything, what was right, what was wrong. He loved me enough and trusted me to be the one who would keep the secret. I felt so grown up and set apart. I was aghast that I had the gruesome task of sorting my recollections, such evilness, out in my younger years.

I found myself hating the fact I didn't stop him or tell anyone. Self-loathing was overpowering much of the anger I had felt towards my brother. I was too busy blaming myself for those awful days. Did the fact that I obeyed my brother that summer, by participating in the sexual games, make me his accomplice?

I wrestled with the fact that, because he never penetrated me, that made it less of a violation, right? In my twisted rationale, growing up, I actually thought, because he never entered inside me, that proved his love and concern for me. I figured he knew his penetration would have caused me pain, and, in his love, he spared me. Now I questioned if that was his way of protecting himself.

Then, in a giant leap, my mind would inadvertently switch mental soundtracks to my brother's sexual assault at the hands of the ruthless babysitter. I could hear him pleading for mercy, begging her to stop inflicting such pain. As though I was listening to a tape recording whose volume I could not turn down, I would hear the demands from her lips for him to remove all of his clothes. I would cover my ears in a futile effort to stop the sounds of his wailing from long ago.

I recalled her telling him to touch himself and then her. If he didn't obey, I would hear the striking of her hand against his bare skin while making him chant his apologies. He begged her repeatedly to stop pulling, which at the time I had no knowledge of what she was doing. I could hear him continually say "Please stop, it hurts, it hurts, it hurts...." She would demand he say certain phrases and that he had to make requests of her. Again, if he refused or begged not to, I would hear her hit him ensuring his obedience. The sounds of my brother's sexual torture would roll inside my head with no way for me to stop them.

I could see in my mind's eye my sister and I with our ears fixed firmly against my brother's bedroom door. Too scared to speak, we would look at each other in complete desperation not knowing what to do. Before the assault became violent, my sister and I would nervously giggle upon hearing what was going on behind the closed door. When the babysitter began the torture, we were horrified and gasped; then, we quickly covered our mouth with our hands so she wouldn't hear us. As a child, to hear your brother crying out in agony and feel so powerless to help him defies all human comprehension.

In my seven-year-old state, I wanted to leave but felt as though some imaginary glue had fixed me in place. When would it end? Suddenly, without warning, the babysitter opened the door. Terrified, my sister and I looked up to see her staring down at us. In horror, I wondered if I would be next. *Do I run or do I stay?* I wanted to escape but felt utterly immobilized as though I was a measly statue set in cement. In an icy authoritative tone, she told us that we were never to tell anyone what we just heard.

"If you try and tell someone, no one will believe you. If I find out that you have told, I will come back and kill you."

Not knowing what else to do, my sister and I nodded our heads in complete submission.

These flashbacks made me feel sorry for my brother and excuse his sexual misdeeds towards me. I reasoned the recollections were enough evidence to conclude that I was not allowed to hold him accountable for his crimes against me.

It felt as though I was losing my mind. I never wanted to think about the evil, perverse events of my childhood. Why was God allowing those thoughts and images to torment me? At that point, I wasn't even bothering to pray. A Heavenly Father to forsake His daughter was more than I could comprehend. Then He would speak to me. *"Veronica, I know you think I have abandoned you but trust Me, I have not. Remember I told you? There was a four-step process to true healing; well, this is step three, and it is the hardest one of all. As a matter of fact, most people refuse this step altogether. Nevertheless, it is of utmost importance that you go through the "Dealing" portion of the journey. I haven't left you, I AM here, I have always been here. But, if you're not willing to feel the pain, then I can't give you the healing that is rightfully yours. I want to heal you. I want you to be free."*

"God, this is barbaric! No one should have to endure this. How am I going to survive this step? I didn't even know it was possible for me to hurt so hard or so deep."

"Veronica, these feelings are not new. The wounded emotions have been in you the whole time. I have always known the pain the traumas have caused you, and it's my desire to release you from their torment. However, I can't take something away that you won't even admit exists. Feel them, grieve for them and acknowledge the pain; it is all a part of the process."

With those words, I lay on the sofa sobbing, clinging to a pillow as if it was my floatation device in a sea of emotions. I couldn't stand that I had to feel the pain. My body would shake violently with images from those first two boxes. Nothing seemed to stop the inner torment. I hurt in places I never even knew existed. It felt as if my heart was truly going to break into a million different pieces.

Ultimately, I said, "God, I will trust You; I simply have no other choice." With that inner vow, I dozed off for a couple of hours and then was awoken by fright of another terrifying memory. There was no place of escape in the recesses of my mind. Day after day and night after night, this would be my fate. Whether awake or asleep, the memories would require my undivided attention. They demanded to be seen, felt, and understood for the horrifying events that they actually were.

I needed a fellow soldier to help combat the attack mounted against me. Knowing who it was, I picked up the phone and called to make an appointment with Dr. Storm. I was in way over my head; no one was meant to do this alone.

Now all the recollections that had been stored in their own individual boxes were beginning to unpack themselves. The lids were popping off one by one. Yes, freedom was something worth fighting for. I had considered its fee and determined it was worth the asking price. To my surprise, my journey had only just begun.

****

Landing back in Dr. Storm's office, it had occurred to me that I was no longer in marriage counseling—I was in

80

Veronica counseling. Funny thing was that I still didn't know if therapy was a valid choice for a Christian. Holding fast to my dad's belief that Christians were not supposed to need emotional or psychological help, I felt a little torn about it. Either the work at the cross was enough or it isn't. I saw no gray area in this.

If a Christian wasn't experiencing victory in a troubled area of life, then he or she simply didn't know how to tap into His goodness. I always thought that to go get the help of a therapist was like slapping God in the face. Actually, that was not entirely true. I did believe in counseling, just not for me. It was reserved for those who weren't disciplined enough to get into God's Word, work it, and patiently wait for the results. If you didn't have a strong inner constitution to walk by faith and not by feelings, by all means, get counseling.

It seemed to me that I was in this battle because I didn't admit to myself that negative feelings and God could inhabit the same place. Never giving myself permission to be hurt or angry had almost cost me everything. If ever a bad thought or memory tried to surface, I would simply pray it away. Singing praises was a great temporary distraction, but the inner turmoil still raged. It was like a temporary high for an addict in need of a fix

God had called me to a place He referred to as *"Dealing."* What was this place and how was I to navigate through it? No longer seeking temporary fixes or highs, I insatiably hungered for real answers. Determining not to pray the contents of the boxes away, I would face them with the grit of a warrior.

Sitting across from Dr. Storm, I was resolved to be my true self. His office was proving to be a safe haven from the illusionary world I created. He would be able to see past the lie of my artificial appearance of a woman who had it all together. Knowing he had no connection to my social circle, I spoke without inhibitions.

"I had a great week. I was calm, happy and sleeping for the first time in weeks. I know this sounds kind of odd, but I feel like I have met Veronica for the first time."

Dr. Storm smiled. "You feel like you met yourself for the first time? That's incredible, Veronica. What's that like for you?"

"I don't really know how to explain it. It's as if I'm getting to know myself and understand some things I never did before. But then I started having horrible flashbacks."

Before I could continue with our conversation, it happened. Those stupid, sharp, uncontrollable shakes started to take over. It was like electrodes were being shot through my body. My body began to quake and quiver at the mere thought of my recollections.

"I can't seem to stop this. My body starts to shudder when I think of what we talked about last time." I sat on my hands trying to override the circuits in my brain that sent out the shockwaves. "The flashbacks are consistent and totally unmanageable. The thing is, I don't think I'm supposed to control them. I do hate the trembling though. When do you think it will stop?"

"There really is no time line on things like this. But, the more you are willing to talk about the events, the faster it will pass. All these memories have been bottled up for so

long; they are in need of a release. Your body is simply trying to expel the effects of those incidents in the only way it
knows how."

"Can I ask you something?" I inquired.

"Sure, what is it?"

"Well, I've been thinking about what my brother did,
and I think I totally overreacted. I mean, calling it molestation seems a little over the top. Perhaps it was just a child's
sexual curiosity and not molestation. I feel we were a little
hard on him."

Dr. Storm seemed concerned with my vacillation.
There was a certain way he handled himself when he
needed to clarify something that always reminded me of
a teacher. He would become incredibly serious; appearing as though he was concentrating on choosing just the
right words so, he could adequately relay his point. His
eyes would turn thoughtful; then he would lean forward
in his chair, look me in the eyes and begin his explanation.
With a studious expression, he said, "There are several differences that distinguish between simple childish behavior and what is classified as molestation. In your case,
there is over a two-year age difference between you and
your brother. He was a teenager and you were only
eleven. The age difference is the first thing that always
comes into check. You also said he had done several
things earlier that summer to lure you into what would
take place. That's a huge red flag. Another thing that calls
his behavior into question is the fact he knew it was wrong
and swore you to secrecy. Your parents left him in charge
that summer while everyone was away. You were vul-

nerable and trusted him. He took advantage of the situation and you."

I was unable to abandon my own feelings of blame. "I didn't fight him off, I should have, but didn't. It was all so confusing at the time. I feel like I am also responsible. I shouldn't have allowed him to do it."

"Veronica, what were you supposed to do? You trusted him; no one would have expected you to fight. He was your older brother, and you loved him. It would have been way too complex for you to handle at that age. You were introduced to a world that no eleven-year old should be introduced to."

Still unable to partner the two words, brother and molester, I continued to defend him. "Well in some ways I feel grateful to my brother. I mean, he could have completely overpowered me, you know? But he didn't. The babysitter brutalized him, so, if he wanted to, I knew he could have taken me by force. Because he didn't, in some ways I thought I owed him. I know that sounds twisted, but it's true. He controlled himself from being violent. For that, I really am grateful."

Dr. Storm sat back in his chair and didn't appear shocked at my reasoning. He sort of smiled and said, "Yeah, like if a burglar came up from behind you with a gun, pointed it at your head and told you to hand over your money. You obey and give him your money. He takes it and runs away not having pulled the trigger. You actually think you owe him your life because he could have killed you, but he chose not to. That now makes him the good guy. Is that what you mean?"

"Well, yeah I guess so. And by the way, I would be thankful if someone held me up and didn't pull the trigger."

"I know you would, but he still robbed you. The fact that he didn't pull the trigger does not make him the good guy."

His words offered no comfort. I have decided that more boxes needed to come down. Some of the containers I chose were decorated in a glorious array of colored paper. However, one of the boxes was actually wrapped in very plain paper. It is the least adorned package in my storage room. The only exception, on top is the most magnificent bow. This container is unique in that it has a ribbon, cross-hatched, coming up on all four sides. All other boxes with ribbons only have the ribbons on two sides. Looking at all the other packages with their beautiful wrapping paper, one could wrongly conclude this was the least favorite of all my containers. The opposite is true. I treasured this box and its contents more than any other package I have in my inventory. The contents inside are precious, and there was no need to have them hide behind the false covering of beauty.

Unpacking one of the beautiful boxes, I saw some of my conduct during my teen years. I needed to place these artifacts under the microscope for further examination. The contents of these particular boxes were not hard for me to discuss. They involved my behavior, so there would be no betrayal of loyalty.

"I think what happened to me that summer might have started some dangerous actions I had as a teenager."

Looking interested, he asked, "What behaviors?"

"Starting in seventh grade, I began pulling my hair out, strand by strand. I pulled it out so often I actually created a bald spot on the top of my head. A friend noticed it and asked what happened. I was embarrassed, so I told her my hair got caught in the door. That didn't make me stop pulling though. I just learned to pull it out from underneath. Believe it or not, I still have to fight the urge to pull my hair out when things get rough. It has always been some kind of unexplainable release for me."

Then with utmost care, I began to unpack the package. Trying to control my grief, I continued. "Life at home started getting harder. Two years later, my uncle was responsible for the death of his two kids. We were pretty close to them. They only lived about twenty minutes away, so it was really hard on my family."

Dr. Storm sat straight up with this information. "Your uncle was responsible for the deaths of his children?"

"Yes, it was July, so he took his kids to the lake and drank beer the better part of the day and was drunk. When it was time to leave, he loaded my cousins into his camper. They were sleeping on the bed that was on top of the cab of the truck. The witnesses at the scene of the accident said he was driving precariously and they knew he would eventually crash. He did. He lost control of the camper and wound up rolling off the freeway down an embankment. My cousins were thrown out of the vehicle through the camper window. The paramedics figured that my oldest cousin was the first out the window because she had multiple lacerations. Her younger brother was thrown out right behind her. It was awful, the truck landed on top of him and he was pronounced dead at the scene. His older sister was rushed to a hospital. They did all they could to save her, but she was too severely injured. She died later that day."

"That's terrible!" he gasped.

"I know. It was incredibly tragic, as you can imagine. He originally told us a truck had pushed him off the highway. The family believed him. That was, of course, a lie. The next day we went to the airport to pick up my grandparents who had flown in for the funeral. Walking through the airport, we saw the headlines of all the local papers in the newsstands. Right there on the front page: '*Drunken father kills his two kids in car accident*', or something like that. My mom flipped out! She broke down, started crying and wailed, 'He did it, he killed his two kids!' Lots of people were staring; it was quite the scene."

"Then what did the family do?"

"I think it was pretty much a taboo topic. I mean, how do you go to the grieving parents' house and say the children would be alive if it weren't for you? What made it even more unbearable was my aunt's family was there as her support. Can you imagine, being part of the uncle's family when he is the one responsible for the death of their two precious children?"

Choking up, I continued. "The funeral is something I never will forget. Tragic doesn't begin to describe that horrible day. The church was packed with people. It was a large Catholic church and was overflowing with grieving friends, neighbors, and relatives. As customary at funerals, we entered last to help protect our privacy. I can remember walking into the church the day of the funeral like it was yesterday."

I paused momentarily noticing that I could taste the salt from my tears as some rogue drops streamed down my face, past my nose, and into my mouth. I hadn't realized I started crying. I grabbed a tissue from the little sofa table beside me and began to dab my cheeks. Almost in a daze, I continued. "As I entered through the side door, my eyes glanced across to the front of the church. It was adorned with the most beautiful flower arrangements I had ever seen. Then I saw them—two small white caskets. The first thing that popped into my mind at the time was, 'I didn't know they made coffins that small.' My knees buckled; then I collapsed onto the pew. I couldn't move. My mom had my brother push me down to help make room for the rest of the family."

"You could hear the audible sobs from the attendees behind us. There was simply no way to prepare a thirteen-year old girl for such an event. I was practically blubbering sitting behind my aunt and uncle. Did I tell you the age of my cousins when they were killed?"

"No, you didn't Veronica. How old were they?"

"She was five and he was only three. Her little casket had a big pink spray of carnations on top and his had blue ones. Knowing what was lying beneath the pretty flowers was anguishing. The songs and music that were played during the service were absolutely breathtaking. But the real kicker, as sad as it all was, I never saw my uncle crying."

Aghast Dr. Storm asked, "Wait, he wasn't crying?"

"Nope, not that I could see. Pretty unimaginable, huh?"

"Are you sure he wasn't crying?"

"Absolutely," I assured him. "You didn't know my uncle."

I placed the delicate figurines back into their rightful container, lacing the ribbon up on all four sides. This ensures no harm can come to them. I had appointed myself their protector in their death because I didn't feel they were protected in life. I cautiously placed the precious box back up on the shelf that only houses their memories. They are never to be exposed to the other packages in my storage room. It is my duty to keep them safe from cross contamination.

It was becoming apparent I was going to have to unpack more boxes to help Dr. Storm understand. No outsider can comprehend a family like mine without great assistance. I had to usher this kind man into the dark places of my past, so I could answer his probing questions. For some strange reason, I held myself responsible for him having to deal with the unusual contents in my packages. I always have felt the need to protect others from my family. Uncertain if the doctor was ready, I anxiously began to unpack more boxes.

CHAPTER SIX

The Throne Room

Explaining the behavior of a family member to a regular person had always been a great challenge for me. Knowing Dr. Storm would respond in an educated way, would actually work against him. Trying to categorize the behaviors of my family into a typical psychological profile could not be done. I would try to lead him in the direction his mind needed to go for him to be able to analyze my situation correctly. Historically, this proved to be unsuccessful. While trusting him with my carefully guarded secrets, would he think that a family's bloodline is a tie that cannot be broken?

With only half of the session over, we continued our conversation.

"I never did see my uncle cry for what he did. He had to go to a rehab center as part of his sentence. When he finished his required time, he returned to court to face the judge. My mom went with him. She said my uncle stood before the judge completely unremorseful. The judge looked down from his chair and rendered his ruling. He informed my uncle that never in his history on the bench had he seen someone who was so cold and unapologetic for his crime. 'You are responsible for the death of your two kids, but you don't seem to care. If I had my way I would send you to prison.' You see, the laws were different back then towards drunk drivers. So, the judge told my uncle that he had to release him with "time served.'"

"Maybe your uncle was just too devastated to come to terms with what he did? Perhaps it was too overwhelming?"

"I don't think so, but I guess that's a possibility. All I know is, I think my mom was totally different from that day on."

"How was she different?"

"She told me that while she was listening to the judge talk to her brother, it occurred to her that no good comes from her family line. I seriously think her personality changed after that day."

"Really, how so?"

"Depression set in like a haze in our home. She was so sad and upset and didn't seem to feel the need to try to contain her temper. I was on the receiving end of that temper most of the time."

I wished to change the subject off my mom and back to my own behavior. It had always been easier to reveal facts about myself rather than her.

"Anyway, like I was telling you earlier, it was worse in the home at that time. One day I came home from school with a terrible headache. As usual, I came home to an empty house. I took some extra strength pain reliever, but it didn't make a dent in the pain. Desperate, I remembered my mom's prescription for her migraines. I knew I wasn't supposed to, but I got some of her pills and started taking them."

"Started taking 'them'?" he repeated. "How many did you take?"

Thinking for a while, I admitted, "I don't know how many. I remember at the time I thought the pain reliever and the prescription pills could be a deadly combination. I really didn't care."

Dr. Storm waited for me to continue the story.

Obliging, I said. "When my mom came home from work that day, I was passed out on the couch. She must have been trying to wake me up for some time, because, when I did wake up, she was shaking me. She looked at me sternly and asked what I took. I told her I took a couple of pain reliever pills. She could tell I had ingested more than that, so she demanded to know what else I took. I began crying while explaining to her how my head had hurt so badly when I got home. Then I told her that I got into her prescription pills. She asked me how many pills I took, but I didn't know. That was the absolute truth. I really didn't know how many I took."

"By now, my mom was pretty upset with me. She looked down on the couch and said, 'Veronica, you could have overdosed. Do you want to die?' Much to my mom's dismay, I couldn't answer the question. I wanted to say 'no,' but I couldn't get the words to come out of my mouth. This seemed to upset her. Obviously, I didn't give her the answer she was looking for."

"Then what did she do?"

"She told me to get up and make dinner."

Dr. Storm's face became stern and then he remarked, "Your mom thought you almost killed yourself and she told you to make dinner?"

"Yes," I muttered. "That pretty much sums it up. In keeping with the standard protocol of our home, it was never discussed again."

Dr. Storm began writing in my file and asked, "So when you were only thirteen you didn't care if you lived or died?"

"Nope, not at all. I would begin calculating my death from that point on."

"You began to plan your suicide?"

"Yes, actually I was totally obsessed with it."

"I'm glad you didn't go through with it, I'm sure many people are glad," he assured me.

I really don't know if that was true or not, but that was so kind of him to say.

Changing subjects one more time, I said, "I grew up real fast. I even looked old for my age. By the time I was thirteen, I looked sixteen or seventeen. This freaked my mom out, I guess. One day, she called a family meeting when I was fourteen. She said they had done a good job on raising my brother and sister, but they had failed on me. She told me I wasn't allowed to be with friends or keep attending my youth group at church. She claimed I was out of control."

"Why did your mom classify you as out of control?"

"I don't know. It was totally random and unexpected. I was only allowed to go to school and then I would have to go straight home. No phone calls, no friends, no church, no activities. She never would tell me what I did to be on such stringent restrictions. I talked my sister into sneaking notes back and forth to my friends. She secretly agreed. She said if our mom ever found out, she would deny she had any part of it. I told her I would never tell."

"How long did this last?"

"I don't remember how long exactly. It was several months though. One Friday night I was home with my parents. Of course, my brother and sister were out with their friends. My mom walked in while I was crying. She asked me what was wrong. I complained I didn't understand why I wasn't able to go out like my brother and sister always did. I told her I was lonely and I didn't know what I did to get in trouble. She got upset with me for calling her into question. She barked, 'Welcome to my world; I'm lonely too.' She then turned and walked out of the room."

"So you really have no idea why she placed you on restrictions?"

"No, like I said, I often found myself at the receiving end of her anger. She was the mom and didn't feel the need to give me a reason. After several months, I was suddenly released from the punishment. As strange as it sounds, I went from house arrest to practically no limitations at all. Then my philosophy on life became, 'If you have to do the time, you might as well do the crime. I became completely out of control."

Dr Storm was scribbling in my file. He asked, "What do you mean you had 'no limitations'?"

"Oh that's easy, I went out all the time. When I was barely fifteen, I had a boyfriend who was almost nineteen."

Dr. Storm's head snapped up from his notes. He looked completely shocked. His eyebrows were raised, his eyes grew bigger and his mouth opened slightly with no words coming out. I was a little shaken at how disturbing it seemed to him. Again, I found myself using another person's surprised expression as my compass on what was considered abnormal.

Stunned, Dr. Storm exclaimed, "Your parents knew about your boyfriend? They knew how old he was?"

"Sure, they knew."

"Where was your dad while all of this was going on? You only tell me about your mom, where was your dad?"

"My dad was there, he just wasn't very involved."

"Wasn't involved?!" Dr. Storm, objected. "It seems to me, he was totally asleep at the switch! Why would he allow you to be in harm's way like that? No father should allow his teenage daughter to be in that kind of a dating relationship."

Casually, I said, "Gosh, that's nothing. When I was sixteen, I was dating a twenty-five year old. I guess my dad never considered what the man's intentions might be. As you said earlier, my brother introduced me to a world where no young girl belonged."

No sooner had those words left my mouth that I started to understand Dr. Storm's reaction. Why hadn't it occurred to me earlier that this was so absurd? It would *never* enter my mind to allow my teen girls to do anything like that.

"Veronica," cautioned Dr. Storm, "It concerns me that you say your father was the safe one in the home. He was supposed to protect you. Allowing you to be in such inappropriate relationships, never knowing what you were up to is very unacceptable. Fathers show love to their daughters by making sure they are safe. Your life was al-

95

ways in danger, both in the home and out."

This was proving much harder than I originally thought. Trying to explain how our family dynamic worked seemed to be impossible. It's like speaking Swahili to someone who only understands English. In this case, it was like trying to get a normal, healthy person to see the dark side. Too weird and unreal, surely the contents of my hidden container would frighten him away. He might think I was just like the other members of my family. Maybe I could get him to understand without having to reveal what I had chosen to keep in secret.

****

At that point in the session, my brain felt like it was in a cramp. I was defending a brother who molested me and a dad who didn't protect me. How did I get to such an emotionally bankrupt place where I had to choose the lesser of the evils? It was a funny thing to be smack dab in the middle of a behavior that always seemed normal, but then in that office, seemed completely twisted.

Continuing to defend my father, I said, "My dad was the nice one in the family. When my mom was in a bad mood, she would target me. I would try not to crack with the innuendos and her cruel actions. I never wanted her to know she could get to me. Finally, after awhile, I wouldn't be able to hide it any longer. She would see the pain she had inflicted and it seemed to gratify her. I think that satisfied her temporarily because she would back off for a while."

"To be perfectly honest, when you think your mom gets pleasure from your pain, it's pure hell. My dad would never do anything like that. He simply wasn't capable. He would buy me ice cream cones when we went out on errands. I know you might think that the price of loyalty should exceed the price of a treat, but it meant the world to me. Then there is the matter with my sister."

"Your sister was involved too?"

"Yes, my sister had pretty low self-esteem. When she was feeling bad, all she had to do was say to my mom that she wished she was like me. That would set the wheels in motion. My mom would sing her praises and tear me down. One of the worst things she would say was that my sister was beautiful on the inside and that I would never know beauty like that. My sister was also naturally thin. So of course, she would remind my sister of how I would always have to watch my weight. She would say to me with a smile and wink, 'Sorry kid, you got the wrong end of the gene pool.'"

I hated that the subject of my weight came into the session. Looking down, self-consciously, I said, "Not that it matters, I suppose, but I was only a size seven at the time. I always felt like an ugly 600 pound whale by the time they were finished."

"Were there any other times your mom would attack you?"

"Oh sure, she would often tear me down if something good happened to me. It was as if she thought it was her duty to make sure that I didn't think too highly of myself. If something good happened to me, I would need to be reminded I wasn't that great. My happiness wasn't allowed, especially if my sister wasn't happy."

"So, you see Dr. Storm, with a mom who got pleasure from hurting me, a sister who set me up to be insulted so she could feel good about herself, it was intolerable for me. My dad and brother might not have protected me, but they were never out right cruel to me."

Dr. Storm addressed my mistaken conclusion. "Your father should have been keeping a closer eye on you. In the eyes of God, he was responsible for you. He allowed you to be in dangerous dating relationships. By allowing that, it gave you the wrong impression about your worth. Not to mention your dad did nothing to protect you from your mom. A daughter needs her father to keep a safe watchful eye on her and defend her. Trust me; he was not the nice one."

Dr. Storm began his prosecution of my brother. "I know you feel your brother was only seeking his own pleasure and never intended to hurt you, but that concerns me as well. You didn't see him as a threat to you, and maybe you should have. Do you still think you shouldn't confront your brother about what he did?"

"Absolutely," I shrieked. "I will never approach him about it. It would mortify him. It all happened so long ago it's hardly worth bringing up now."

Compassionately he conceded, "OK, Veronica it's entirely up to you."

Our session was concluding, so Dr. Storm would do what we would refer to as *pushing the domino*. This was a question or thought he would pitch for me to contemplate between sessions. I had a "love-hate" relationship with the domino. They were always useful in getting me on the right path, but often my findings were troubling.

"Are you ready for the domino?" Dr. Storm offered.

"Yes, give it to me." I beamed.

"You're probably not going to like this one, but I feel it's necessary."

Puzzled, I stated, "Go ahead, I'm ready."

"You will need to get in touch with your anger towards your father. He let you down, and you have a right to feel hurt by it. Your brother used you for his own pleasure without taking into account what path he would lead you down in your life. His actions set you on some hazardous terrain in your teen years."

"I don't understand. Why is it so important to you that I get angry with them?"

"Because Veronica, a girl bases her self worth on how she is treated by her father. If he didn't protect you or stop the attacks in the home, then you probably don't think you have any value. Essentially, you see yourself through the eyes of your dad. In order for you to know your significance, you have to acknowledge that he didn't keep you safe. Also, you will need to find a way to hold your brother accountable. This might push some buttons this week, but it will get you in the right direction."

Flippantly I declared, "Don't hold your breath. I have no intention on getting mad at the only people who weren't intentionally cruel to me during those years."

Our session was over, and my uncontrollable shakes had, for the time being, stopped. I knew the images were bound to return and my body would rebel at their sight. I had to contemplate the subjects that were discussed in this session later. There was a much grander issue on my mind.

I was determined to find out how to handle the *"Dealing"* part of my journey. I wanted the peace to return. With that in mind, I left his office with another appointment on the calendar. A warrior in the making, I walked out his door.

****

Knowing nighttime was just a few hours away, I began my plan of action. The flashbacks would return; I was sure of that. The emotional, mental and spiritual battle was raging. Now I was a woman on a mission, and nothing would divert me from my cause. I had tasted a sampling of inner peace. I would not be denied tranquility to remain a constant in my life.

If the actual events in my childhood didn't kill me when they happened, I wouldn't give them the award of slaying me now. The contents of the boxes were no longer in need of a manager; they were in need of a conqueror.

Knowing not to deny the memories existence, I felt that it was imperative to find a way to have peace and the recollections co-exist. On the upside, I was fighting mad enough to be counted as a soldier. The downside was that I was not only mad at the pain of my past, I was infuriated with God. The dilemma was that I needed Him, but I didn't trust Him. Now what was I supposed to do?

God's requiring me to "*Deal*" with the memories, sad to say, placed Him in the "sadistic" category with me. Wasn't it enough for me to endure the pain the first time, now He required that I face it a second time? I could honestly say I had never blamed Him for the events in my childhood. Evil is a real force, and it alone should be judged. Even in my childish capacity at the time, I knew who was responsible for my sorrow. In my estimation, the perpetrators of the deeds were solely responsible for their own actions.

It never occurred to me that God should have stopped the babysitter, or any member of my family, from operating of their free will. That would make all of His creation puppets and He the Chief Puppeteer. Now I found that I was at odds with His methods. Necessitating my involvement with the road to recovery seemed an unjust sentence. This would have to be an area where I chose to "agree to disagree" with my Maker.

Oddly, like all my other relationships, I no longer desired to pretend with God. I had been jumping through hoops my entire life trying to get Him to be on my side. I kept my end of the deal; memorizing scriptures, praying, staying faithful in my marriage, raising my kids to know Him and being active in the church. It was never enough, *I* was never enough!

This was a new chapter in my relationship with God. His authority in my life brought great fear to me, not a sense of safety or protection. I felt He thought I deserved to be punished, but for the life of me, I didn't know my offense. If true intimacy in a relationship is only found in transparency, then honesty was crucial for both parties involved.

It occurred to me that it was not just OK if I showed anger at God—it was mandatory! When I'm close with a person and he or she has wounded me, I let that person know. If I don't, then ultimately the insincerity or distrust of the un-resolved offense affects the relationship.

I wanted to build a new bond of trust with Him. Now, I would see if He could be trusted with my anger.

The second part of the *"Dealing"* process appeared to be acknowledging that the evil happened in the first place. For whatever reason, it seemed essential to be willing to see the trauma like a video on constant rewind. Dr. Storm said that the more a person is willing to talk about it, the faster the sting of the event disappears. I was coming to terms with the knowledge that having to mentally revisit the place where the pain was inflicted was an obligatory part the *"Dealing"* process. While this was a very important step, it was critical that I didn't set up camp there. I don't claim to know much, but I did know this; hurtful memories left un-managed would be the soil for bitterness to grow.

I tried to pull from whatever resources I could to know how to tackle those tasks. Deciding to turn to the book of Psalms, I began reading the pages in search of the truth.

I believe the Old Testament of the Bible is not only filled with stories, it's packed with patterns. If the reader prop-erly examines the inspired writings, life applicable nuggets can be mined.

I began by analyzing the writings of David when he was besieged with grief or overwhelmed with fear. David never seems to withhold any true emotions while talking with God. In fact, he outright explodes on occasions. God never seemed offended with David's supplications; on the contrary, there is great intimacy between the two of them. I wrote some scriptures that aligned with my own feelings of abandonment.

Ps. 42:9 (King James Version) David writes to the Lord, *"I will say unto God my rock, Why hast thou forgotten me? Why go I mourning because of the oppression of the enemy?"*

Ps. 10:1 (King James Version), "Why standest thou afar off, O LORD? why hidest thou thyself in times of trouble?"

Ps 13:1-2 (King James Version), "How long wilt thou forget me, O LORD? for ever? how long wilt thou hide thy face from me? ²How long shall I take counsel in my soul, having sorrow in my heart daily? how long shall mine enemy be exalted over me?"

Ps. 22:1-2 (King James Version), "My God, my God, why hast thou forsaken me? why art thou so far from helping me, and from the words of my roaring? ²O my God, I cry in the day time, but thou hearest not; and in the night season, and am not silent."

Jesus Himself called out to His Father in His time of torment. "My God, My God, why have You forsaken Me?" Why would I hold myself to a standard that Christ Himself did not hold to? If He cried out to His Father in a time of despair, shouldn't I?

Deciding to try what I had learned, I began to work my

part of the *"Dealing"* step. I had never been honest or real with God. I was raging with what had happened to me and with the fact that I had to relive it. I would no longer be timid about my approach. I desired closeness and transparency. I would be open about the depth of my despair towards a God I longed to know. He wanted me to *"Deal"*; well, let's see how He handles it!

With reckless abandon, I entered into the Throne Room of the Holy of Holies. Fist clenched, both barrels blazing I prepared to make my emotional assault on my Creator. I feared no retribution. What could He do to me that He hadn't already done?

With unrepentant rage, I began. "How dare you!" Why are you doing this to me? What have I done that has made you unleash Your wrath? You expect loyalty in exchange for cruelty, faithfulness for abandonment. I can't do this with You anymore. *Dealing*, You call this step *"Dealing?"* Why should I have to *deal* with the evil choices of others? It was horrifying enough to have suffered through it the first time, now You require me to emotionally revisit my place of suffering? You seem clueless in the way of love."

"In no way do I think I have been the perfect mother, but even I know not to do that to one of my children. I would never require them to go through what You have required of me."

"I'm dying—why don't you see that? Those awful, gruesome images taunt me and mock me in my effort for peace. How long will it last, how long will I have to endure this step? My heart is broken beyond repair, and I still have so long to go. You allow my body to betray me as it recounts the horrific assaults on my innocence."

Knowing He was aware of the grotesque contents of the ominous box I had sworn never to open, I persevered in my accusations. "You saw what they did to me; you know I can't go through it again. I won't, do You hear me? I won't! I know Your ways are higher than mine, but now I feel the need to teach You in the way of compassion. What makes it worse; I feel You have deceived me. I thought we had a deal. I was never to look back. All I asked of You was help in washing the memories away. It worked for so long, now You deny my simple request. How can I trust You? I want to know this God of the Bible that loves unconditionally."

Fully enraged I cried out, "Who are You and why are You mad at me?"

My heart was pumping, and my blood continued to boil as I waited in stillness to hear a reply. Would I be punished for challenging His authority on what He was requiring of me? Is it true intimacy He desires or mindless servants who are terrified of His presence? Wondering if He would answer my charge, boldly I dared to be silent and listen.

Softly, ever so softly I heard Him. *"I'm sorry you're in pain. I have always been grieved by your heartache. You think you are alone on this journey and I have relented on a pact, but I have not. I never said you wouldn't have to deal with the sorrow of your past. That was a product of your design, not Mine."*

"It's hard for you to see right now, but I was there when they chose to violate you. It angered Me, and justice will be served. Even the box you refuse to open, I saw the contents you had to place in there. My heart was breaking with yours. In sadness, I witnessed the abuse, betrayals, and rejections you endured. Nev-

ertheless, I can mend the broken hearted and set free those who are captive.

I know you don't trust me; you never have. You have confused Me with another one's authority and betrayal. Always longing for your honesty, I'm glad you've trusted me with your anger. I can handle it, Veronica. I see your heart and know your confusion. I desire for you to know Me in ways I want to be known. Please believe I keep my promises. I will use your pain for your benefit and My glory as only I can do. Trust Me to work these things together for good in your life. My oath to you was beauty for ashes, the oil of joy for mourning. It's time to release the sorrow to Me so the divine exchange can begin."

In awe, I sat still and tried to comprehend what had just taken place. How could I have been a Christian my entire life and not know the One I served? I realized I didn't know the true character of God, but with earnest desire I longed to.

Yes, brazenly with fists clenched I entered boldly into the Throne Room of the Most High God daring to be authentically real. To my amazement, I was met with a Redeemer who knew me. His arms were wide open and there was healing in His wings.

CHAPTER SEVEN:

Reality Check

Morning had come and reluctantly I looked at the clock. I couldn't believe it! I slept ten hours straight! I had never been so excited to have had a good night's sleep. In no rush to have the moment pass, I remained for another hour.

I was aware that this was only a momentary reprieve. Too many boxes had been opened in the past forty-eight hours to make me think the involuntary shakes would remain quiet. Uninvited mental tapes would surely show themselves in a matter of time. With Jerry at work and the kids off to school, I had the house to myself. I basked in the quiet as I reflected on the events of the last few days. While enjoying the silence, I knew I needed to mentally explore the session with Dr. Storm from the day before.

I never intended to go into to my mental storage unit as often as I had in the last session. He was still unaware of the container that housed one of my greatest family secrets. I was also concerned about my husband. With everything that was coming out, would he doubt his decision of marrying me? Guilt and fear had overridden my decision to let him be a part of this process.

How did it get this far? I had lived in the company of a

husband and four children who I adore, and yet I felt alone. No one knew me; no one would be able to comprehend why I had lived in secret for so many years. I was finding that I trusted a counselor with my secrets because I knew he was bound by law not to tell. Even he didn't know the greatest classified events of my past and yet what he knew was surprising to him.

I was reflective about the two boxes that were to remain untouched. One contained contents that I feared would cause people to question my true self. If revealed, would some think I was the imposter, and not the one who turned away from what I was destined to be?

The other was an ominous box that I kept securely on the top shelf. It held the most grotesque articles of them all. I would never allow Dr. Storm access to that container. There was too much pain, betrayal, and heartache for me to allow that box to be examined.

It was difficult to sift through the memories as I knew I should. The fact that I couldn't see my memories the way Dr. Storm did bothered me tremendously. I was also facing the truth that my psychological profile seemed a complete contradiction. One part said that I had to keep secrets. The other part seemed to have classified all the incidents as normal, so why be so secretive? Even I know that didn't make sense. I questioned my ability to have such a double-minded perspective. Why had I not seen the total discrepancy between the two rationales?

I began contemplating my dating practices while a teenager. That being barely fifteen and allowed to date a nineteen year old was shocking to say the least. The weird thing was that, even though my parents knew about it and condoned it, my mom acted as if I was a loose girl for going out with him. When we went out, my mom treated me like a girl who had done something horribly wrong. I was encouraged one minute, then down-graded the next. I felt like I was being set up and encouraged to pursue a relationship and then was on the receiving end of spiritual judgment when I got home. It was hard to live with so many mixed messages. I always seemed to lose in the game of psychological warfare. I was simply no match against her.

Dr. Storm said that every daughter bases her self-worth on the way her father treats her. Did I see myself through the eyes of my father? Like in many homes, my mom was in charge. With her state of mind at the time, I think my dad was trying to keep peace. In my estimation, he simply didn't want to cause waves in an already uproarious sea of emotions in our home. It had never occurred to me to doubt his love for me.

Then there was the matter of the twenty-five year old that I was allowed to date when I was sixteen. To be truthful, I would turn seventeen in a month. By that time, I was already self-medicating. Drugs, alcohol, and cigarettes were a regular part of my life

I also had to admit that it felt so unsettling to have defended my brother for molesting me. When left alone with my thoughts, I could see the rationalization and understand my conclusions. I had been doing it for years. Every Christmas, birthday, Easter, Thanksgiving, and family gathering, I chose to think of something else while I was with him. Admittedly, whenever I was with my brother, I would always remember what he had done to me. Mental images would flash across my mind, and I would intentionally erase them from my mental screen. I would wonder if he thought about our past as much as I did. I always waited for him to bring it up, and hopefully apologize, but he never did. Several times, I almost brought it up so we could put it behind us. Never having the nerve, I would let the moment pass. It's a bizarre thing to have a closely guarded secret between two people. No one in the room would suspect the dangerous facts that lie beneath the surface. Two smiling faces, families of their own, yet a dark truth remained unsaid.

I had lived with an unspoken assumed contract between my brother and me. My part was to show him respect by allowing his secret to remain hidden, his part was to show respect by knowing what he did and living with the guilt of his actions. A perverse partnership birthed in hell that no person should have to abide by. How painful for my brother to have this cross to bear. I found myself actually feeling sorry for him.

My brother had been considerate to me in my teen years. I mean, I did not for one minute think what he did was right, but he was never outwardly mean to me. Why would Dr. Storm say he was one of the worst offenders? He loved me; I was sure of that.

Then I began to remember some not-so-pleasant memories about him. I was around thirteen, and I went bowling one Friday night with my brother, sister, and some friends. In the lane next to us were a couple of guys who kept flirting with all of us girls. As the night progressed, one of the young men started making it known he was interested in me. Trouble was, he was in his mid-twenties. I was actually frightened by him because he was coming on so strong. He asked for my telephone number, and I told him I was only thirteen. Of all things, he smiled and said that age was not a problem with him. Scared, I looked over at my brother and sister to see what I should do.

My sister had been disappointed that one of the men did not pursue her. She is over three years older than I am, which made her think she was the reasonable choice. She was visibly upset with me and was too distracted to help. My brother was consoling her for the lack of attention she received. My sister was so distraught; she left and went to her car. Just like many times before when she got upset, my brother and friends went after her to try to comfort her. Meanwhile, I was trying to end the unwanted conversation. Although he was persistent, he finally believed I was serious. Alone with the stranger, I left to make my way to the car and hoped he wouldn't follow me.

The drive home was hell. My sister was crying about how she had not been approached by one of the men. She then continued to tell me how I made her feel ugly and how hard it was to have me for a sister. My brother remained quiet as my sister went on with her lamentation. Not knowing how to answer such accusations, I remained silent and perplexed in the backseat, unclear as to why her anger was directed at me and not the men.

To defend myself would have made matters worse. It would have shown a gross lack of compassion on my part. So I let her say what she needed to say. It was bad enough to have her angry with me, but it cut deeper that my brother chose silence. I truly thought he, of all people, would defend me. I had always felt that, after that summer when I was eleven, my brother owed me, and I mean owed me big. If I protected him by keeping his secret, the very least he could do was protect me from my mom and my sister.

When we got home, I went to my room to get ready for bed. I could hear my brother and sister talking in her room, so I snuck up to the door to listen. I wanted to know what they were saying. My brother was comforting my sister and telling her she was beautiful too. Then he said something that shot an arrow through my heart. He told my sister that the only reason the guy liked me and not her was because he thought I was "easy."

"Just look at her," my brother told her, "She purposely dresses in a way to draw attention to herself. You're not like that, you choose to be good and sometimes it gets unnoticed." He continued to tell my sister how pretty she was and how one day the right one will come along. He also told her that I was not worth being jealous of.

I looked down at what I was wearing to see if this could be true: a vest buttoned all the way up and a pair of blue jeans. An ordinary tank top would have covered less. Questioning my wardrobe choice, I tipped-toed away quietly.

My mind was trying to resolve the complete discrepancy with what had just happened. He chose me when I was eleven, that would mean I'm special to him, right? He was only trying to make her feel better; surely, he didn't believe what he was saying. My heart began sinking at the possibility that I was so utterly irrelevant. He must love me, why else would have he crossed such a dangerous line of moral civility? Although typical for my sister to go out for a compliment at my expense, it shocked me that my brother didn't defend me. Why didn't he simply say to my sister that she didn't have to worry, that she was pretty too? It seemed unnecessary to insult me in an effort to compliment her.

He told her I appeared loose and that's the only reason they were attracted to me. It was appalling that he considered me seductive. Up until then, my brother was my only sexual encounter. He molests me and I'm the harlot?

It occurred to me that every demon in hell must have been celebrating with the unfolding events of that night. A thirteen-year old girl doubting her very self-worth, because her brother, who she thinks has preferred her, said she was an insignificant girl not worthy of envy. For me to have confused love with an act of evil was a perversion that can only be contrived by the Prince of Darkness himself. While my friends were playing typical childhood games like tetherball or riding bicycles, I was being introduced to a world I never knew existed. The inability to differentiate between good and evil is the burdensome baggage one carries when sexually violated by the one they trust.

The reminder of this event had sent me seething, looking for other boxes. How could he have done that? Could it be possible that he thought I wanted him to do what he did? I was only eleven at the time and I was the temptress? I quickly and in rage opened more boxes of my brother's betrayals. I was no longer his chief defender—I was the prosecutor. I found a box which contained articles that were placed in there not too long ago. Infuriated, I looked at the articles, unable to comprehend how I had never seen them this way before.

Now with a clear head, I began my careful examination and recalled a conversation between my brother and me.

A few years ago, while at a family gathering, my brother and I were talking about our teenage kids. He was saying how strict they were with their kids, not allowing them to receive phone calls from members of the opposite sex. When I commented that I wasn't as strict, he said, "You are hardly the example to follow as a teen. We wouldn't want them to make the same mistakes you did, now would we?"

I looked at my brother and was too stunned to speak. My mind was a flurry of words that couldn't find their way into a complete sentence. He was accusing me, in my own home, of being the out of control teenager. If I wasn't mistaken, this is the same brother who at age twenty or twenty-one was coming into my room to do the unthinkable to me, and he didn't want his kids to turn out like I did? Remembering my role as the "secret keeper," I once again remained silent. Understanding he was referring to my party ways and ultimate promiscuity, why did he not see he was the one with his foot on my dangerous teen accelerator?

My brother, my molester was standing in my house, and I found myself unable to speak. I began to believe he might be correct. Maybe I was the bad one during those years. He always seemed so unscathed by our past; why did it still haunt me? Not willing to be the one to ruin the event, I pretended not to get the slight. Dinner would be served, presents opened, candles blown out and the house would be filled with the tune of "Happy Birthday."

I was looking at the memory in complete disgust. The shakes were beginning to return at the recollections of my brother. Still trying to sift through all of the contents, a thought came to mind. What if he thought I liked it and what if he thought I was a willing participant? Oh no, this couldn't be! Could I have made a huge miscalculation of the past three decades of my life? For the first time the thought came to me that, my brother was disgusted with me! He was not my defender—he was my critic. I think he concluded that I was a willing member in his evil game. Was he able to reconcile this in his own mind?

As I remembered my teen years again, apparently my brother was unaware of my repulsion every time he would set me up to fall into on of his traps. Literally, months would pass without him being a deviant. I would think that he had grown up and changed. I had really convinced my-self that, because he was so nice to me, apparently he knew what he had done was wrong, and he vowed never to do it again. Then, unexpectedly, he would call me to the back of the house. With my guard down, I would walk in on some-thing so disturbing I would be too shocked to move.

There were times when I thought I was alone in the house. I would inadvertently walk past his bedroom while his door was open. Having no clue that he was actually in his bedroom, I would glance in, and to my shock, I would see him masturbating. Never did he jump or act embarrassed. He would just sit there, pants down, and give me an intense stare. Why didn't he just close his door if he was going to do that? I hated it when I wasn't smart enough to know that he was there. Never speaking out, I now feared he mistook my teenage silence for permission.

At that time in my life, I could not handle him being mad at me too. I had enough strife in the home to manage. So I made a decision to remain quiet and leave it alone. I would gladly exchange his nice behavior when he was good for my oath of silence when he was deviant. It was a high-ticket price, but it was all I had.

Dr. Storm said the "domino" would throw me for a loop this week, and it did. He wanted me to think of a way to hold my brother accountable, which I thought was laughable at the time. Now, this had changed everything. How was I supposed to be in the same room with my brother and not have a reaction? I felt physically sick with my new revelation.

With the recollection out for me to see, I began crying at the betrayal; not that of my brother but my own. When did I become so insignificant in my own eyes? I concluded that he was never sorry for what he did; he was amused.

More boxes of his betrayals could be unpacked, but why bother? This was more than enough evidence to convict. Only yesterday, I had defended his actions, and now I found myself sickened by them. Sobbing and trembling at my own self-deception, I didn't know what to do. It was all happening so hard and fast. How had I missed it all these years that he was one of my worst offenders? Could I have been so blind and desperate for the love of a family member that I would not see the humiliating truth? I tried to recover, but I couldn't.

One more illusion was being ripped away by proper examination. My whole life appeared to be a lie of my design. Defending the indefensible had been my method of operation for the sake of my family. If he, too, was one of them, what did that make me? Can it be possible I was the only one who escaped?

My children would be home soon which meant I had to regroup. I was determined not to allow this to affect them. There were already enough casualties in this twisted saga; they were not to be among them. Having been raised in a home with a mom who was depressed and emotionally out of control, I swore I would not do that to them.

As usual, I went upstairs to my bedroom to pull myself together. Doing my hair and make-up, trying not to look any worse for wear, I could see the desperation in my eyes. No amount of mascara and lipstick would be able to cover my exhaustion. The reflection in the mirror was a woman I no longer knew. With a fake smile on my face, that day would be no different from any other day. I would drive carpool, help with homework, make dinner, all the usual activities to keep the family in order. I still appeared to be able to live a dual mental existence. One minute completely devastated—the next minute Suzy Homemaker. This ability was beginning to scare me. How had I mastered the art of deception?

After the day's commotion had subsided, nighttime had come, and the butterflies returned. I knew my sleep would be interrupted by the terrible night frights once more. Seeing my brother's behavior as evil and not merely a nuisance had sent me spiraling into despair. It was a harsh reality to think that three out of the four family members were cruel to me. It would be one thing if their behaviors were equally distributed to all other members of the family, but that wasn't the case. For some unknown reason I was singled out. Does this kind of targeting happen in all families, or just mine?

It was time to put all the contents back into their proper boxes. Before placing the items in their appropriate containers, I was watchful in making certain that they returned to their rightful place. Good memories and bad memories never dwell in the same packages to insure no cross contamination took place. Having a family that didn't always distinguish between good and evil, it was up to me to separate the two when I located the difference.

My memories about my brother being supportive were once stored in a container that housed good memories. Perhaps he was only nice to me to ensure my loyalty to the secret. I had the painful task of placing his artifacts on the shelves where the other evil contents were held. I didn't do this for the sake of judgment, only for clarification.

When the boxes were safely returned to their shelves, it was time for bed. Tears began streaming down my cheeks at the remembrance of the day's findings. *Would I ever be normal?* I wondered as I dozed off to sleep. It wouldn't be long before I was awakened by a heartache no words could describe. I loved my brother and never wanted to betray his trust. However, I couldn't live with the notion that he thought I had asked for it, or worse yet, might have wanted it. I had to find out the truth about whether or not he was remorseful. *Veronica*, I admitted to myself, *You know you have to confront your brother.*

****

The alarm clock went off, begging for a new day to begin. I wished I could stay in bed and pull the covers over my head. I couldn't bear the thought of going out today. But, alas, the day's duties were calling my name. It was time to get up and get going.

My usual technique of dealing with life's messy issues was simply keeping busy. When my calendar was full of meetings, speaking engagements, and Bible study dates, there was just no time left for reflection. The art of distraction had served me well for many years. However, I was finding it exhausting with my current state of being. I also knew that too much time left alone would prove to be harmful as well. As all-consuming as it was, I didn't think it wise to stay locked up in my home. Too much time left for mental inventory would quickly turn a good practice into a self-serving one. It seemed important to try to maintain some sort of balance in this process.

The first item on my list for the day was breakfast with my Bible study group. Trying to get my mind off my brother was a futile exercise, for they all asked how things were going. I tell them I was still in the thick of it. The restaurant was a local favorite, so seating was at a minimum. Unable to find a suitably sized table for all of us, the nine of us squeezed into a table more befitting a party of six. No problem, that made the sharing of food all the easier. Each one of us reached across the table sampling each other's menu choices.

They asked a multitude of questions concerning my counseling. I readily shared everything that had been coming out in therapy. It was still baffling to them that they had known me for so long and yet really had not known me at all. I was only able to stay for about forty-five minutes, which is short considering we could usually kill a good two hours together sharing our stories. Needing to make the second appointment on my calendar, I said goodbye and rushed out the door. I had a church luncheon for leaders to attend. On the drive down the coast to the restaurant, I once again found myself obsessing over the revelations of the night before.

The choices I made in my teen years were starting to haunt me. I went to church; I knew better but did them anyways. The thought of my wildly inappropriate dating relationship with a married man made me loathe myself even more. I was pretty certain I was disqualified from ever teaching in church again. Furthermore, I never wanted to be in a position of leadership again. Honestly, why would anyone ever have listened to me in the first place?

Rage over my brother's actions both back then and present day was taking over. I began sobbing and screaming at him although he was nowhere near. How could he do that to me? He came off as so self-righteous, and *I* was the one in need of cleansing? I wouldn't ever be able to be in the same room with him again without having held him accountable.

Close to the restaurant, I began to second-guess my decision to go to the luncheon. I parked in a space where I wouldn't be seen by others to freshen up my face. Looking into the mirror, I wondered if my eyes would give away the secrets beneath the surface. Hating the promise I made to be there, I got out of the car. I began silently praying that the Lord would show me mercy and have me sit next to a person who would be easy to talk to. I didn't know all the women, and I didn't have the energy to make idle chit-chat.

I wound up sitting next to a woman I had met once or twice and across from the wife of a pastor at our church. Dreading the next two hours, I forced a smile on my face and began with the casual conversation. The gal next to me said, "There is something I have wanted to tell you for a long time but I never had the opportunity."

"What is it?"

"Well, years ago you came to speak at my mom's group at church. The topic was 'Celebrate Marriage.' Problem was, my husband and I were on the verge of divorce. He wasn't a Christian, and I had just started going to church myself. I had cheated on him several months earlier. It wasn't a full-blown affair, but I did let the man kiss me. My husband and I were already having troubles but when he found this out, I thought my marriage was over. You talked about marriage in such a way that it got me excited. I bought the tape of your teaching to take home to my husband. Not only did he listen to it, we both did repeatedly. We practically wore the thing out. This piqued his interest in church, so he went with me one Sunday. In a matter of a few weeks, he gave his heart to the Lord, and our marriage was radically changed."

"But that's not all," she continued. "He ended up going

back to school to go into the ministry. He is now a pastor at church and loves it! When we reflect back on that terrible time in our marriage, we both remember your message and how the Lord used it to totally transform the life of our family."

God's love was so amazing! I had to restrain myself from throwing my arms around her neck and bellowing out at the top of my lungs, "Thank you!" Not able to give her the rightful boisterous response, I just politely smiled and told her that her story had meant the world to me. The Lord had used me to help save her marriage. Now, the Lord was using her to help save my life. I taught that marriage message so many years ago, and God waited until that day to have our paths cross. The Lord was so merciful to have orchestrated this divine meeting. It was exactly what I needed.

Our conversation continued as we talked about God's mercy. I divulged that I had made some pretty significant mistakes of my own; not the least of which was an affair with a married man while still a teen.

Joanne, the sweet woman across the table looked at me. "You weren't bad; you were merely working on your testimony. Some of us take more time than others do to work on it. But, trust me, Honey, in no way should you feel bad today about the decisions of yesterday. It's forgiven; all you have to do is forgive yourself."

The rest of the lunch conversation was filled with laughter and stories. We openly shared about our mistakes and what a Redeeming God we serve. Driving home, I wondered what tomorrow would bring. I had a lunch date with my sister. It would be the first time seeing her since all of this stuff came out. She knew I had been in marriage counseling but had no knowledge of where it had led me. I contemplated whether I should tell her. I also wonder if I was the only sister my brother chose for his sexual misdeeds. Did she escape his touch?

CHAPTER EIGHT

Ricochet

My sister had always been one of my greatest sources of confusion. She was supportive one minute. Then on the next visit, whatever support she offered the last time was quickly revoked.

One such instance was two years ago. I made the decision, because of an incident that happened between my parents and me, that I would no longer be in relationship with them. My sister found out what they did and totally supported my decision. It wouldn't be long before she would change her mind and tell me I needed to reconnect with our parents. To excuse her inconstancies, she would usually say she had prayed about it and now thinks differently. My sister would inform me of God's plan in the situation, and that I needed to comply in order to be in His will.

The incident that happened was two years ago. Father's Day was approaching, and my mom emailed me letting me know they were coming down for a visit. Before that time, although I had been in contact with my mom, it had been a year since my mom initiated any contact with me, except for a short call on my birthday. I had no idea why she had been so aloof and was too afraid to ask.

They came down for Father's Day all right, but it was no celebration.

Both of my parents were noticeably distant towards us the entire visit. Although I am used to such emotional assaults, my mom made a crucial error on this particular visit. She was never to have my children be on the receiving end of her emotional punishments.

Even though we had made the trip to my brother's house expressly to see my parents, they avoided talking directly to us the entire time. That took some skill considering the only people at the barbeque were my brother's family and mine. The evening was ending and it was about time for us to leave. My mom saw that we were wrapping it up. She got up and said she was tired and was going to bed. Not acknowledging us, she walked past me and then walked past my children. She went straight for one of my brother's children, hugged him, and told him how proud she was of him. She looked past my kids for my brother's other kids and did the same to them. She never spoke a word to my children who were standing right next to her. My mom then went to her room for the remainder of the evening. My daughter looked at me and shook her head in disbelief. Not willing to let this one go, I questioned my dad as to why she didn't say goodbye to any of us. He said she was tired and simply forgot to. I countered his explanation by telling him my kids were right next to the other grandchildren while she was saying goodnight to them. My dad said she was tired, and the subject was dropped.

On the drive home that evening I told Jerry that I had enough. I was willing to remain silent when she was cruel to me, but I would not allow her to mistreat my children as a way of getting her point across.

Several weeks passed; I knew it was only a matter of time before I would get a phone call from my mom. When she was successful in inflicting pain to get her point across, she would re-engage the relationship. If the emotional beating took, it would give her the boost she needed to get back in touch and act as if nothing ever happened. I had vowed that this time would be different. I would hold her accountable.

Like clockwork, she called a few weeks later to shoot the breeze. She left a cheery and cordial message on my machine saying she was calling to catch up.

Having a backbone for the first time, I picked up the phone and returned her call. I got their answering machine too. Ready for battle, I began my response. "I got your message and I must say considering how you acted towards me and my family I'm a little shocked you have the nerve to call and act like nothing happened. The children and I are hurt by the way you treated us. If you want to discuss your behavior and apologize, I would be happy to accept your call."

Knowing this would be like walking into a wild hornets' nest, I anxiously waited for my mom's expected furious response. The phone rang. Too afraid to pick up, I let the answering machine receive the verbal assault. She did not disappoint. Her ranting would go on for several minutes, which exceeded the allotted time for the message, so the machine cut her off. No problem with her. She simply called back not missing a beat and picked up where she left off. It appeared scripted and well rehearsed. She did say she was *so* sorry to her grandchildren and that she would never want to hurt them.

Then she blasted, "But, *you*, Veronica, I offer you no apology. You are the one to apologize to me. You have no idea how hurtful it is to have you as a daughter. You are so cold and distant; it is impossible to get close to you. I have never done anything to you, but you pretend to be the victim. Your message on Mother's Day was so short, how do you think that made me feel? I deserve so much more from you! So if you want to talk and tell me *you're* sorry, you may return my call." With that, she hung up.

Replaying the condemning phone messages, you would have thought I had just received a death threat with the way my heart was pounding. Even being a woman in my early forties, I was still terrified of my mother. Completely panic-stricken, I had Jerry listen to both of the messages so I could get his opinion.

Jerry advised, "Veronica, you have no need to feel guilty for holding them accountable. You are allowed to stand up to them and let them know they hurt you and have been hurting you for years. Tell them you would value being in relationship with them, but it has to be based on mutual respect. Any good and decent parent will see that this is the only healthy way to be in relationship with their child, whether young or old."

Truth be told, if my mom hadn't used my kids to get to me the night of the barbeque, I would never have had the nerve to stand up to her. Now she was no longer dealing with her daughter, but an enraged "Mother Hen." I was willing to keep the family creed at my own personal cost; however, the dues were never to be collected from my children.

With mammoth trepidation, I picked up the phone to make the dreaded call. My mom answered and had my dad get on the other phone. What started as a calm and tense conversation would turn into a screaming match within minutes. Accusations went flying from both ends of the phone. She would not stand to be held accountable for how she treated my children and me. She insisted I was the one who owed both of them an apology for my lack of involvement in the family.

There would be no way to clearly know what was said next. The two of us were screaming at the top of our lungs at each other. I had never in my childhood or adult life ever raised a voice, let alone screamed, at one of my parents. This was something much unexpected and not tolerated from the once submissive daughter.

My father firmly and with a loud voice announced, "Quiet. It is my turn to speak." I am no match for my dad, so in stunned silence I was the good little girl and obeyed. He told me of my complete disrespect and dishonor to my mother. He continued by saying they had done nothing wrong by treating me the way they did at the barbeque. It is what I should have expected for being the kind of daughter I am. If I'm not mistaken, I believe a few Bible verses were thrown in for good measure. Children are to honor and obey no matter what malicious conduct the father and mother choose to dispense. The Bible has clear-cut commandments, and I was sure I was breaking one of the big ones.

This cut me to the core. He was my father; he expected me to obey without question. My mom tried to continue the blasting. I interjected that she would have a chance to defend herself, but first I need to be able to complete a sentence without being yelled at.

She would have none of that, so she continued to yell at me. Totally out of character and to my parent's utter surprise, I hung up. I was shaking I was so furious. As far as they were concerned, I got what I deserved at the barbeque. They called back immediately. I told them I could no longer handle their accusations or yelling. I informed them that, from here on out, they can only contact me through emails. Even the sound of their voices by this time would send me into a frenzy.

In emails, I reminded my mom that she too had to separate from her mother because of the cruel treatment she was receiving. "How can you not see you are doing the same thing to me that your mom did to you? You were so hurt when your mom was continuously mean to you—why are you repeating the behavior with me? Your mom was nice to all the other children and singled you out unfairly. How can you justify your actions as the mom when you condemned them as a daughter?"

With strong encouragement from my brother and sister, we exchanged emails for the better part of two months. Time after time, I would try to make my case for why I had felt so wounded over the years. Outlining a clear pattern of behavior, I would bring up example after example of how inequitable the treatment was for me compared to my siblings.

They had no problem making their case too. I was the

unforgiving daughter who claimed to be the injured party, and they were the godly parents who had loved me unconditionally. Once in awhile, they would throw in an apology, but I usually didn't know what they were apologizing for. It appeared they wanted the subject closed, so they would use a one-sentence defense in response to a three-page email. Most emails would conclude by informing me of their prayers for our relationship and the need for reconciliation.

After several months the emails stopped. Reconciliation was not a possibility, so I ended communication with my parents.

When first informed of what happened during the Father's Day visit, my sister offered her sympathy and support. I had been telling her for years that the closeness she and my mom enjoyed was something I had always longed for. She was sad that the family was unable to be under the same roof at Christmas and was disappointed the dynamic had forever changed.

The compassion would only last for a while, then came the preaching and telling me to forgive and forget. "You need to honor and respect your parents Veronica. Can't you see how divisive your actions are? It is not only affecting you, it's affecting all of us." She would inform me of her prayers for reconciliation. Then she would tell me that she had asked God to give me the ability to forgive as He intended me to do. The conclusion of the conversation was usually, "I'm not concerned about me; I just don't want you to remain in bitterness."

My attempts at convincing her that forgiveness and relationship were not synonymous terms were unsuccessful. I would ask her why she was preaching at me and not mom. She never did answer that question.

Now, pulling up to the restaurant, I wondered if this time she would be safe. *Do I trust her with my information regarding our brother?* Not knowing exactly what to do, I got out of the car and went in to meet my sister.

****

With my internal butterflies in full flight, I walked into the restaurant and saw that my sister was already checked in with the hostess. Whoever came up with the saying "Anticipation is half the fun" didn't know my family. Laying all fears aside, smiling, I embraced her in our usual greeting. Unsure of how to bring up the subject of our brother, we exchanged the usual pleasantries for the first several minutes of our lunch.

The server greeted us, took our orders and gave us some bread to start. With the interruptions now at a minimum, my sister asked how my marriage counseling was going. Thrilled that she was the one to bring up the topic, I began to fill her in on our counseling. I knew this would be the perfect segue for me to open up discussions on our family history. I eagerly began telling her about the session where Jerry and I had to describe each other's childhood.

My sister looked a little puzzled as to what this had to do with anything. She asked, "What did Jerry say about our family?"

"Oh, he pretty much nailed it. He watched how our

family works through the years so he was able to tell Dr. Storm pretty much everything."

"Like what?"

"Well, he told him how mom treats me and how I'm not even in relationship with my parents anymore."

This seemed to pique her interest. If there was anything she liked to talk about, it was how I have split the family in two. Trying not to look too interested, she casually said, "Oh, what did Dr. Storm have to say about it? Does he think you should try to reconcile and work out your differences?"

Knowing this would catch her off guard, I said, smirking, "Not at all actually. He agrees with my decision to stay away."

My sister was baffled at the doctor's seemingly divisional approach. She actually flinched. She blinked her eyes, cocked her head slightly, and put her bread back on the plate. "Is he a Christian counselor?" she implored.

I, on the other hand, felt no need to stop eating. I took a bite of my bread and smugly replied, "Yes, absolutely, he is a Christian counselor."

Now seeing the need to undo the damage done by the doctor, she began her spiritual counsel. "Veronica, I know you have been hurt, and I'm thrilled you are in counseling. I hope it gives you the answers you need so you can get better. You have to let it out, and then you will be able to see it more clearly."

Completely insulted, I returned, "Are you inferring that I am the one who needs to be fixed? Do you think that this is all about getting me better so I can see the errors of my ways and the family can get back together?"

Maintaining her position, my sister continued. "Well, I'm just saying it would do you good, that's all. You seem so tied to the past, maybe your doctor will help you know how to let it go and get on with your life. I know I've said it before, but you just seem so bitter."

Trying to not go flying off my seat to wrap my hands around her neck, I spat out in disgust, "I am not the one who needs fixing in this family; I can assure you of that! I trust you with information about my counseling and you use it against me? I hate it when you do that! You act all concerned, but what you're really doing is getting facts that you think you can use later."

She snapped, "Why do you think it's all Mom and Dad's fault, Veronica? They want to work it out; Mom is so hurt and upset. Why can't you just reconcile? It takes two to fight you know!"

"Oh yeah? Name one thing I have done to bring this on myself. What is my offense here other than not allowing an abusive relationship to continue? The only thing Mom and Dad can say against me is that I didn't keep in touch enough. I already explained to them that I tried to fly under the radar in an effort to stay out of trouble. Apparently, it didn't work!"

With the direction this was going, obviously I was not going to tell her about our brother or inquire as to whether he involved her in an incestuous relationship too. The waiter had tried to approach our table several times, but he would divert his path when he saw we were still fighting. Neither one of us seemed to care what the other diners around us thought of our heated exchange. We went at each other as though we were in the privacy of our own homes. I had wished the server would just "man up" and refill our water glasses. I desperately wanted the distraction and knew we were both in need of something cool to calm us down. Back on the defensive, I answered her allegations once more.

"You are driving me crazy with this! Why do you always insist that because I am not in contact with them that automatically means I haven't forgiven them? When grandma pulled her crap on mom, we all applauded her for walking away. Then you wouldn't speak to grandma for years because she was so mean to you."

My sister never liked when I brought that subject up. Our grandmother was in no way nice to my sister. My sister was the target of some nasty insults, and, at times, she seemed completely invisible while in our grandmother's presence. When my sister became an adult, she walked away from the already fragile relationship, which was no loss to my grandma. I saw how hard it was on her, so I had always supported her decision to leave the toxic relationship.

Seeing this was upsetting my sister, I added, "I am sorry that Mom is so hurt by what is going on. If she wants to be in relationship with me, all she has to do is admit there is some terrible dysfunction and be willing to stop the attacks. I really don't think I'm asking too much."

Unrelenting, she persisted. "They have said they were sorry, Veronica; you are the one who won't accept their apologies. I'm worried that you are going to get trapped into bitterness and this will affect your relationship with

God. It's not something you want to play with. I did for-give Grandma, and I allowed us to be reunited."

"Oh brother," I laughed. "You weren't in contact with her for years and when you did get back in touch, she was sick and had lost all ability to talk. I guess you did feel pretty safe then, huh? Not much an old women can do to you when she is unable to speak," I said still smiling.

Now furious, she countered. "I didn't wait until she was unable to speak; I just knew that I needed to take the high road and allow God to heal me. I wasn't going to let grandma come in between my relationship with God, so I forgave her. It was the hardest thing I have ever done, but I know it was God's will. I think you need to do the same and allow God to heal you from all your past hurts."

The smile now returned to her face. "Besides, Veronica, you didn't have it that bad in the first place. You are hardly the victim here."

Her words echoed in my mind, ricocheting off the cor-ners and back again. Responses like these always caused me to question the validity of the contents of my boxes. Yes, I know my memories to be true, but perhaps my analysis of them was not legitimate. When a member of my family will admit to the behavior but quickly dismisses the harmful ef-fects on me, I tend to bend to the pressure. My categoriza-tion of the recollections become blurred once more.

My sister would never give up her place in the family as the "victim." It has been her defining role, and it most cer-tainly was worth defending. She always thought no one had it more difficult than her, and she was willing to take me to the mat to prove it. Always making sure I remembered that, in her opinion, I had it so much better than she, she was aghast at the thought I should ever feel bad about my treatment in the family.

"Trust me," I contended, "Mom and Dad are not coming in between my relationship with God and me. I will stand before God one day, and I'm not concerned that He will be angry that I chose to leave an emotionally abusive relationship. Why is it so hard for you to see that our family is so screwed up?"

Still combative, my sister continued. "Veronica, our family is no worse than any other family out there. Every family is dysfunctional. There are no perfect families."

This made me wonder if she even remembered the sexual assault of the babysitter, her own deviant sexual history, or the depression of our mother. I conceded to myself that this was a losing battle.

"I think our family has its own unique problems, and I do think we have some pretty bad generational curses going on here. Furthermore, I have no intention on getting back into relationship with our parents until the issues can be resolved. And by the way, I'm hurting badly too in case you were interested."

She did not like the insinuation that she was being unconcerned. This actually sent her on the warpath.

"Veronica," she barked, "Where in the Bible does it say that you are supposed to be divisive? God tells us to love and forgive! You think you are so spiritually superior; well you're not! You will never convince me that what you are doing is right and that God actually approves. The Bible does not say that it's OK to tear a family apart. I see it in your face when I mention Mom and Dad's name. Bitterness and un-forgiveness is written all over you!"

And there you have it. In our family, the Bible wasn't used as source of comfort and instruction; it was used as a weapon of mass destruction. Whenever my sister felt like she was losing a conflict, she would use the tactic that was taught to us by our parents: simply refer to some biblical principles and go in for the kill. The rationale was that it might be easy to fight against a family member, but who can fight against the Word? Just counter with a Bible verse, and it leaves the opposition speechless. Well, at least usually. That time it would backfire on her entirely.

Practically snarling, I chided, "You do not want to take me on where the Bible is concerned. That is the one area you will lose every time with me! I have no intention of letting you misquote or manipulate the scripture to obliterate me. Try actually keeping one of those scriptures in context that you insist on referring to and see how far it gets you! I'm so tired of having you think you can teach me a thing or two regarding the ways of the Lord. I could bury you in my knowledge of the scriptures!" Admittedly, that was combative of me, but it was true. I always hated who I became when I was with her. To say she always brought out the worst in me was like saying the sun was a little hot.

Then much calmer and almost muttering, I explained. "As far as my face-changing expressions when you talk about Mom and Dad, you're right. However, let me assure you, you are not seeing bitterness—you are seeing pain. Has it ever occurred to you that I, too, am hurting? I seriously want to crumble when you talk about them. I long to have them show their love and support to me as they do to you. However, what pours salt on the wound is your insistence that I am the one who is ripping the family apart. When grandma did the same cruel treatment to you and Mom, everyone knew she was the one at fault. Now that I stand up for myself, everyone blames me for not taking it, not Mom for dishing it out."

That turned the conversation into more of a quiet exchange. She backed down and said that, although she didn't agree with my decision to not talk to our parents, she would respect it. We ended on a good note, but, as far as I was concerned, not much had been accomplished. My sister had also mastered the art of keeping the family creed. Only with her, I think she believed it.

After such altercations with a family member, I felt like a part of me simply vanished. Reaching out for support but being met with rejection was something I never got used to. I didn't just feel the pain of rejection; it was as though it inhabited me. It became my mental dwelling place until I could discern what it was about me that they found so unworthy. Why wouldn't they just let me go? If I was that awful of a person, why did they insist on being in relationship with me at all? I wanted so much to be free from them, but they were all unwilling to let me walk away from the family.

Exhausted and spent after the lunch with my sister, I entered my home with a tremendous void inside. Alone again in my house, I found it safe for the sadness to envelop me. In my private moments, I morphed into a woman I hardly knew. Grief overtook me, and the trembling returned. To have family members hurt me relentlessly, then show me contempt when I acknowledge the pain made it hurt even more. I never knew what hurt worse—the act or their devaluing its effect on me.

At times, I felt there was a black pit of despair that was calling my name. Thoughts of suicide started to torment me. I did not want to take my life in the present, but I regretted my unsuccessful attempt as a teen. If I had ended my life back then, I would not have to deal with the grueling realities today. If successful with the deadly deed, maybe my family would have understood that one person is unable to withstand the attack of so many.

I tried in vain to wrestle these thoughts. Guilt flooded my very being and feelings of ingratitude shamed me. It was not that I didn't want to live; it was that I didn't know how to live with my boxes unpacked and the contents out for me to see. That was why I had kept them safe on the storage shelf of my mind for so many years. While beautifully wrapped and properly stored, the gruesome contents were something I never had to face. But everything had changed, and I had never felt so all alone. Still unwilling to allow my husband to know what a toll this had been on me, I waited until he was in bed before I allowed the tears to flow.

Knowing that my sister would not be my ally in this fight, I was left with only one person who I thought could help me. He was not my friend or family; he was actually a stranger to me—Dr. Storm.

My confidante was a professional who was paid to do so. This knowledge was not a source of comfort but of humiliation and isolation. I was not certain if there was anyone on this planet more pathetic than I was. Although I hardly felt like the warrior, I had no choice but to fight. Fortunately, I had an appointment with Dr. Storm the next day. Maybe he could help me shuffle through the wreckage that had become my life.

CHAPTER NINE:

Broken

I awakened from a dreadful night's sleep. The inventory of my mind was in total chaos. Everything was happening so fast; I was barely managing to keep up with the pace. Many of my containers had been opened with contents spilled out to see. In order for me to have peace of mind, I had to make sure the storage room was pristinely organized. I began to work at a frenzied pace with the stockpile of memories set before me. There was not much time to accomplish this task. I would leave for a session with Dr. Storm in a couple of hours.

The drive down to his office usually proved to be reflective and calming. The stereo would remain off to ensure no distractions took place. When I arrived in his office, as always, I sat in the waiting area waiting for Dr. Storm to greet me. At this point in the counseling, I was unusually antsy. I would sit quietly so I could listen for his footsteps so his arrival would not alarm me. It was easy for me to have an exaggerated reaction to an unexpected noise. Since my counseling had begun, my nerves were on hyperactive mode, and it was a useless exercise to try to compose them. My involuntary tremors had returned, which they usually did before a session. Hearing his steps, I looked up intently at the doorway to make sure it was Dr. Storm.

"Hello Veronica," he said with a smile as wide as Manhattan. "How are you doing today?"

We walked down the short hallway to his office and entered the room. His office is what you might expect a therapist's workplace to look like. Only with this doctor, you get a killer view! His office was located on the tenth floor of a beautiful executive high rise near Pacific Coast Highway. When you walked through the door, you were met with a large picture window that faced you as you entered. From his vantage point, he could see the beautiful Pacific Ocean. From mine, I saw the rooftops of tract mansions that lined an exclusive golf course. It was a stunning sight to behold every time I entered. Sometimes, on a beautiful day, I could be distracted by the awesome view. If the session became too difficult, I often found myself engrossed in the magnificence of the landscape right outside his window.

If the view wasn't distraction enough, I heard the voice of the exclusive shopping center right across the street that often screamed my name during the session. I have always found comfort in shopping. Throw in lunch at a sidewalk café with a friend and you have the makings of a perfect day.

He sat on one side of the room and I sat in my usual spot, right-hand corner of the couch, grabbing the decorative pillow that waited my arrival. He also had a smaller sofa that was against another wall. Every single time I saw the one pillow on the couch, it threw me. For the life of me, I couldn't figure out why there was only one pillow. He had one large couch and one smaller sofa, but he only had one pillow–why? It felt so off balance to me. I actually had the paranoid thought that perhaps it was a test. I mean after all, he was a marriage counselor. Maybe he was keeping score who would get the pillow each visit–the husband or the wife. I considered buying him two matching pillows to replace the one, but knew that would be crossing the line. It never ceased to amaze me how such superficial things could actually make my world seem slightly off kilter.

The first time I entered his office, I inwardly chuckled when I saw the sofa. How cliché, I thought. All therapists on TV programs have a couch with an unraveling patient lying down, hoping for the psychologist to cure them. Then it occurred to me that he was a marriage counselor, so he would need a large sitting area for couples to sit next to each other. It wasn't nearly as funny when I connected the dots, but it was fun while it lasted.

Dr. Storm began. "So I see your body is still trying to get your attention."

"Yes, it is. I thought this would have ended by now. You remember the domino you pushed last session?"

He smiled, "Of course I remember. Have you come to any conclusions regarding your father and brother?"

"OK, about that domino, yeah, well, it kicked my butt! I left here last time thinking what my brother did was no big deal and now I'm so mad at him I could scream!"

Dr. Storm was surprised. "Wow, you work fast," he laughed. "What made you do a complete turn?"

All I could think was that he was being very gracious to say I work fast. If he meant my quick three-decade journey to come to this conclusion, then yeah, I'm a regular Speed Racer.

Still steamed, I answered, "Oh, I just started remembering some insinuations my brother threw at me over the years." I filled him in on the bowling alley incident and several other times, even in our adult life. "There's no way I can go on as though nothing has happened. I see now what you were trying to tell me. If I think he is sorry, why don't I give him the chance to apologize?"

Seeming satisfied, Dr. Storm remarked, "Well, someone's found her voice! For you to have gone from excusing him, to being angry and wanting accountability in less than one week, that's huge progress Veronica. You were violated; you are supposed to be angry. Holding him accountable isn't just in your best interest; it's also beneficial for him and his family."

"Oh, I wish I were just angry," I bellowed. "I'm completely and utterly furious! However, the anger isn't just for him; it's for me. I'm disgusted with myself for not thinking I deserved any better than what he dished out. Celebrating that I had the privilege to choose between the lesser of the evils is horrifying to me."

"Still, you have come a long way in a short time. Have you been able to get angry at your father yet?" probed Dr. Storm.

"No, I'm not angry with my father. I have no reason to be," I said with tears welling up in my eyes.

Instantly, the mood changed dramatically. No longer focusing on my brother, I felt a great sorrow flood the room at the thought of my father.

I begged, "Why is it so important that I get mad at my dad? Honestly, after the past week, he is all I have left. What is the harm in believing he was good to me? I want to hold onto, even if only an illusion, that he had no clue what was going on. It's my only anchor right now."

Compassionately, yet firmly, Dr. Storm began, "Because, Veronica, you have chosen to live in the truth and not the lie you created. Your dad was supposed to protect you and be there for you. He was there physically, but he was not the father you needed him to be to keep you safe from the hazardous world you lived in. Because of his complete inattention, your brother had full access to you, and he turned a blind eye to your mother's emotionally crippling behavior towards you."

Trying not to crumble in the floodlight that was shining brightly on my past, I said, "Trust me when I tell you, Dr. Storm, that I know he wasn't the best father in the world, but I can't say this strongly enough: he didn't try to hurt me. Don't you get it? You have no idea what it was like for me growing up in that house. Never feeling safe, feeling as if I was living with an emotional terrorist. The mental and emotional games constantly being played and you are the only one who doesn't own a copy of the stupid game instructions or the rulebook. Yes, maybe he was lacking in his parenting skills, and he should have stepped up to the plate more often, but he remains my childhood hero. Why won't you just let it go?"

Relentlessly Dr. Storm reasoned, "If your earthly father doesn't show you that you were worth protecting, it's hard for you to think your Heavenly Father feels any differently.

It's natural for us to project our dad's relationship, whether good or bad, onto our relationship with God. Because your father didn't esteem you in the way a good father does his daughter, you probably think God doesn't love you and that He is constantly distant from you. If you acknowledge the emotional abandonment of your dad and allow yourself to get angry, it will be the gateway into a deeper under-standing of your Heavenly Father's pure and unconditional love. You can't have one without the other, I'm afraid."

Tears began rolling down my cheeks. I understood for the first time what the doctor had been trying to convey. What he said stung like the snap of a towel on bare skin. I had always felt God was angry with me or completely un-caring about my life. Trying to win His favor and get into His good graces had been an endless quest of mine since I could remember.

Timidly, I said, "OK, I promise to try and be honest about what my relationship is with my dad. If I find that he, too, is responsible for my pain, I will hold him account-able. That's the best I can do for now."

Dr. Storm assured me that it would be a worthwhile en-deavor and then radically changed directions.

"So, how is your relationship with Jerry going? Are the two of you doing OK?"

Smiling at the mention of my husband's name, I said, "Sure, it's going just fine. He's being very supportive."

Digging deeper, he asked, "Does he help you when you're hurting? How does he handle it when he sees you crying or trembling?"

"Well, that's a little complicated. I don't let him see me

cry most of the time. Jerry didn't ask for any of this nor should he have to deal with it. This is my garbage, and I am the one who is responsible to manage the mess. To be perfectly honest with you, I'm not altogether convinced he would have married me if he knew about my past before hand."

Dr. Storm was ready for this response and was well aware of the dynamic. "Veronica, you have to let him in. He wants to help you, I promise. You do not have to do this alone. The weight of what you're carrying is entirely too much for one person to bear. Trust him with the information. All the things you have chosen to share with him up until this point he has handled beautifully."

With tremendous sadness, I said, "I don't know how to let him in. I have been living in emotional seclusion for my entire life."

Dr. Storm shocked me with his question. "Do you trust me Veronica?"

Without the least bit of hesitation, I amazed myself by saying, "Yes, I do trust you." Crazy as it seems, I hadn't trusted a man in authority my entire life.

Dr. Storm then asserted, "Good. Then trust me when I tell you that you can trust Jerry. God has given you a wonderful husband who loves you more than you seem to know. Let him in Veronica; it will help you in your healing. Jerry doesn't want you to do this on your own; I don't either."

Marveling at my ignorance, I asked, "What does that look like? How do I do it?"

"It's easy," he encouraged. "When you start having

your night tremors or begin to feel the overwhelming sadness, don't hide from Jerry—seek him out. Wake him up if he is sleeping and tell him you're afraid and that you need him to hold you. You will not be bothering him, I assure you."

A little off the subject, I said sheepishly, "I know this is not what we were talking about, but I'm having trouble in an area of my marriage right now."

Struggling to get the words out, I dared to take on a taboo subject. "I'm finding it hard being sexually intimate with Jerry during all of this. We used to be so passionate and enjoyed such a great sex life. Now I cringe at the thought of him touching me or trying to get close. The very act itself is repulsive, and I don't know how to get past this."

Sympathetically, he said, "That's to be expected, Veronica. You have accomplished a lot in such a short time. You'll be ready again to make love to Jerry; it will just take some time. Be patient with yourself. You are expecting entirely too much, not enough time has passed yet. God created the sexual union between husband and wife. He will restore you in this area too."

"I guess so, but it all seems so dirty to me, and the thought of it freaks me out entirely. I'm terrified I won't ever get over this. I want to be close to him, but I jump when he touches me, even just to calm me. It's all so unfair."

Dr. Storm continued with his encouragement. "The reality of what happened between your brother and you only came out about four weeks ago. That's not nearly enough time for you to have emotionally processed it yet. Give yourself time. Jerry is a patient man. He wants you to feel

148

safe, and I guarantee that he will wait until you are ready. God won't abandon you in this area; sex is a holy thing.

Without thought, I laughingly burst, "Holy, are you kidding me? Oh Dr. Storm, you're killing me!"

I can tell you right now, he did not see the humor in it. He looked at me and, with complete seriousness, said, "Yes, it is holy, Veronica. The problem is sex was introduced to you at such an early age that you have never been able to see it that way. Having witnessed a sexual assault at the age of seven and then starting to be molested at age eleven, your healthy development was hindered. You knew of no other way to express yourself. It was a little like giving a toddler a machine gun. It was an act of perversion and not of holiness because it was taken from you from someone who had no ownership, but that is not how God intended it to be. God created making love for a husband and wife's pleasure; Satan is the one who distorted it. When you're ready, it will be the close intimate act that you have longed for it to be."

His words cut like a surgical knife in search of a cancerous growth. Needing healing in this area it was imperative that the toxic memories be removed so healthy understanding could replace them. The very thought of the sexual union as an intimate and spiritual act was not one I ascribed to. Sex had only been a pleasurable physical act to me and nothing more. In my teen years, I never considered sex intimate and most certainly not holy. Having been used, I would use; it was a vicious game where all players were defeated. There simply could be no winners in a game manufactured out of hell itself.

Once again, I found myself on the receiving end of an unsettling revelation. I felt as though I had been robbed of a precious gift. What made it all the worse, I didn't know this gift even existed.

Dr. Storm continued to be my instructor on the most basic of life lessons. Much like a father teaching his daughter, he mentored me on how to distinguish between normal and abnormal, good and evil behavior. My emotional and developmental deficiencies were painfully obvious during our sessions.

With the ominous box that remained unopened, there was a nagging question that I wanted to ask him before our session had concluded. The contents in that box are so barbaric that I was uncertain how I mentally survived this long without an emotional breakdown or worse.

"I have a question for you."

"Sure, what would you like to know?"

Somewhat tentatively, I continued. "If my background is really as bad as you and everyone else seems to think, then how am I not crazy? Last night I was watching a show where a journalist was interviewing a woman about her life story. A family member molested her when she was only a child, and it completely threw her over the edge. She ended up becoming an alcoholic, drug addict and wound up living on the streets. Even more appalling, she became criminally insane and killed her baby while washing him in the bathtub."

"Yes, that can be the sad result of this tragedy," Dr. Storm commented.

"But that's my point. I mean with the babysitter's assault and what my brother did to me, the traumas in my life seemed so much more significant than hers, and yet I'm still here. I'm not at all discounting that God's grace has saved me and if it weren't for Him I wouldn't be here, but there must be something else that I'm missing. How did I endure all these years without having to deal with my past until now?"

"That's a great question, Veronica." Cautiously and with great care, he explained. "You did what some people do to survive a violation when they are unable to process it, you fragmented. That's when an individual is so traumatized that they are powerless to handle it, so their personality fractures; it splinters off into many different pieces."

"What in the world are you saying?" I grimaced.

Carefully he clarified. "It is similar in some ways to multiple personality disorder. Instead of completely coming up with different personalities, which could be either male or female, you took your own personality and fractured it so you could be what you needed to be in any given situation. You were dangerously close to multiple personalities though. I would classify you as borderline. Probably, one more trauma, and you would have crossed over."

Too astonished to speak, I sat and listened to the doctor tell me something that rocked my world. *I'm broken, that's what he is telling me: essentially I am broken.* What was even more chilling was I knew exactly what he is talking about.

Hesitantly I said, "I never referred to it as fractured. It's called 'switching gears,' and I do it all the time."

****

The dictionary definition of fragmented is as follows: Existing or functioning as though broken in separate parts; disorganized, dis-unified, an incomplete or isolated portion, detached, *a fragmented personality.*

Hardly knowing where to start, I proceeded, "You're saying I am broken? That's what fragment means, you know—broken. I thought everyone 'switched gears.' It always came so natural to me. That would make me either stupid for not knowing it wasn't normal or crazy. I'm not too sure which is worse."

As if walking on thin ice, Dr. Storm tried to soften the blow of the dynamite just ignited. "Veronica, let me assure you, you are not stupid or crazy. It takes someone with pretty high intelligence to pull off what you did for so many years. Your mind was incapable of managing all the traumas you endured. No one could have survived it without the help of coping mechanisms. You were in a perfectly unmanageable, unhealthy living situation. You could have chosen drugs, alcohol, multiple affairs with men, any number of ways to cope; however, your mind chose fragmentation because you were smart enough to achieve it. Housing all your memories in boxes and separate containers to keep yourself sane is nothing to take lightly. God gave you that ability; coping mechanisms are his way of helping humanity deal with the inhuman.

The good news is you've already begun the 'integration' process. A few weeks ago when you said you felt as though you had met Veronica for the first time, well, you did. You blew me away with what you discovered on your own. While going through your mental inventory, you inadvertently saw many of the facets of your personality. It was as if you placed each individual splinter on the table and introduced them to each other. It was fascinating to hear you explain something you had no knowledge of."

Not as convinced as he was that I would be OK, I was still trying to figure this out. "Only in the past several weeks have I been concerned with my ability to change gears. One minute I am totally unglued and incapable of communication or rational thought and, within a split second, if the situation demands it, I switch gears and become calm, cool and controlled. It's not as if I'm pretending; I really am genuinely in high spirits at the moment of the 'switch.' It's as if I become another person entirely. It literally takes less than one second to achieve it."

Mentally going deeper into the concept, I began to think aloud how it affected other areas of my life. Then it hit me.

"Oh no, this is what I do when making love with Jerry. I have always switched gears when being intimate with him. It's a little like role-playing, I guess. I become this other woman. She has always been a necessary part of our relationship, but make no mistake, she is not me. I do it every time. It has helped me have an enjoyable sexual relationship with him. It was really the only way I knew how to do it."

It had never occurred to me until that moment in his office that it wasn't normal to have needed the other woman that I had created. Then the revelation came to me, that, unbeknownst to my husband, he had loved her thinking it was me. I began mentally to picture all the different personas I had created over the years. I loved them and felt as though they were a part of me—they were me. I knew who to switch to in any given situation. Sometimes it was an intentional switch; other times, they involuntarily took control. Either way, I loved them and felt I needed them.

I sat on the sofa in a psychologist's office and heard the most shocking information regarding my personality and life. "I don't want to be broken; I want to be normal and whole," I pleaded. "I thought everyone switched gears. Is anything in my life or personality normal, for crying out loud? How am I supposed to function without being able to switch gears? That's how I get from moment to moment and situation to situation. I have no clue to how to stop doing it."

Dr. Storm tried to calm my unraveling nerves. "Veronica, it was how you were able to manage so many roles without breaking down. Like I said, you have already begun the integration process. You are learning to deal with situations as they arise and to allow the feelings and reality to sink in. By not denying the emotions and 'switching gears' as you call it, you remain in the moment and don't splinter off. Eventually all the separate splinters of your personality will begin to work together and not separately. It takes some time, but you'll get there."

Dr. Storm looked at his watch and told me it was about time to wrap it up. "Are you ready for another domino for this week?"

Feeling as if nothing could upset me more than what just took place, I said, "Sure, why not. What do you have?"

"This might not make sense at first, but give it time and it will help you find the path you need to be on. So here it goes: what if the reason you don't stand up to your family is because they will say you are the crazy one and they are all normal? Are you concerned that others will believe them and that's why you remain silent?"

Already knowing the answer to his question, I told him I would consider it throughout the course of the week. I picked up my purse and started to head for the door. Before leaving, I stopped and looked back at him. "Will you do me a favor?"

"Sure, if I can, what is it?"

Almost in desperation, I said, "Please don't give up on me."

Too quick to answer for my satisfaction, he replied, "I won't give up on you," as he continued to collect his things.

Not willing to let it go, I reiterated my concern. "I mean it, I don't care what I say or how I act, I don't want you to quit on me. I'm not even sure who I am or what I'm doing anymore. I need to know that you will see this through. So, please - please promise you won't give up on me, OK?"

Hearing the seriousness of my request, he stopped for a moment. "Veronica, I told you we are not through here until you are free. God has picked this time in your life, for whatever reason, for you to be healed from your past. I won't consider my part in this accomplished until you have achieved your freedom. God is doing the work very quickly with you, I'm really not doing that much. You have come such a long way in a short period of time. I feel very privileged to be a part of it. So, I promise—I won't give up on you."

The Lord was able to use those words to empower me

to cross the threshold of complete suspicion of Christian men to trusting one for the first time. Dr. Storm was ushered from being a stranger to the first man I have ever trusted, Jerry would be my second. Two men in a world of millions; it would be a start. It would appear to be such a small beginning; however it was huge to me. I was embarking into what I had always considered cold and dangerous waters. Although scared out of my wits, I had never felt so bold or courageous in my life.

As I left his office, my mind was entangled in the words: *fractured, integrated, broken, trust, holy,* and *splinter,* all of which were foreign to me. I wasn't looking for any easy solutions; however, things were being put on my emotional plate that I never would have chosen to dine on. Realizing confrontation with my brother was inevitable, I felt the thought start to eat away at me like worms devouring an apple. The tragedy of life can sometimes be life itself. It continues to go on as if nothing has changed, when the reality is everything has changed. Although still a wife, mother, church leader, and friend, I was unable to go day to day as though nothing out of the ordinary was happening. I was losing the family of my birth and the false realities that I had clung to. One other casualty might be my soundness of mind.

Saturday came, and I had been invited to a high school graduation party of one of my friend's son. The chore of mixing and mingling with complete strangers exhausted me before it even began. Feeling completely robbed of so many childhood things, I was infuriated when past events robbed me of my present happiness as well. Two for the cost of one, evil got a double prize. I went to the party but could only last for thirty minutes. I was unable to pull off a celebratory mood right then.

After being at a volleyball tournament all day, Jerry arrived home later that evening with our daughter. Greeting them with a hug and kiss, I asked her how her team placed in the games. She was beaming as she filled me in on the details of a victorious day on the courts. Jerry asked how I was doing and wanted to know if we could slip away to catch up. Glad to accept his offer, I told the kids that we were going out for a while and would return in a few hours. Ensuring they were clear on bedtimes and house rules, we headed out on a late night date.

While in the car, we tried deciding where we should go. We didn't want to be concerned about having our conversation overheard at a restaurant, so we wound up spending our date in the car at an empty parking lot. Trying to get comfortable, we reclined our seatbacks with our legs outstretched in front of us. We kept the car stereo on with soft rock music playing in the background.

Jerry reached over to hold my hand and asked, "How did your day go? Are you doing any better?"

"I can't stop thinking about how I'm going to confront my brother and how it will impact my family if I do. I really can't believe this is happening. It's all going so fast."

Jerry continued on the same subject. "What do you think your brother's reaction will be if you confronted him? Do you think he will admit to it or deny it?"

I pondered his question and then had an out-of-the-blue

epiphany. "He won't remember!" I declared with certainty.

"What makes you so certain?"

"Shoot, I can't believe I haven't remembered this until now. A few months ago when he was at our house, I asked him about something that had happened several years earlier. He didn't have a clue what I was talking about. When I tried to remind him of the event, his wife chimed in and told me to give it up. 'Veronica, your brother doesn't remember what happened five minutes ago let alone five years ago.' This is terrible Jerry!"

The two of us sat quietly looking at each other not knowing what to do. I felt totally deflated.

"This changes everything. He doesn't remember; I know he doesn't remember. I actually conjured up enough nerve to confront him but it's too risky now." Thinking that all my unpacking of my preciously concealed containers had been in vain, I sat motionless unable to comprehend the change of events. Nothing was the same for me, yet everything remained unchanged in the overall functioning of my family. I wanted the masquerade to be over and every member of my family to remove their facades. How could I make this happen?

Reaching out to Jerry for support as promised, I asked, "Will you go to Dr. Storm's office with me tomorrow? I need to talk to him about how to proceed."

CHAPTER TEN:

Failed Memory?

The family ties that bind are no less restricting than the shackles around the wrists and ankles of the toughest of criminals whose hearts have turned to stone. It's a difficult thing to decide to walk away from your DNA. The blood that flows through the veins of my loved ones flows freely through mine as well. My efforts to simply vanish from my family had been unrewarded. They wouldn't let me go, yet they seem to abhor me. It's a slippery slope to confront religious people who appear above reproach. Once you step out, there is simply no way to scale your way back up that muddy hill.

Jerry and I returned to Dr. Storm's office, which had become my home away from home. With every molecule of my being, I wanted to be whole, and I would work with tenacity to make it happen. Right on time, Dr. Storm peeked around the corner with his usual greeting. His eyes bright, a smile sprayed across his face, and his right hand extended for a cordial shake, he welcomed us back to his office. His smile was always outrageously contagious. Even when I was in my lowest state, I couldn't help but to smile in return. Always enjoying seeing us as a couple, he was thrilled that Jerry would join us in our session.

"How are you guys doing?" he raised with genuine curiosity.

When asked that by the average person, the replies are pretty basic: Fine, thank you, how are you? When asked that by a psychologist, it is one loaded question.

Jerry looked in my direction for me to respond. "Well, it's been a difficult couple of days again. I was considering your domino question in the last session, and I have come up with my answer. I don't remain silent and hide my family from everyone for fear they will call me the unstable one. They already do that. So my conclusion is, I'm not afraid of them; I'm terrified of me."

"Really?" Dr. Storm asked. "Why are you afraid of your response?"

"Because I can be totally secure about who I am when I'm not with them, but, while in the company of one of them, I am completely insecure. It's like I'm a different person entirely. They really do hold a power over me. It's crazy but true."

"Veronica," Dr. Storm implored, "They don't have any hold on you that you don't surrender to them. You are the decision maker about who you are, not them. You are a grown woman with a family of your own. If people continuously hurt you, you are allowed to walk away."

His explanation sounded so reasonable, but it was completely out of my mental grasp. The boxes on the shelf of my mind began to quake at his suggestion. I felt as though my very salvation was dependant on my ties to the family. Is it possible that brainwashing, normally only attributed to religious cults and governments, can be used in families as well?

Religiously authoritative parents can walk a dangerous line if they abuse being spiritual advisors to their children. Proud in their convictions, they praise their ability to do both God and their child a favor by using the Bible to inform them of their inadequacies. Little do the self-righteous parents know they have chosen the wrong partner in the spiritual realm and have caused the dark side to cheer. Bullies with Bibles—never a good combination. They carefully choose verses and scriptures to give them permission to dominate whom they consider the lesser of God's creation, their offspring. Their unjust crusade blemishes God's original intention of parenting although they give Him top billing for their cause.

The child carries the heavy weight of deciphering between what is God's standard and what is the parent's selfish motivation. The promise of God's blessing if obedient or cursing if rebellious—which would you choose?

The truly godly parents view their roles as a sacred responsibility to teach the love and ordinances of God and not as an excuse to exalt themselves above the family. They are motivated out of love to discipline their children so they can walk in the fullness of God's plan. They are not concerned what others think of them or their child; they are only concerned with their child's character and view of God. They know that the child, whom God has entrusted to them, will in their childish mind, view them as God, so they walk cautiously to convey His true heart of love and grace.

Fathers, who proclaim that they are the priest of the household for the sake of silencing their children from having contrary opinions, speak as if they are the voice of the

Almighty. Such fathers cloak their uncontrolled temper in the disguise of righteous indignation and their insecurity as divine inspiration. They use the scripture "Honor your father and mother" as an instrument used to gain their own way and not as a holy decree for them to adjust their behavior to be worthy of honoring.

How many children who are raised in homes like these have turned their back on God and the church? Only God knows the exact number, and He will judge those parents accordingly. On the other hand, perhaps equally as bad, when grown and parents themselves, they continue this selfish style of parenting. He must not take lightly a mortal man proclaiming to be His harsh voice of discipline when, in fact, the father has spoken for his own selfish gain. Yes, evil empires and mind-controlling cults could stand to learn a thing or two from religious parents like these.

"Perhaps my family is right, and I am the one to blame for the ruin of what they call a solid family. What if they are correct and God does want me to stay in their tight circle? I am constantly under the microscope of suspicion, not only with them but also with myself. If I confront my brother, and he doesn't remember, what am I left with? They will all come at me with spiritual fury. It will be my word against my brother's."

"I'm telling you right now: the fact that it might be true won't enter into the equation. My parents will be more concerned that this information will tarnish their reputation. My sister will have to admit that perhaps she isn't the only one in need of compassion. Everyone will have too much to lose; they will all try to dismiss my claim, so I won't disrupt the family roles and dynamic. I seriously don't think I'm worth it to them. My mental and emotional condition will hardly be a factor. It doesn't matter anyway; I cannot pull away from them."

Appearing as though this was out of the realm of possibility, he said, "What do you mean, you can't separate from your family?"

"I've tried not returning phone calls and coming up with excuses for not being able to make it to family functions. It's totally ridiculous. My mom condemns me about who I am as a person, and then she gets mad that I don't desire her company. The hardest part is: she's so unpredictable."

Smiling, I added, "Do you know the Lucy and Charlie Brown football cartoon? You know when Lucy holds the football and tells Charlie Brown that she will hold it for him to kick. She always pulls it away while he is running full speed and is in mid-air. At first, Charlie Brown says he is not going to fall for it again, but she's successful at convincing him that this time is entirely different. Choosing to believe her, he runs with all his might and goes full throttle for the ball. Of course, Lucy pulls the ball at the last minute and he winds up landing flat on his back. I never know who is at fault: Charlie Brown for believing her or Lucy for being so cruel. That's pretty much how I feel every time with my family. I trust them and then *wham*, they pull up the ball and I land flat on my back."

"When has that happened?" he asked.

"Well, not too long before I stopped talking to them, my mom came to visit us for a couple of days. As always, I was a little suspicious and scared it might be a set-up. I was right. She arrived while the kids were at school, and, to my surprise, we actually had a nice afternoon visit. When the children got home mid-afternoon, they were excited to see their grandma. I went into the kitchen to begin cooking dinner while they began their visit. Everything appeared to be going well. I actually started to feel guilty that I had thought she might be up to something."

"While we were eating dinner, the tide totally turned. Suddenly she changed from being conversational to cool. I sat there paralyzed and watched her work her pre-orchestrated plan. She invited my kids out for ice cream. 'I love my grandchildren,' she announced, 'I've come all this way to be with them.' Then with a smirk on her face, she looked across the table at me and said, 'Not that I don't want to be with you, but this time it's not about you. I want to spend all my time with them and not have any interruptions.'"

"My mom then told me I wasn't invited to go with them to get ice cream. She hated spending money on me. I guess she thought it must have sounded rude, so she backtracked and said I could come, just not in her car. It got more ludicrous as she went on. She actually told me I could follow her in my own car, but that she would not pay for my ice cream if I chose to go. 'I'm only buying it for them,' she said to make it perfectly clear I understood."

"She actually said that?" Dr. Storm asked abruptly.

"Yep, I'm not even kidding you. I just laughed and told her I never asked her to buy me ice cream. Right after dinner, she loaded my kids into her car and away they went. They were only gone for about a half hour. When they returned, everyone went to their bedrooms. It was so weird; no one said a word when they came in through the door."

"I could tell by the expression on my children's faces, it didn't go very well. My mom usually stays up to the wee hours of the morning watching television. To my surprise, my mom told me goodnight and headed upstairs. No hugs and no 'thank you;' she was quickly going to a bedroom to be alone for the remainder of the night. It was only like eight-thirty or so; for a woman who never usually goes to bed before midnight, I assumed I was being sent a message."

"The first thing in the morning I came downstairs and found her waiting on the sofa with her bags packed and ready to leave. Shocked, I asked if she was leaving. Without looking at me, she said her visit was over, and she was ready to go. We had originally planned on spending the day together. I had no clue what was going on. Feeling the cold wind of her wrath, but, pretending not to notice, I thanked her for coming. Then I leaned in to kiss her goodbye. She quickly turned her head to avoid the kiss. That about knocked me off my feet."

"I couldn't believe she actually had the nerve to be that obvious with her rejection. I told her I loved her. She stood up, said thank you to my 'I love you' remark, and headed for her car. To this day, I have no idea what I did to make her so angry with me. She definitely wanted to let me know I didn't deserve her love, let alone an ice cream cone."

"When the kids got home from school, I asked what happened when grandma took them out the night before. My older girls said it was so awkward. They told me that while in her car, my mom began telling them what a wonderful mother she was to me and how blessed I was to be part of the family. My mom said that although her mom abused her, she stopped the cycle of abuse and what a privilege it was for me to be raised by two loving, Christian parents. She kept going on and on about how kind she was when I was growing up and how she prayed all through my teen years."

"They didn't know what to say while in the car listening to their grandmother talk about what a fantastic mom she was when they just witnessed what had happened at dinner. They felt like a captive audience who just got duped. I have to admit that I was thrilled they noticed the hypocrisy of her claims in contrast to her behavior."

Dr. Storm sat back in his chair. "You must be exhausted trying to keep up with them. Keeping score and making sure you weren't the one who messed up, which would mean you actually deserved such treatment. The problem with that way of thinking is you seem to believe they would be justified to treat you horribly if you really did mess up. Either way, you bear the burden of their actions, not them. That has to wear you out."

"You have no idea," I said with a sigh. "Of course, I ducked out of sight for a while after she did that. Nevertheless, she continued to call and be nice, so I thought she was sorry."

Trying to describe what it was like to live like that, I began. "You never know when one of them will start to act up. It's like walking down a calm quiet hallway, minding your own business, and then suddenly, without warning, someone comes up from behind and shoves you into the wall. When you finally catch your breath, you look to see who did this to you. Painfully enough, you see a family member who looks at you as if you have no reason to be hurt. They endearingly embrace you and encourage you to walk with them the remainder of the way. They might even volunteer to pray for your safe passage."

"You don't know if a violation even occurred because they show no remorse or sign of any wrong doing. If confronted, they tell you that you are over reacting. Unbelievably, I actually don't know who is right, them or me. It's four against one, you know."

Thinking before I spoke, I continued. "It's just that we all serve the same God, you know? How can they all be wrong, and I'm the only one who sees the evil in our family line? Maybe I am the nutty one, and they all really do love me and want what's best for me."

Concerned with my lack of confidence, he tried to affirm me. "It sounds like a whole lot of work with no return on investment. No one should continue to set themselves up to get hurt by people who have proven over time to be unsafe. It doesn't matter if they are family or not, God does not want any of His children to be abused."

Backtracking on what I said earlier, he probed. "You said you were afraid your brother might not remember what happened in your childhood. What makes you think he doesn't recall what he did to you?"

"Easy, I remembered last night that my sister-in-law once joked about what a bad memory my brother has. If that is the case, he won't remember about the babysitter or how he molested me. There's no benefit in confronting him knowing he probably doesn't have any recollection of it."

"Why would that change anything?" he asked unwavering. "You know what happened and that's all that matters. It's not just about him repenting and offering you an apology; it's about future generations. If this is allowed to be kept in the dark, it's pretty typical for the behavior to go down to the next generation. At this point, it is about you, your brother's children, and your future grandchildren. You can't undo the sins of the past, but you can have an impact on your future."

Seeing the look of skepticism on my face, he tried another approach.

"Veronica, your brother very well may not remember anything about his childhood. It's not at all uncommon for a young child who was sexually assaulted, like he was, to shut down his memory. We have no way of knowing how he coped with being a victim. What is more injurious, however, is that he knew your parents were informed about the attack and they chose to do nothing to help him. That will usually make survival kick in quickly."

A nine- or ten-year-old boy has no natural abilities to deal with such an act of violence without proper medical help. If you decide to confront him, but his coping mechanism was to block it from his memory, then if approached, it might trigger his recollection as well. It would be a hard reality for him to face, but God wants him whole too. Remember, the Lord has been in control every step of the way. Not only did He prepare you for this moment, He has been preparing your brother too. Whether or not your brother has been receptive to the Holy Spirit's leading is between God and him."

"I guess I never thought of it that way."

Dr Storm finished with his train of thought. "What concerns me is that you seem to be so incredibly connected to them even though you don't want to be. Believing them when they say that you are at fault for the family being divided is not a valid conclusion. I can't emphasize this enough: they have no hold on you except what you give them."

Statements like these made one of the containers in my mind jump at his argument. Needing to constrain my inventory, I tried to divert his attention by changing our topic of conversation. "So you still think my brother really might not remember his childhood?"

"It's a possibility. Life in your home seemed to have been a tough challenge for any child to navigate. You mentioned in one of your earlier sessions that you actually wanted to commit suicide when you were a teenager. So, tell me: how old were you when you planned on doing it and what were you going to do?"

This was not at all a burdensome topic for me to discuss. Regrettably, when I retrieved this box from the storage shelf it was housed with the good memories and not the bad. Placing the wonderfully wrapped package on my mental table, I looked inside at the contents that I felt at the time were my only way out in the vast wasteland of my teen years.

"I had it all planned out perfectly. I was sixteen and decided it was time for me to die. Then, because of a miscalculation on my part, something unanticipated happened and everything went all wrong."

****

"I can't seem to remember why it was I chose that day to commit suicide. It's not like one day was particularly worse than another. Maybe it was because my boyfriend and I broke up; that's all I can think of anyway. It had all been planned out in my mind for months. I decided trying to kill myself before school would have been a mistake. My mom was always home in the morning. Well to be honest, by that time she was home most of the time. She really didn't have any friends or activities in her life. She was in full-blown depression by then. Because of this I figured she would have found me entirely too early and the suicide might not have been successful. So, the logical choice was to wait until after school. For some reason I knew I would be coming home to an empty house that day."

"At school, as awful as this sounds, I was in such a good mood. Finally, in control, I would be the one who decided something about my life. I would be able to send my family a message. Thinking I would never see my friends again, I took extra care in seeing everyone that day. When I got home, I cannot begin to tell you how nervous I was. My heart felt like it was going to beat right out of my chest."

"I walked into my bedroom, put my books on my desk and contemplated writing a suicide letter. I really didn't know what to say. I thought the very act itself was message enough. However, I couldn't bring myself to point the finger of blame at any individual; that would have been cruel. It had also occurred to me that if I wasn't successful in my suicide attempt and someone found me in time to revive me; then there would have been hell to pay. On the other hand, by not leaving a note, I was a little afraid that they might categorize my death as a tragic accident. I'm not too sure how anyone could spin the fact that I drank a glass of poison and died, but, if anyone could pull it off, it would be my family."

"I was excited and terrified all at the same time. It's a horrible thing to admit, but it's true. With the decision made that I wasn't going to leave a note, I got up from my bed, with my heart pounding and went into the garage to get the glass. It was a little like everything went into slow motion."

Dr. Storm was leaning forward to listen and then asked, "You went to the garage to get a glass? What kind of glass?"

"You see, there was this glass in our garage that had been there for at least six months, maybe even a year. My dad had a mixture of gasoline and turpentine in it that he would use to clean paintbrushes and tools. I figured I could just swallow the mixture, go back to my bedroom, lie on my bed and let the poison kick in. I made an inner vow that I would not panic and call 911. The mixture would burn like the devil himself, but I thought I would eventually pass out and then die."

"That would have been a horrible way to die, don't you think? What happened, did you decide it would be too painful?" asked Dr. Storm.

"Gosh no, I couldn't find the glass! I was frantic. It had been there for months, but I couldn't find it anywhere! I looked to see if my dad had simply washed it out so he could mix a new concoction when he needed it. I couldn't find the empty glass either. I was furious! I had finally gotten the nerve to commit suicide, and I couldn't find the stupid glass with the gasoline mixture. When each member of my family got home, I asked them if they knew where the glass in the garage went that had the gasoline mixture in it. They all said they knew about the glass but had no idea where it went."

"I began to wonder if God was trying to save me somehow. As far as I was concerned, it would have been a mercy killing if He allowed me to die. I knew He wouldn't see it that way though. At the end of the day, I had enough God in me to know that He had just spared my life. Glasses don't just magically disappear you know? I figured if God loved me enough to make sure I didn't get my hands on the deadly mixture then I should stick around for awhile."

Dr. Storm readjusted his position on his chair. He leaned back and extended his legs while crossing them at the ankles. He smiled and asked, "Did you ever find the glass?"

"Nope, never did," I said smiling in return.

Jerry chimed in, "I'm pretty sure when Veronica gets to heaven there is going to be an angel who pulls out the glass from behind his back and says, 'Were you looking for this?'"

Looking at Jerry, I said in wonder, "Wouldn't that be incredible? I guess I should be more thankful that I had angels watching out for me back then, huh?"

Jerry looked a little concerned. "You *are* glad you weren't successful right, Veronica?"

Hesitantly, I replied, "Sure, I'm glad. It's just that if I had been able to kill myself back when I was sixteen; I wouldn't still be dealing with this crap when I'm forty. I wouldn't have gotten married and brought four kids into this drama. Think about it Jerry: you wouldn't even have had the chance to meet me. You would have met someone else and had children, which means you wouldn't have to be sitting here dealing with this mess. I would be dancing on the streets of gold without the looming probability of confronting my brother. Maybe my family would have known they pushed me too far, and, if nothing else, it would have blown the whole 'perfect family' illusion out of the water."

"It might be hard for you guys to understand this, but there hasn't been one day, for over twenty years now, that I haven't asked myself the question, *What is wrong with me?* All these memories have always been there; I just didn't talk about them. Don't get me wrong: I've had some great years and good memories too. It's been difficult having my family in my life and being entangled in the same old emotional games without acknowledging our true history."

Jerry became even more concerned. "Wait, I haven't thought that you might be in danger of hurting yourself; was I wrong? Should I be concerned Veronica?"

With complete conviction, I assured him. "Absolutely not. I would never do anything stupid like that, I promise. I love you and the kids more than you could possibly know. I'm just saying that sometimes I think it would have been easier and a lot less painful if I had succeeded. That doesn't mean that I think it would have been better." I reached for his hand. "Trust me, I'm not going anywhere. I'm here for the long haul."

Dr. Storm interjected. "I can see where it might be easy to contemplate what it would be like if you never had to face any of this. It would be hard not to imagine what would have happened if you were successful. That doesn't take away from the fact that you are happy and grateful to be alive."

"Yes, thank you, you're exactly right! That's all I was trying to say. But you know what's weird? I have never been able to figure out why I didn't just pick another way to kill myself. I mean, I could have gotten into my mom's medicine cabinet and taken a fist-full of pills or something."

Surprisingly Dr. Storm answered, "That's one of the mysteries that the psychiatric community is still trying to figure out. A person decides to die, contemplates it, has a plan and then the plan fails. There simply isn't a plan "B." For instance, let's say someone jumps off a bridge to kill himself, hits the water, but doesn't die. When an officer arrives at the scene to save him, the man fights and tells the officer to leave him alone. After struggling with the distraught man for a while, the police officer finally pulls a gun, points it at the man, and says 'Get in the boat or I'll shoot.' That should be music to the man's ears, right? No, the man will become furious and tell the officer not to shoot and then get into the boat. No one knows for sure why the person who wants to commit suicide is more intent on the plan than his or her death."

Dr. Storm continued. "So you knew you shouldn't kill yourself, but you still had to deal with your life and family.

What did you do after your plan failed? How did you manage to go on day after day?"

"If leaving this earth wasn't an option, I thought maybe leaving the house was. My best friend was also so unhappy at home. For months, we would talk about it down to the last detail, but, as you can guess, we never actually did it. The fantasy that we might actually run away was enough to keep me going."

Dr. Storm thought and then asked, "Didn't you say that your brother and you were close during that year?"

"Yes, he was the nicest one in the house at that time."

He continued. "The Lord could have used your brother to save your life. He is willing to use the most unlikely of things to help one of His children. Although it was a twisted relationship, you would have not wanted to hurt your brother by attempting suicide again. You always were his protector; you probably even wanted to protect him from your death."

Jerry choked out, "Well, at least that's one thing we could thank him for, I guess." Then he looked at me. "What did he actually do to you when you were eleven? You never have said what took place that summer. It must have been pretty bad though for you to have all those night frights."

Stunned, I look over to Jerry to see if he was serious. The inquiry seemed to have come from out of nowhere. It felt like a machine gun was firing rounds into my heart. I always knew it was just a matter of time before Jerry asked me that dreadful question.

CHAPTER ELEVEN

Amazing Grace

Thinking he deserved an answer, I struggled to have the words come out. "I ... I ... well ... you see ... he was."

For the life of me, I couldn't get the words to formulate into sentences. I didn't want to paint the mental picture for him that would forever be like a mural in his mind to see.

Instantly, tears welled up in my eyes as I choked on my words. I tried to contain what I feared would be a total emotional eruption. As if venom were flowing through my veins, I began to violently tremble and wail. It felt like being back in the place of the violation. The images flooded my mind, and I shook my head back and forth to stop the mental video. "I was minding my own business," I howled begging them to believe. "I never wanted it to happen. I didn't even know why he was doing it! I wanted to be left alone; why wouldn't he just leave me alone?"

Jerry, regretting having asked the question, reached out in an attempt to comfort me. His touch sent me into a fright and I inadvertently flung my arm to protect myself as if hitting a ghost from my past. Now in complete hysterics, I continued to cry uncontrollably. The mental images were more than I could manage. Fearing that Dr. Storm was writing admission papers to the psychiatric ward, I tried to regain some resemblance of composure, but I was wildly unsuccessful.

My uncontrolled sobbing went on for several minutes. I wanted to become invisible and crawl away on my hands and knees with nobody noticing. How could I stop this? My emotional explosion was completely unexpected and most certainly unwelcome. I wanted more than life itself to have my body stop its uncontrollable shaking. Eyes remaining closed, head down in shame, I wanted the session to end.

Still sobbing, I was exhausted and began to slouch down on my corner of the sofa. *Please let me melt into nothingness and simply vanish.* Afraid, I finally open my eyes and was relieved that the men in white coats, carrying a straight jacket, hadn't been summoned to carry me away. I was pretty certain that a break down of this magnitude was worthy of a minimum two-week stay in a psych ward. The only upside was I might have finally gotten my hands on some medication to help ease the pain.

In my tears, I looked at the two men in the room and began to regain my control. With a restrained quiet tone, I said, "You are never to ask me that question again, do you both understand? I will never tell what happened that summer! I promise you, I will take it to my grave."

With great distress and still shocked at my reaction, Jerry nodded his head not knowing what else to do.

Dr. Storm leaned forward and said, "Veronica, I know it's hard, but you have been able to talk about everything else that happened to you this far. You have to get it out of you; it is all part of the healing process. You don't have to tell me or Jerry. You can choose a trusted female friend or minister if that would make you more comfortable. If you are unable to do that, then just write your brother a letter and tell him how much you were affected by what he did. You don't even have to give it to him: just writing it will be good enough for now."

Looking Dr. Storm dead in the eyes to make sure he completely understood my position, I said, "NO! I will NOT tell anyone or write any letter. Like I said, this one is going with me to my grave. I have done everything you have told me to do up to this point. I won't do it and you are never to ask me again. I will not budge on this one, I promise you!"

Dr. Storm not actually agreeing with my position, said. "I'm sorry that question upset you so much. I was a little worried with your outburst. Are you going to be OK?"

Still slumped and hiccupping, trying to catch my breath, I murmured, "Yes, I'll be fine. I just don't know why he chose me, you know? I was just minding my own business. I never wanted anything to happen."

"We don't know what your brother was thinking Veronica. I do know this: an eleven-year old girl isn't chosen because of her actions. You were chosen for convenience. Because he was sexually assaulted at such a young age, he probably had to do something to cope with it. It could have been that he splintered too. He very well might have been into pornography or something like that which would have heightened his sexual curiosity. That would explain why one minute he was the kind, supportive brother and the next minute the deviant."

"What little you have shared about the molestation, he did have some knowledge on the subject. More than what the average fourteen year-old boy would in that day and age. However, when he came into your room when he was in his early twenties, by then you probably weren't his sister; you were a prop. He wanted access to a female and you were it. You were the one he had access to."

What an odd thing to say. I wasn't a sister: I was a prop. Those words twirled around in the recesses of my mind trying to find a place to land but such a place doesn't exist. It was a freaky kind of relief to hear Dr. Storm qualify the situation like that. A prop? I'll take that over some of the other possibilities. I would have rather been an inanimate object over being a sister back then anyway. To be something that has no heart that could break, no soul that could be damaged and a total lack of capacity to feel pain, would that have been better? A sister who is being molested or a mere prop in his sick imaginary mind—I didn't like my choices.

My body was still trembling, but it was time for the session to end. Both Dr. Storm and I knew a "domino" was out of the question with that visit. He didn't offer one, and I most certainly didn't have the strength or desire to ask for it. With another appointment on the calendar, Jerry and I thanked Dr. Storm, and left. I noticed when I stood up that I was actually weak in the knees; Jerry placed his arm around me for support. Leaving his office, I told Jerry that I needed to go the ladies' room before we headed to the car. When I walked into the bathroom, I noticed that I was alone. Exhausted, I leaned against the wall and slid down to the floor with my hands covering my face. Tears began flowing out from the well of my broken heart.

Sitting on the floor, my mental inventory began once more. I saw the ominous box safely on the top shelf, out of reach for either Jerry or Dr. Storm to retrieve. How would I ever be able to face that container when I was having such trouble with the ones I had already opened? I remembered all too well the day I placed those grotesque articles in that container. That box was the most beautifully wrapped in my entire inventory. I tried so carefully to camouflage the true contents of what could cause my mind to break beyond repair.

My heart felt like a foreign member who was only there to notify me of my pain. Could freedom be worth such a price as this? For a brief moment and the first time in decades, I desired death more than life. I knew it was wrong and even untrue. I was just so incredibly tired. I truly couldn't imagine unpacking more boxes.

I picked myself up off the floor and washed my face and hands. I wanted to rinse away the tears that reminded me of what took place in Dr. Storm's office and of the emotional work ahead. I walked out of the restroom to the waiting arms of my husband. With Jerry embracing me, I looked up and reminded him, "I came here for marriage counseling." Nothing more needed to be said. He knew exactly what I was talking about. I often referred to the fact that it felt as though I didn't come looking for this; it came looking for me.

Still one unanswered question plagued me. Why did

the grace that sustained me all of these years suddenly stop working? As soon as we returned home, I ran upstairs to email my friend Denise. She had been a psychologist. I asked her if we could meet for lunch.

Several days later, we met at a resaturant on the beach halfway between our homes. It was another beautiful spring day with weather that screamed that summer was right around the corner. She was easy to spot, slim build with long, gorgeous blond hair flowing down her back. We sat on the patio under the shade of an umbrella with the ocean waves breaking right beside us. The sea sparkled with as many facets as the most spectacular diamond I had ever seen. The crowds had gathered for sun and surf, and we were both grateful to have found parking spaces so late in the day.

The soup of the day was New England clam chowder. Never one to pass on clam chowder, I ordered a bowl that would be served with some freshly made sourdough bread. Denise decided on a fresh garden salad with dressing on the side. Hers was definitely the healthier choice, but I was sure mine was the more delectable of the two. We both sat back in our chairs, taking in the sun and waited for our food to arrive. Denise asked the usually benign, "How is it going?" and was in for a surprise with my answer.

I didn't waste any time and began to fill her in on the events of the past month and a half. I knew that because of her former profession of psychology and her faith I could tell all the grave details and trust her counsel.

Denise listened with compassion and told me she was sorry to hear what had happened. I appreciated her empathy, but I was not looking for compassion; I was looking for answers. She was true to her former profession and call. Her words brought comfort and confirmation to everything I had been learning.

Still, there was one question I wanted to run by her. "Denise, I'm wondering about something. I know God's timing is perfect, and I probably couldn't have handled dealing with my past until now, but there is one thing that I can't figure out."

"What is it?"

"I have understood and applied the scriptures that tell us God's grace was sufficient. I mean, for years whenever I was hurt or was confused, I could just lean on His grace and it was more than enough. What am I missing? Either His grace is enough or it isn't. My doctrine seems to be off, even though it worked for so long."

With no effort at all, she smiled and said, "Well, Veronica, it doesn't sound to me like your doctrine is off; your definition is. Grace isn't God enabling you to never look back and face your past; grace is God's power to help you look back and deal with all of your hurts with His help. You see, His grace is sufficient; you just need it in a different way right now. God always wants us to be healed from whatever hurts us, but He will allow time to pass so we can better deal with the pain. The measure of relief you have experienced over the past years of your life was merely temporary. It was always His intention to deal with the pain of your childhood. His grace brought you up to this point, and His grace will carry you to the completion."

"Veronica, a lot of people struggle with thinking they're

not even allowed to think about the past once they become Christians. But that's not how God handles our past or our pain. He wants it to be out in the open, and He yearns to have the opportunity to bring His grace and mercy into the situation. Once it's been dealt with, then you can go on towards the future with a whole new outlook. I know the process is painful, but you'll see, it will be the best thing that has ever happened to you."

I also shared with her the angst I had about confronting my brother. She confirmed Dr. Storm's sentiment and said that I was not to view myself as his secret keeper.

"Your brother has made choices along the way with how he wanted to deal with it. You are at liberty to make your own choices, one of which is getting the secret out in the open. You have to be free, and often confronting the offender is one of the necessary steps. You have no moral obligation to remain silent."

We continued talking as the server refilled our water glasses several times to ward off the heat. After we finished our lunch, he brought us our check, and Denise graciously picked up the tab. We walked along the pier and enjoyed the warmth of the sun and the rest of our visit. With a hug and a "thank you," we parted company and promised to keep in touch.

My day went on as normal. All the usual daily tasks still required my attention. In the midst of the everyday chaos, I noticed that calmness had started to set in. Although I was still hurting from all the admissions and exposures, there seemed to be a tranquility that was settling in reminiscent of a warm gentle breeze. My trembling began to subside, and I was enjoying talking to Jerry with the transparency I had only now begun to take pleasure in. Just when I didn't think I could stand it one more day, God's mercy flooded my soul like a healing ointment on an open, oozing wound.

My children thought we were still in marriage counseling and had no clue what was emerging behind the closed doors of our sessions. It wouldn't be fair to let them in on all the secrets at this point. It was more than the adults could manage, and it would be entirely too much for them to sort out.

Things were starting to calm down, and, although there was so much left to do, it was not as overwhelming as it was at the beginning stages. The pattern was becoming clear. I reveal what was concealed, then I deal with what was revealed, and, without fail, healing came as promised.

Healing didn't feel like I thought it would. It wasn't as if I imagined I would want to go skipping through the tulips, and I most certainly didn't think I would see pixie dust floating around. I did, however, think it would be a little like making it to the top of a mountain—battle weary yet victorious! Perhaps even the "Rocky" theme would be playing in the background. I don't mind telling you, it's nothing even close to that experience.

It was more of a peaceful knowledge that I didn't have to be in control. Slowly, I was beginning to feel a calm presence of mind in contrast to having the constant mental inventories. The memories didn't hold nearly the amount of power they once had. I was basking in being my genuine self. The house wasn't kept in its usual perfect condition, but I didn't give a crud if anyone thought I didn't measure up anymore. I'll just let them know right up front—I don't measure up at all, no ifs, ands or buts about it. Now that's freedom!

Another unexpected perk, at least for my husband, was that my need to shop had greatly decreased. I no longer seemed to have the void in my soul that only shopping could fill. In fact, even though my sessions were next to the most wonderful shopping center on the planet, I hadn't gone once. Sometimes, when I didn't want to go to the counseling appointment, I promised myself that after it was over I would reward myself with a shopping spree. I always planned on going, but, when the session ended, all I wanted to do was go home and crash.

Taking pleasure in being quiet and at rest was completely alien to me, but I was enjoying every minute of it. I never knew how exhausting it was to have to stay busy all the time. The busyness would distract me from the voices within, but I had answered their cry, that was all they had ever wanted. They didn't want to torment me: they only wanted to be known.

Patience wasn't such a difficult aspiration any longer. I had hardly arrived by any stretch; however, many parts of my personality were changing before my eyes. Character traits that I had tried to achieve for years were taking care of themselves now that my secrets were being exposed. I had also become enraptured in the revelation that desperation was my ally. It led me to the foot of the cross, not a bad place to be really.

Only just a few months earlier, it was never enough. More money in the bank, a larger home, clothes filling every square inch of my closet, and don't even get me started about shoes. Jockeying for the best place in leadership at church and yet the insatiable emptiness remained. How could shopping, busyness, leadership, public speaking and accolades ever be a replacement for this new tranquility?

This newfound freedom did not have me jumping from cloud to cloud in a constant state of euphoria. However, I was completely treasuring this feeling of being very satisfied with where I was and yet still hungry for truth and wholeness. Life was such a paradox—it was both painful and sweet all at the same time.

My day was about over. The kids were safely in their beds, and Jerry called it a night and went to bed also. Living in a family of six is wonderful; however, I still craved time alone with my thoughts. I was sitting on the couch enjoying a late night snack and then it hit me. A mental picture I didn't ask for but relished just the same.

While I was contemplating the "domino" Dr. Storm gave in the last session regarding the lack of anger I felt towards my father, a vision began to play out on the screen of my mind. In this scenario, there was a mother and daughter standing in the middle of the street. No one was around; they were alone together. Quite unexpectedly and without provocation, the mom lashed out at her daughter with uncontrolled fury. The daughter, terrified by her mother's actions, reacted in confusion. She didn't understand what she did to provoke such anger. Then I saw him. A man was standing along side at the curb watching the whole drama unfold. He was so much larger and stronger than the mom who was measuring out such pain to her daughter. He saw the girl hurting and trying with all her might to defend herself but her adversary outmatched her. Still observing, he stood silently, with no emotion, watching the defenseless child as though it was out of his control to save her.

It would take but one word from his mouth to call off the brutal attack from the mom. I looked in anger at his ambivalence to her actions and wondered how he could be so cowardly or cold. He seemed completely unmoved by the horror show he witnessed as if no human emotions should come into play.

The fictitious drama of my mind sent chills up and down my spine. Who had committed the greater evil, the mom who lashed out on her daughter or the man who stood by so apathetically, not willing to interfere and rescue the girl when it is in his power to do so? Remembering that the opposite of love is not hate, but apathy, I questioned my father's love for me.

I finally saw what Dr. Storm had been trying to convey to me over the past month and a half. How could I have possibly excused such intolerable cruelty? I wanted and felt I absolutely needed to have my dad's love and relished the thought that I was the apple of his eye. Oddly, I was not nearly as upset or undone as I thought I would be with this revelation. Nothing seemed to shock me about my family anymore. I seriously didn't think I could survive letting this illusion go. Fortunately, holding on to the delusion required more strength than embracing the truth. If accepting the fact that my dad really was the greater offender got me to the finish line faster, I would let the truth do what it is intended to do—set me free.

Sleep was beckoning and I gladly answered its call. Grabbing Jerry's arm and wrapping it around me, I held on tight to his hand and fell fast asleep. After a full seven hours of uninterrupted sleep, my alarm clock woke me with songs that would remain in my head the rest of the day. Knowing that I had another appointment today with Dr. Storm, I did a quick check of my inner inventory to see if all of my containers were present and accounted for. I felt there were only two boxes that were still in need of protection. The rest of my packages had either already been opened or could be opened at any time during the session.

I was actually excited about seeing Dr. Storm that day. He would be happy that I had been able to come to terms with the relationship, or lack thereof, with my father. Now that I had seen it for what it really was and had stopped the denial, the second step would be forgiveness. I had come to terms that those were the necessary steps to take if I wanted to be freed from my pain.

Grabbing a cup of coffee and my purse, I quickly headed out the door to make it to my appointment. If I had known that Dr. Storm was going to locate one of the two boxes I had kept closely guarded, I don't know if I would have gone. Yes, a quiet inner peace was emerging from the darkness, but how was I to know it was the lull before the storm?

CHAPTER TWELVE

No One Escaped

Pulling into my usual parking space, I began to wonder if I would miss counseling when I had finished the necessary sessions. It had become such a part of my life, and Dr. Storm felt more like a friend or even a father than a counselor. Funny thing is, he was nowhere near old enough to be my dad, but he definitely exuded the heart of a father. That's a pretty typical response, I think. You have a person in your life that knows more about you than any other person on the planet, how can you not feel they are more than just a professional doing their job? That notwithstanding, I had grown to appreciate his wisdom and compassion during our 1 ½ hour sessions.

Sitting in the waiting room, it felt like I was a student checking in with all her homework complete. Thrilled that I could tell him about the progress I'd made in between sessions, I waited for Dr. Storm to greet me.

While sitting there, the thought struck me that there had never been anyone else in the waiting room when I arrived. Another psychologist shared the executive suite and had an office just down the hallway from his. They seemed to have coordinated their schedules so their patients would never have to sit in the waiting room with each other. If that was the case, that was mighty thoughtful! I sat on the comfortable cushioned chair listening to the classical music that was softly playing in the background. Before I knew it, I would inadvertently begin humming along with the orchestra. Relaxed and reading a magazine, I heard him walking to the waiting area. Peeking from behind the wall and smiling, he said, "Veronica, as usual, you are right on time. How are you doing?" he asked while shaking my hand.

Probably one of the first things you notice about Dr. Storm is his unique voice. It is unusually low, in a tone that is reminiscent to me of a late night disc jockey on a jazz or blues radio station. I shook his hand, returned his smile and told him I was doing fine.

We entered his office. Filling him in on the lunch with Denise was the first item on my list. He knew that I had been wrestling with the whole "grace" question. Right doctrine, wrong definition, worked for me!

Quickly changing subjects, I moved on to the topic of my dad. Sharing the imaginary plot that I had witnessed unfold before my eyes had Dr. Storm completely engaged in my discovery.

"Once again, you have made such progress. I can't get over how fast you work."

Almost laughing I said, "I don't feel like I work fast at all. I spent several weeks on this one."

"You're right," he assured. "It took you several weeks, but most people take months to come up with the answer. All the ground you have covered in a few short months, it would take the majority of people a year or two to accomplish. You probably don't rest until you get the answer you are looking for, right?"

"Yeah, I get pretty consumed by it. I just want to be better, you know? I figure it's worth a few nights of missed sleep and a whole lot of mental inventory to get this over as fast as possible."

"That's good. Have you had any more night frights or trembling? You seem pretty calm today."

"I feel great today. I'm always good when I get answers to my questions or am able to successfully tackle a 'domino.' This past week has been exhausting but peaceful."

"Good, then if you don't have anything you want to discuss right away, I thought you could tell me a little more about your family. We have talked a lot about your immediate family, but you have only mentioned some of the extended family members. I know you have an uncle, and you have also referenced a grandmother. I am curious to see how far back some of these generational patterns go."

"Sure, but I don't know any further back than my grandparents. I think I met my great grandparents on my grandma's side of the family; however, I can't remember them. I was very young when I met them."

"No problem, let's start with your grandparents and work our way down."

One of the two boxes that I had been protecting started to quake with this line of questioning. The box, whose contents shook when we discussed family history, was dangerously close to Dr. Storm's reach. If opened, I might be under suspicion as being one of them. I am never to be considered one of them. "OK, well here goes. First, there is my biological grandfather. I never actually met him. From what my mom tells me, he was a very abusive and dangerous man. He beat her and her brothers all the time. He also began sexually abusing her at a very young age. The last time she saw her father was when she was seven years old. He pulled her out of bed one night and brought her into the family room where her brothers already were, crying."

"How many brothers did she have?"

"She had two at the time. I think one was older and the other one was younger. They were all pretty close in age though. Anyway, her dad was holding a shotgun to her head and telling her mom that he was going to kill all three of the kids and then her. My mom and uncles were terrified. My grandmother was no saint either. She just yelled back that he didn't have the balls to pull the trigger and she dared him to do it."

"Of course, the kids were hysterical, so a neighbor finally called the police. The police arrived but this was back in the 1940s so domestic violence wasn't taken too seriously. As long as it was in your house and going on behind closed doors, they simply wouldn't interfere. When the police got there, they told her dad to put down the gun and go out for a while to cool down. Apparently, he said he would go and cool off but he never returned and do you know he never did? That was the last time she ever saw him."

"Well actually that's not entirely true, that was the last time she ever saw him in person. She said that when she was around twelve years old she saw her dad on TV as being a wanted criminal."

"Your grandfather was on the FBI's most wanted criminals list?"

"Beats me, I don't know for sure what list he was on, but she said she saw him on TV. They had a real unusual last name, so she was concerned when she went to school the next day that everyone would know."

"Then there was my grandmother. She picked up where he left off when it came to the abuse. The only thing that stopped of course was the sexual abuse, but she would smack the kids around and yell at them all the time. My grandmother later remarried when my mom was a young teenager and that is the grandfather I know. I guess he didn't abuse her or anything, but he most certainly didn't protect her either. My grandmother remained mean and unsafe even through my mom's adult years. My mom would periodically have to write her off for years at a time because she was so malicious to her."

Dr. Storm was totally engrossed with the information and was busy writing away on his tablet. I often wondered what he was writing down, but I knew better than to ask. It could be unnerving at times to watch. I became silent and waited for him to catch up jotting down all the details.

I too was writing; he just didn't see my mental tablet. Because my mom and sister would often take what I said during a previous conversation and twist it around to use it against me, I learned to keep careful track of any important dialogue. This didn't indicate at all that I didn't trust Dr. Storm. My mental documentation of our conversations was not a reflection on his character; it was a reflection of mine. I didn't do it intentionally; it really just came naturally. It was a skill that I found essential in helping me to survive whenever a family member tried to rewrite history.

Finished with his writing, he looked up and said, "OK, what about your mom's brothers? Did they ever get married?"

"Oh sure, they got married. There is my one uncle that I have already told you about. You know the one who was an alcoholic and killed his two kids in the car accident? His wife was my favorite aunt." I laughed., "She was my only aunt on that side of the family, so I guess she got the title by default. But she really was nice; I loved her very much. After the accident, she stayed with my uncle to everyone's utter surprise. They tried to have more children but were unsuccessful. She later divorced him and now I have no idea what has become of her."

"My uncle totally flipped out though. You know how I told you he was never remorseful for the death of his two kids? Well, he stuck to that till his dying day. He ended up being a real creeper. He would write different family members the scariest cryptic letters telling them that his two kids came to his room the night before with a message for them. He said his dead children would come and keep him company in the nighttime hours. He continuously told family members that God used him as the instrument to bring his two kids to heaven. Thereby, the accident wasn't his fault; it was God's. He was as serious as a heart attack when he said it."

"He died at a relatively young age; I think he was only in his early sixties. By the time he died, the only people left in his life were my grandparents and his younger brother. He passed alone in his bed and wasn't discovered for several days. Only a handful of family members went to his funeral.

Then there is my other uncle. I guess I knew him the best out of all my uncles. He was married and had three children. I don't remember my aunt's name or what she even looked like. They divorced when I was real young. During their separation, my uncle panicked that he wouldn't be able to have custody of any of their children. So, one day, he took his youngest daughter and left town without telling anyone where he went. He literally went into hiding with my cousin until he could get his wife to agree to let him have her. Can you believe she agreed to it? I don't know how long he was in hiding, but it was a while, that I do know. So I was able to get to know that cousin but I don't remember the older two."

"Did he ever get into trouble for what he did? I mean, he kidnapped his daughter from her mother."

"No, not to my knowledge. That was all worked out in the divorce agreement. My younger cousin, although she had an older brother and sister, grew up as an only child being raised by a single father. She didn't even see her mom again until she was a young adult. Now you have to understand that my uncle was a womanizer from the word go. He had many live-in girlfriends, and it seemed almost all of them had teenage sons. As you can imagine, this does not have a happy ending."

"Did the boys get to your cousin?"

"Yes, they most certainly did. But here is the real kicker: she told my uncle what was going on, and he didn't believe her. He said she was just jealous because she was so used to having him all to herself. So she kept getting molested until her dad would eventually tire of his girlfriend, and they would break up. Being in between women didn't last long for him though. He would get a new girlfriend, and she would move in and invariably bring her teenage sons with her."

"How long did this keep happening to her?"

"I think it was for several years. One time, one of the boys got caught molesting my cousin. Either my uncle walked in on it or his girlfriend did, I don't remember which. However, my uncle told my cousin that it wasn't that big of a deal, and she would eventually get over it. I think he did breakup with his girlfriend after that."

"My cousin, while in her teens, ended up trying to commit suicide. She took a bottle of Tylenol, but my uncle found her in time, and she was rushed to the hospital. Later, she had a boyfriend who she really liked and got pregnant with his child. By then, she was in her late teens. They eventually married, and she had another child. Their first child was a boy and their second was a girl. She was married to him for several years but then divorced him because he was abusive."

"The divorce was pretty nasty I guess. I'm not really close to my cousin so everything I heard was from my mom. My cousin was a single mom for a time and then she starting dating an older man. It turned out that he was an old time friend of her father's, so you do the math. Admittedly, everyone who met the new boyfriend liked him even though he was so much older. He was very kind to my cousin and loved her two kids as his own. They eventually married and were together for many years."

"Then, last year, you won't believe what happened. My cousin decided the marriage wasn't working, and she left her husband and wanted a divorce. Well, much to her surprise, her daughter, who was thirteen at the time, said she didn't want to leave her father. It was her step-dad, but she loved him. My cousin told her daughter that she could stay with her stepfather for a week, so she could get used to the separation. After a week, my cousin told her daughter it was time to leave and come join her and her brother in their new home."

"My cousin's daughter had a fit. I heard my cousin finally laid the law down with her daughter and told her she had to come with her. She explained that he is the stepfather and that she needed to be with her, the mother. Her daughter would have none of it. My cousin started to become suspicious and began to ask her daughter questions about the step-dad relationship. To her horror, she found out that her husband had been molesting her daughter for years and that's why her daughter wanted to stay because of their 'special relationship.'"

"Her husband was investigated and tried last year for child molestation. He was found guilty on multiple counts; I think it's like twenty, all against my cousin's daughter. I was told that he had started molesting her when she was only two years old. Last I heard, my cousin was back in another relationship and living with another man. It's all so sad."

Dr. Storm was completely enthralled by these new findings. "Are there any other aunts or uncles I should know about?"

"Well, I have one more uncle who is my mom's youngest brother. He is her half-brother; it was her mom's and stepfather's child. I've heard from my mom that he isn't doing too well either. I haven't seen him in years but get updates now and then. He never got married and lived real close to my grandparents for the longest time. When I was in middle school and was visiting my grandparents, we went to my uncle's house for a visit. The walls were covered with pictures from *Playboy* and *Penthouse*. I was mortified. I didn't know where to look. At one point, he got into a terrible motor cycle accident that about killed him. He was on disability for years and was never the same after the accident. I think my grandfather still helps him financially."

"Last, but not least, is my step-grandfather. My grandma passed away about four years ago from Alzheimer's disease, and he stayed by her side to her dying day. Everyone in the convalescent hospital sang his praises for being such a wonderful, supportive husband. When my grandmother passed away, to my family's total shock, my grandfather made the announcement about a week later, he was engaged to a woman no one had ever met. Seriously, my grandmother's body was barely cold when he made the announcement. It turned out that he had been having this long-term affair with a woman in the mobile home park where they lived. To top it all off, she was a good friend of my grandmother's. Honestly, soap operas have nothing on my family."

Everyone in the family was incensed that he was so unapologetic about his unfaithfulness to his wife. My cousin went to my grandpa's mobile home to help clean out my grandmother's things. She found lots of pornographic material that was my grandfathers. Later, when the woman he was having an affair with was introduced to the family, it turns out that she was a Christian who had been teaching Sunday school at her church for years. She, too, was completely appalled by the family's lack of support. It was totally ridiculous."

"My mom came blazing at the other woman with scriptures and threatened her with exposure if she didn't apologize. The two women engaged in what they thought was spiritual combat for months, fully armed with scriptures in hopes that they could annihilate their opponent. Boy, they had both totally met their match. My mom would call me and fill me in on all her sermons and scriptures she used to get this woman in line. It was hilarious to me. They all eventually kissed and made up and are in relationship with each other. From what I understand, my grandfather's new wife immediately had all the money from my grandparents transferred to her. If that was true, trust me, it wouldn't be much."

"Then there is my sister who I have already told you about. She has often referred to having gone to counseling and she says that she has some trauma in her past as well. My sister informed me about how some guy, in either middle school or high school, did something to her when they were alone in the classroom. I have never gotten any of the details. To be perfectly honest, I didn't want them."

"I also cannot remember a time when my sister wasn't sick or suffering from some kind of injury. I mean, she always has some kind of physical ailment. The same thing can be said about my mother too. They both seem to go from one disease to another. It's tragic but a little weird too. It's really no exaggeration that, in over thirty years, I haven't known them to be without some ailment or injury of sorts."

Between the two of them, they have had everything from cancer to gum disease, hypoglycemia, blood clots, cysts, infertility, car accidents, muscle problems, eye problems, tumors, broken bones, arthritis, hip replacement, neuropathy, allergies, various skin cancers, migraine headaches that require trips to the emergency room, lumps in the breast, and even a kidney transplant. The combined surgery count for the two of them is well into the double digits. When my grandmother was alive, she was usually chronically ill and had a multitude of surgeries too. "

"I know you don't need me to go into my brother's information again. I think that subject has been pretty much dissected over that the last several weeks. I guess that pretty much sums it up. My family doesn't leave me with many bragging rights as you can plainly see."

Unpacking so many of my containers, I took inventory of what was left. The articles were all spread out, and it would take me some time to place them back in their rightful packages. I really didn't mind; it was what I did best.

Dr. Storm was still feverishly documenting all I had revealed. He was unsettlingly quiet. After what felt like an eternity, he looked up from his notes and asked, "Is this everyone? Are there any other family members you have left out?"

"Yeah, that about covers it. There isn't anyone left."

His silence was deafening as he continued to survey his findings. Then with a look which could be thought of as concern, he said, "But no one escaped. Everyone has a story. This is unprecedented; I've never seen anything like this." Again, he looked down at his paper and my heart began to race. He was a seasoned professional—why was he so unsettled?

I looked on, anxiously waiting for his response, and then, to my complete amazement, Dr. Storm found my vulnerable container that was not to be touched. Looking at me with complete certainty, he inquired, "Veronica, what member of your family was involved in the occult?"

****

How did he know? Will he think I'm one of them? Oh no, will he turn me away in fear? My mind sprinted immediately to my mental inventory. Although the box on the top shelf remained untouched, the box on the lower shelf that I wanted to keep from his grasp had its lid blown to smithereens. I scrambled to collect the figurines that were too delicate for touch and was unnerved by Dr. Storm's certainty. His gaze met mine and I knew I could no longer hide the contents of my package. With my blood pumping at an unnatural speed and adrenaline racing through my veins, I reluctantly answered his question. Fearing this could change everything, I was intent to study his response. I had come to know him well enough to judge his facial expression, so I could discern for sure. Without warning, my tremors returned. With my body shaking and with great apprehension, I said, "My grandparents were involved in the occult. My natural grandfather was a high priest in a satanic coven and my grandmother was the head witch."

Still looking at Dr. Storm with careful scrutiny, I looked in his eyes to see if I would be judged as one of them. He seemed surprised at the revelation but looked as though he was sympathetic towards me. Although he appeared to be unsettled with his findings, he did not give the impression that he distrusted me.

I realized that this revelation had opened a door that no man could close. Trepidation mixed with courage, I chose to walk through it, and Dr. Storm was right on my heels. One of my greatest fears had always been that people would think I'm an imposter. I feared their judgment that no one could escape a family line like mine. My genetic pool would link me to a family tree I wanted to keep in secret. Now exposed for the doctor to see, nothing would remain the same. This session had just unleashed a chain of events that no one could have predicted. With the contents of this box unpacked, Dr. Storm, Jerry, and I were all about to embark on the ride of our lives.

CHAPTER THIRTEEN:

War

Ephesians 6:12 (King James Version)

[12]*For we wrestle not against flesh and blood, but against principalities, against powers, against the rulers of the darkness of this world, against spiritual wickedness in high places.*

How could he possibly have known? There was absolutely no uncertainty in his question concerning my family. Dr. Storm didn't ask *if* a family member was involved in the occult or *has* any family member participated in the occult. He came out and asked, *"What* family member was involved in the occult?" He knew, he absolutely knew!

With the contents of my container out for him to see, I could not believe I was discussing this with Dr. Storm. This was never to have come out of my inventory. How would he take what I was about to uncover to him? To be honest, I didn't think anyone was equipped to deal with the contents of my box.

"Your grandfather was a high priest in a satanic coven?"

There simply was no going back. I answered him with a sense of dread. "Yes, he was."

"Your grandmother was the head witch?"

"Uh huh"

"When did you find out about this? How do you know?"

"Well, remember when I told you my mom was seriously depressed when I was a teenager? She always told us about how her dad left the home in such a violent way when she was seven. The stuff about the coven didn't come out until after I was married."

"In my earlier years, she taught Bible classes on how to overcome abusing your children. My mom would tell everyone that although she was abused, by the grace of God, she didn't abuse in return. The problem was, when the past started to surface, she was powerless to deal with it by herself. My dad thought it went against Bible teachings to get outside help. To be perfectly honest, I think he thought that it somehow discredited his abilities as a husband."

"I didn't understand that, though. I figured, if she had been diagnosed with cancer, she would have gone to an oncologist to get treatment, not a minister. I mean, she would have gone for prayer to the pastor and then the doctor for treatment. It makes no sense to me that because it was an emotional ailment, and not a physical one, she should only go to a minister. Why on God's green earth would a person think that someone who holds a degree on the Bible is a substitute for a person with a psychiatric degree?"

I continued. "It seems to me that many Christians hold the belief that if you are in a crisis, whether marriage or emotional trauma, you should go to a pastor for counseling. Isn't that a little like choosing to take your car to a CPA instead of a mechanic? It would have been better if the ministers my mom went to had just offered their support by prayer, then handed her a phone number of a qualified therapist. Not to have that be the standard protocol borders on misconduct, if you ask me."

"Well, being the wife of a Christian man, she thought she wasn't allowed to defy my dad and get the help she needed. The downward spiral began, and it was an ugly one. I think she compared herself to her parents, and, because she never kicked me or threatened to take my life, she was a great parent. By the time I was in high school, she practically went into total seclusion. They didn't even belong to a church during my mid-teen years."

"To her credit, she seemed to have dealt with her anger and sadness until I was in middle school at least. Then when I got into high school, all hell broke loose. She was so angry and upset all of the time. It was as if she thought she was entitled to her anger. What was done to her was inexcusable, but I had nothing to do with it. She kept telling my dad that something was wrong with her, but he would not cave. Our family's reputation and his reputation were of the utmost importance. No matter how uncontrolled her anger or sorrow, we were all to act as if we were still the perfect Christian family. Then she got to a point where she could no longer deal and she went into counseling."

"What changed in your family or father's mind that she could get the help she needed?"

"Within a one year period of time, my parents had an empty nest. My sister moved out and into her own apartment, my brother graduated college and moved, and I got married. I have always thought that once she didn't have me around for the emotional release when she got angry, she cracked. I'm not even kidding you, I had been gone for less than a year and then she puts her foot down and goes to get the counseling she needed."

"I can't say I was thrilled with her timing. It would have been splendid if she had gotten help when I lived in the home. But I really did think the whole 'better late than never' philosophy applied in her situation. My dad was reluctantly on board with the idea. He really had no choice by then. She was completely losing it."

"It wasn't long into the sessions before the counselor tapped into her childhood. And, as the saying goes, the rest is history. When dealing with the events of her childhood everything unraveled for her. She was completely unprepared for such intense therapy. She wound up losing a great deal of weight. None of us were prepared to see her diminish like that."

"I remember calling her therapist and telling him, that I was afraid she was in danger of hurting herself. I was so frightened that she was going to commit suicide because she was so sad and depressed by what was coming out in the sessions. After a few more sessions, she was admitted to the hospital. After that, she was released to a halfway house where she received intense therapy and group sessions. I was out of the house by then so I'm not too sure how long she was under medical care."

Dr. Storm was completely riveted to this saga. "What information came out? What did she have to deal with?"

To answer his question would mean I would have to reveal contents so dark, he had no knowledge such artifacts could possibly exist in my inventory. It felt like I was reading from the worst horror novel ever written. An event so vulgar it defied the imagination. Only the words on this mental notepad were fact not fiction.

"Like I said, my mom's father was a high priest in a satanic coven. Well, when my mom was only five years old, her father brought her into his coven to be offered as the young virgin sacrifice. Her mom was at the coven that night too and was fulfilling her duties as the head witch. They both, in a ritualistic style ceremony, had my mom passed around to the men in the coven to do whatever evil they wanted to her."

"I cannot begin to imagine the horror she must have felt with each and every violation. Her body was brutalized as the worshippers each took turns fulfilling their evil sexual pleasure. That's only the half of it. After the men were done with her, my grandparents placed her on the pagan altar in her broken condition. As part of the ritual, my grandparents, being the ones in charge, sacrificed a goat, and each coven member took turns drinking its blood as part of their devotion to Satan. Then my grandfather took some blood and spilled it on the altar. It was then he made his vow to Satan."

"With my mom as the payment, he told Satan that he would give his undying loyalty to him and then he did the unthinkable. He offered up his family line in exchange for Satan's power. Her dad, with her mom there, made a pact with the devil that, if he would give his power and loyalty to them, Satan could have their family. That was the exchange."

Dr. Storm was listening, but I feared this was too much. How was he to know that the session would take such a turn? I wanted with every fiber of my being to turn back the hands of time and undo what had been said. It pained me to transfer this visual burden to him with such gruesome images.

So many more details could be unpacked about what happened in that coven. Things that I have never repeated once I was told about them. I decided to shield Dr. Storm from any more of the ghastly contents of that box. Placing the untold artifacts back into their package, I sat not knowing where this would all lead. He didn't ask to be invited to this fright fest. There was no need to haunt him with more facets of this crude tale.

Looking at Dr. Storm, hoping to convey the reality of such a family tree, I tried to explain. "You have no idea what it's like to have to grow up in a family like that. As far as I'm concerned, I believe Satan was promised a family, and he would visit every house to collect the debt that was owed to him. Don't you see Dr. Storm? I was promised to Satan before I was ever conceived. You don't know the half of what happened to me when I was young. I'm not sure if I will ever be strong enough to tell you all of the things that I either witnessed or were done to me before I left the home. But, make no mistake, you are a hundred percent correct— no one escaped."

With those words spoken, Dr. Storm's face changed dramatically. He sat straight up, his mouth forming a straight line; he somewhat squinted his eyes, and looked at me silently. It appeared as though he was contemplating asking me to explain, but decided otherwise. With inquisition written all over his face, he seemed no longer concerned with my family history, but with the knowledge that there was still so much about me to uncover. The babysitter, my brother, my mom, my sister and my father—yet he hadn't found the hidden containers that housed my darkest secrets. Thinking he knew the worst of my past, he just found out I was still a mystery that begged to be understood.

I stopped and began to realize the magnitude of what I just revealed. My mind then shifted to the ominous box that was on my top shelf and completely out of reach. I knew that the figurines I placed in there were the direct result of my grandfather's pact. *No one escaped*. Only being five years old myself when I had to begin my inventory, I tried to divert my attention to the conversation in progress. How barbaric of a family line. So much sexual deviance and the robbing of children's innocence simply because of their DNA. I had seen the pattern for years; did anyone else in the family see it too?

It was appalling to know such evil is real. I once heard it said that the biggest lie the devil ever told humankind was that he doesn't exist. I believe that to be true. To be given the truth about where you come from, when it is such a demonic line, is horrifying at best. I had always felt a great deal of sorrow for my mom to have endured torture not befitting an animal let alone a human. It saddened me—no sickened me to know that her past was littered with the level of physical, mental, and verbal violence that it was.

Her survival instincts were to be envied. I don't know how she functioned without cracking as long as she did. In my estimation, she outlasted most people who suffered much less. To her credit, she never did physically abuse me in any way. That was the one area she did appear to master.

In my estimation, to feel as though no admonishment was needed simply because you didn't smack a child is a dangerous view on parenting. Thinking that apologies are not in order for the child who said that they have been wounded by your treatment will make for a lonely relational future. You only have to look at my family to see if this is not so. Funerals for the adult members who have passed usually consisted of five to fifteen people at the most. No relationships can survive, yet alone thrive, when pride is chosen over truth and humility.

The old saying "Hurting people, hurt people" was never so played out as in this case. How deceived people can become, thinking that just because their behavior doesn't directly emulate the behavior they abhor, they are in the clear. Abuse and dealing out pain comes in many forms. Although I have always thought my mom's childhood explained her cruel actions, I don't believe it excuses them.

Jeffrey Dahmer, Adolf Hitler, Son of Sam all have stories to tell. Statistics show that most all wife beaters, child abusers, sexual predators have a sad or horrifying background which caused them to do what they swore they would never do. Should a society look the other way when a person is found guilty of a crime because a crime was committed against that person? Where would it stop? How could future generations have hope that they could be secure in their safety and happiness if we were to pardon brutality based on someone's history?

Now, grappling with the notion that my wicked container had been unpacked, I was terrified with what Dr. Storm's conclusions might be. Will he conclude that I was one of the deceived? Maybe the better question I should have asked of myself: was I one of the deceived? Was he asking himself the question if I was living a double life and was I hiding hideous truths from him?

My whole family said they were a wonderful Christian family, full of faith and good works. I said that I came from a screwed-up heritage where everyone was walking with blinders on. Who was giving the accurate account? Seeing that it was possible to think you were a dynamic believer and in my opinion be so lost, I was constantly questioning my own position of faith.

This had been my motivation for secrecy my entire adult life. Coming from a line like I do, I feared people would believe that it's not possible for one to escape. I'm not even safe within my own family. They think they are healthy, and I am the wayward sheep of the herd. I am nothing like them, and yet I am one of them. How can I be sure that Dr. Storm wasn't suspicious of me?

Dr. Storm waited for me to continue but seemed to realize I would offer no more without his probing, but I wasn't about to just volunteer anymore information. If he wanted to know something, he was free to ask. Understanding this was my standard method of operation, he inquired, "What happened after your mom was in the hospital? Did she get the help she needed?"

"I guess she got some help. I mean, she seemed better but she also seemed incredibly angry. She wound up leaving my dad. Now you have to know my father fully to appreciate how devastating that was to him. His life revolves around her. He was like a walking zombie when she was gone."

"Really, after seeing how she acted after her counseling was finished, I wasn't too thrilled with your profession. She said she never intended to divorce my dad; she just needed to be on her own for a while and reestablish their relationship. She seemed to blame him for most of her troubles. She thought he had been overly controlling and wanted him to know that she wasn't going to live that way any longer."

"One night, the two of them invited all three of us kids back to the house for a family discussion. They were bringing us up to speed on what was going on with them, and then she said my dad was going to apologize. Of all things, my dad said he was sorry for how he had treated us growing up. I couldn't believe the audacity of my mom to have him take all the blame for the way we were treated."

"I did think an apology was in order; it's just that it would have been great if it was his own idea. Also, she offered no apologies of her own. My dad said he was sorry that he created an atmosphere where we were not allowed to talk or have differing opinions. A couple months later or so, she moved back into the house with him. Any chance she had to talk about the past or our childhood, she would say that it was dad's fault that she acted and behaved the way she did."

"I really think that, from the bottom of her heart, she finds herself blameless. She sees herself as the godly wife and mother, and him as the ruthless dictator. I don't think he told her to imply to me that I was fat or only pretty on the outside. Nor was he there the day I almost overdosed at age thirteen on her prescription pills and she told me to get up and make dinner."

"This is all to say, that yes, she was different after counseling, but, in my opinion, she got nastier. It was as if she figured out she had enough grief to last her a lifetime. Her entitlement was off the charts and grew by the day. When she came home, she had my dad buy her a sports car and pay for plastic surgery. She was mad that a business deal of his went bad, for she wanted her fair share of the money."

"I never wanted to have anything to do with counseling after I saw what it did to her. If that's what therapy did, leave people bitter and angrier than when they started, I wanted none of it! If you remember, Dr. Storm, most of the stories I have told you about my mom are from after I left the house. Before then, although I have many to tell, I really don't hold her accountable. She didn't get the help she needed to cope with her devastating childhood until after I was married. Now I have no trouble holding her accountable."

Dr. Storm was trying to make sense of all of this. "She probably got the plastic surgery because she didn't feel good about herself. Maybe she wanted a fresh start."

"Of course, she didn't feel good about herself, who does? I hardly think that was her motivation though. I'm telling you, she was plenty mad at my dad and he was only too willing to make sure to keep her happy. That would ensure she stayed with him."

Changing the conversation's course of direction with no sense of doubt, he asked, "How did you and Jerry break the curse? The two of you have been able to live such a different life compared to the rest of your family. You must have done something to change your life."

All my fear quickly evaporated with his question. He actually didn't count me as one of them. To answer his question, I went back to my inventory for a different set of boxes. I created these to house the memories of Jerry and me. They were not even on the same shelf with my family packages. I have never wanted the two worlds to blend. It was of utmost importance to me to start over and not cross-contaminate my "before marriage" and "after marriage" life.

After sifting through some artifacts, I began. "To be perfectly honest, at first we had just as many bad things happen to us as the rest of them. Some pretty funky stuff took place in our first year together. I narrowly escaped getting raped after our first month of marriage. It was incredible really. All I can say is that it was a divine intervention."

CHAPTER FOURTEEN:

Protected

Revelation 12:11 (a) (King James Version)

11 And they overcame him by the blood of the Lamb, and by the word of their testimony.

"At first we had bad stuff happen all the time. However, you have to understand, when it is your life and it's all you have ever known, you have no basis of comparison. It really didn't occur to me that anything out of the ordinary was happening."

"When Jerry and I were engaged, one night while leaving my house, he said the strangest thing. 'If anyone from my work calls and tells you that they need to come by the house and drop something off, don't give them our address. I would never have anyone come by to drop any work off.' We were going to be married in like two weeks. I had no idea why he was warning me like that.

I asked Jerry if there was anyone at his place of employment that I needed to be concerned about, he said no. He then said it was no big deal and he didn't even know why he brought it up."

"Well, like a month after we got married, as you can probably guess, it happened. There I was, home alone during the day, and the phone rang. When I answered, there was a man on the other end who knew my name. He was so nice and acted as if I should know him. He introduced himself as someone Jerry worked with and said we had met at my wedding. He understood when I said I couldn't recall meeting him because we had over three hundred people there. He described my dress and said he thought our ceremony was just beautiful. He even went into details about our reception. Anyways, he told me that Jerry wanted him to drop off some purchase orders by our apartment but he had lost our address. The man said that Jerry was his boss, and he didn't want to look like an idiot and ask him for his address again."

"Immediately I remembered what Jerry had warned me about a month earlier. I was nice enough, but I told the man that he could just wait and give Jerry the papers the next day at work. He began to get more insistent and then I started getting really scared. After several failed attempts to get our address from me he finally said, 'Veronica, don't you dare hang up. I already know where you live and if you hang up I'll come there and kill you.' Scared half out of my mind, I slammed the phone down and ran out of the apartment."

Dr. Storm wasn't even bothering writing anything down at that point. He was completely riveted to the story. "You must have been terrified. What happened? Did you ever find out who made that call?"

"Yes, actually we did. We called the police to see if there was anything, they could do. A couple of police officers came to our house to fill out a report. After they were finished, they asked me how I knew not to give out our address. That was a little awkward to answer. It seemed completely ridiculous for Jerry to have known to warn me about this a month before it happened. There was simply no other answer to give them than to tell them the truth. They were stunned. They looked at Jerry and asked how he knew, to which, of course, he had to say he wasn't sure why he would warn me about phone call like that."

"The officer said, 'Well you are one lucky girl. The other brides he called didn't know better and they gave out their address.' The officers informed us about a rapist who would read the newspaper and get the information that people placed in there concerning their weddings. He would look at the photo and read all the details the family wrote concerning the wedding. That's how he knew the names of the bride and groom, what they looked like, their parent's names and the all the details of the wedding.

"Jerry and I both knew God had totally protected me from that man. I asked Jerry if he knew what he was saying was from the Lord, and he said he had no idea. The thought just came to him and he relayed it to me."

"Wow, Veronica, God really looked out for you. I know a lot has happened in your life, but God did have a hand on protecting you and you even found a good man to marry. That alone defies the odds."

Dr. Storm gave some reassurance. "You said you always loved the Lord even when all hell was breaking loose. God doesn't physically come down and stop bad things from happening, but He can intervene to help a person come out of a bad situation. It was what you wanted more than anything back then, and He was faithful to help you. So, God protected you in a spectacular way the first month you were married. Did anything else happen that was like that?"

"Yes, if you can believe it. One morning I went to get into my car to go to an appointment and something didn't seem right to me. I had a funny feeling something was wrong. For some reason I decided to look into the back seat to see if anyone was there. When I peeked through the window, there was a man down on the floor. He didn't even see me looking through the window."

"I was scared out of my mind. I went racing back upstairs to my apartment and dialed 911. They got the man out of my car, put him in their squad car and took him down to the police station. I have no idea what happened after that."

"Did that happen right after the phone call incident?"

"No, I guess it was about five to six months later. Then another wild thing happened. One night Jerry had a friend from church over for dinner. Jerry had to leave and told his friend it was time for them to go. His friend had just refilled his coffee and told Jerry he would leave in a couple of minutes. Jerry thought nothing of it; I mean, it was his friend from church."

"Oh no, I don't like the sound of that. What did the man end up doing?"

"Pretty much what you're thinking. I was in the kitchen doing dishes and he came in to keep me company. He was totally disgusting. He began asking about Jerry's and my sex life. I didn't want to come out and totally accuse him of being a jerk because I was afraid to get him angry. He could have totally overpowered me in a second."

"I left the kitchen and told him he needed to go. I went to the door and opened it. He came over, closed the door, and cornered me against the wall. I really thought he was going to rape me. I just looked at him and told him he needed to leave. He smiled at me, and then leaned in for a kiss. I turned away but he landed one on the lips anyways. He remained there for several seconds. To my relief, he walked out the door. Needless to say, that was the end of their friendship."

"Were there any more close calls?"

"Yes, only one more. One night we went to bed, and both Jerry and I checked to make sure that all the doors and windows were locked before going to the bedroom. I'm sure I don't need to tell you, with my past, I'm a freak about making sure all doors are locked before going to bed. Then in the middle of the night, Jerry and I were awakened by a loud noise. We could hear someone was breaking in through our balcony. Jerry went flying out of our room to stop the intruder. When he got there, the sliding door was open and the man had already jumped down. We got up just in time."

"Those things all happened within the first year we were married. Not to mention how we were sick all of the time. Jerry missed tons of work and I did too."

Dr. Storm was in one of his usual positions, leaning forward with his legs extended out in front of him, feet crossed at the ankles with his hands holding my file and pen. "Did you think anything strange was happening? No one has

219

four close calls like you did and not suspect something out of the ordinary is happening, right?"

Thinking how to clarify it, I said slowly, "No, I didn't think it was strange at all. I always had near misses and some that didn't miss at all. As you said, no one escaped. All I can tell you is, it always felt as though I was walking around with a bull's-eye on my back."

Wanting clarification he asked, "How did you make it all stop? What did you and Jerry do to change things? Especially you, Veronica, because this wasn't even abnormal to you."

"Jerry and I were sick again. We were pretty good friends with this guy from church and he asked us what was going on. It never occurred to me that it was such an unusual thing to be as sick as we were. Before the visit was over, he knew about the four narrow escapes."

"He looked at Jerry and said, 'Something is not right about this. For whatever reason, you guys are always under demonic attack. Jerry you need to pray and take authority over your household. God has paid too high of a price for His children to walk in freedom for the two of you to be under the curse like this.' When he said *curse*, I immediately remembered my grandfather. I, of course, never told him about my history or my grandparents' involvement in the occult. To him it was a completely obvious conclusion. After he left, the two of us prayed together."

"That's it? You prayed and it all stopped?"

"Yeah, kind of freaky, huh? It wasn't as if it was an eloquent prayer either; it was pretty basic actually. We had no idea what to do, so we sounded kind of stupid." Acting out the prayer with a dopey voice, I said, "Jerry just said, 'Heavenly Father, thank you for taking care of us and that you paid the price for our safety and deliverance. We believe we are redeemed from the curse and choose to take You at Your Word. Thank You for the blood of Jesus and all that it brings ... Amen.' That was it. Nothing special, but my hand to heaven, everything stopped."

Dr. Storm laughed. "So did he sound that dopey when he prayed it?"

I laughed in return. "I'm pretty sure he did. I'm telling you the truth; it was no big deal. But everything changed after that. We weren't sick all the time, and I never had any more near misses. Think about it: from four in one year to nothing in over twenty-two years."

"That was the first time that I found out that apparently being a Christian wasn't enough. It was our responsibility to know what God's promises are and then ask Him for them. I was raised in a Christian household, and every kind of evil occurred in that home. Everyone in my family is a believer. Jerry and I learned that we had to tell Satan to back off, and we were only able to use the name of Jesus for it to hold any weight."

"Veronica, that's a mighty powerful testimony. I was actually in my office the other day and ran across a teaching series that deals with what you are talking about. If you like, I would be happy to loan it to you. The Bible teacher goes into generational curses and the various scriptures to educate people about evil and how to overcome it. It sounds like you and Jerry are pretty well educated on the subject, but you are welcome to borrow it if you want to."

"Oh sure, I would love to listen to it. I know all too well about generational curses."

To my relief, the subject matter didn't appear to be foreign to Dr. Storm. He most certainly did not appear to be creeped out by it nor was he uncomfortable. He never seemed to be the least bit religious and most certainly not a Bible thumper, but he had no qualms sharing whatever insight he had gained through the years. I thought this little bit of news concerning my family would throw him over the edge.

Dr. Storm continued. "Do you think anyone in your family has ever seen a connection to all the sickness and sexual deviance that occurred in each generation? You said your mom mentioned it."

"I'm not too certain. I do wonder about my brother though. I think that maybe he clued in along the way because he seems to be living a great life. Yes, I would consider his past sketchy, but he is married with four healthy children and all seems well with them. They are what you might consider the perfect Christian family. Both he and his wife are active in their church and community. They are pretty well known in the town where they are living. I think many are envious of their lives."

Dr. Storm remained silent and waited to see if I would speak further. His lack of feedback started me thinking, and his silence screamed louder than any words ever could. Something about what I just said was terribly unsettling to me and him. Had history repeated itself? How does anyone really know anything about people, even family members, if they choose to live in secrecy? He had never approached me about what he did to me. Now a father himself, why hadn't he tried to make amends for what he did?

Dr. Storm saw that I had connected some mental dots. Making the most of this revelation, he knows what "domino" to serve up this visit. "Are you willing to have a 'domino'?" he asked.

"Sure, why the heck not! It's been several sessions since I've had one of those, so hit me."

"Great," he said with a smile. "Here goes. Are you willing to have a face to face with your brother and confront him with your past? If so, how do you think it should transpire, and when do you think it should happen?"

"Ugh, not that 'domino' again," I said, no longer enthusiastic. "OK, I'll think about it and get back to you next time."

It had been a wild session, and I couldn't have been more thrilled that it had come to an end. The grisly contents about the coven were ready to be placed back in their container and returned to the shelf.

Entering my mental storage room, I saw the shadow of a box that I had never seen before. My heart jumped with the new finding. It was somewhat blurry which caused me to doubt its true existence. This could not be possible. I kept meticulous records of my inventory. I had always been the master at inventory control, and my system of managing it was impeccable. Choosing not to give attention to the shadowy container, I exited my mental storage room.

With the usual handshake and fond farewell, it was time to return to my ordinary life outside this office. On the drive back home, I determined to reclaim an area of my life that had been held captive since the first few weeks of counseling. It had been two months of waiting but now sexual intimacy with my husband was the next item on my list of things to conquer.

CHAPTER FIFTEEN:

The Getaway

The drive back home after a session was often a thoughtful one. With the beauty of spring that surrounded me, I wondered what it would have been like to start counseling in the winter months. It probably would have been an entirely different experience. To be smack dab in the middle of the most beautiful time of year had helped me have a certain kind of serenity that only comes through my surroundings. Perhaps it was the splendor of the ocean or the beauty of the palm trees that swayed in the breeze, but I always had a sense of calm when I left a session. The dramatic color of the blooming flowers and the dazzling green that radiated from the grass and trees was a remarkable sight. The sun was hot, but the air was cool with the soft wind bouncing off the sea. If you looked across the beach, you could see some locals on their sailboats and yachts playing hooky from work, taking advantage of such a gorgeous California day.

While in the car, not wanting to waste any time, I plugged in the first CD of the teaching series Dr. Storm had given me. The teacher was speaking with such authority; obviously, he had a passion regarding the content. The instructor had an accent that sounded a little European. The inflection was intriguing which made listening to him completely effortless. The words rolled off the CD and filled the car's atmosphere with information on the spiritual realm that few preachers would ever dare tackle. He was an eloquent orator and seemed very well researched in the matters of generational patterns and curses.

Not wanting such things to be passed down to my children, I listened with great purpose to what he had to say. I desired to be free and live in the life that God had purchased for my family and me. Because of this, I wanted to know all there was concerning this topic. Some of the things he said I agreed with and some I didn't. However, as the old saying goes, "Don't throw out the baby with the bathwater." As long as what he was teaching could be backed up with several scriptures, I really didn't have a problem with it. His lessons were full of examples and applications that had come from his years in the ministry. He had spent his lifetime tapping into God's heart concerning the unnecessary bondage of His children. Simple and basic truths are often overlooked in the church at large.

Pulling into the garage, I left the teaching CDs in the car. Since it took a certain amount of concentration to fully absorb what he was saying, this type of study couldn't be found in my home when the children were back from school.

One thing that continued to preoccupy me was that I found myself doubting the recollections. The thought that I somehow contrived the contents in some sort of a wild imaginary childhood scheme was beginning to plague me. That was actually one of the reasons I found it difficult to confront my brother.

I rehearsed in my mind a make-believe scene where I met my brother. In this imaginary plot, he not only denied having molested me, but he was able to prove beyond any doubt that it could not possibly be true. Of course, in this make-believe scene, my family and Dr. Storm were notified, and all will know I was the crazy one. What would I do with my boxes?

That was one possible scenario. Another was one where my brother denied what happened all together. I feared that I wouldn't be able to tell if he was lying, or if he simply didn't remember because he was a victim too. I could honestly say that I wouldn't know who I would believe at that point, him or me. This fabricated confrontation is actually the worse of the two. The thought that I might have to prove my boxes contained the real history was enough to keep me silent. Not being believed would be like being violated all over again.

I knew Jerry and Dr. Storm would always be in my court and the rest of my friends too; however, I thought that some sort of reservation might exist in their minds as to the validity of my stories. I would not be able to continue with counseling if this were to happen. How could I face Dr. Storm again if I thought he questioned my packages?

Another area that still brought concern was the fact that I still struggled with what was normal. It sounded so ridiculous, but it was entirely true. Sometimes, in a counseling session, I would randomly say something about an incident that happened in my childhood home. Dr. Storm would practically fall out of his chair in disbelief. The only reason I knew that I had said something disturbing was because of Dr. Storm's shocked reaction.

"Veronica, did you just remember that last night and that's why you're telling me now?"

My answer remained the same. "Dr. Storm, I remember everything; of course I didn't just remember this last night."

"Why haven't you mentioned this before now? You need to tell me these things so we can work through them."

My usual reply was, "I didn't think it was relevant."

In somewhat of an exasperated tone, he would reply, "It's ALL relevant Veronica!"

Yeah, that was embarrassing. It didn't just happen when I was in a session either. I would say things with my girlfriends when they asked me how counseling was going. They began to probe into my life with great interest. It was not lost on me that it was all a little entertaining as well. You have to pay good money on a book or movie to get a storyline like this; only with me, it's totally free. Casually I would say something about a past incident and then I'd be met with mouths wide open and eyes the size of quarters looking back at me.

Because I often slipped with my horrifying stories, I really didn't talk to too many people outside that circle. I simply couldn't trust myself with knowing normal from abnormal at that stage. Once being a person who was surrounded by so many people, it could get a little lonely for me at times. Nevertheless, I felt this temporary self-induced isolation was necessary until I could get a handle and properly categorize my memories.

Another critical relationship that was completely different was my relationship with the Lord. Having been used to habitual daily devotions that could last for several hours, I was changing that up a great deal. Praying used to be so easy, but then I found it could be a difficult thing for me to do. It wasn't that I didn't want to talk to Him; I didn't know how. I had spent my entire adult life praying for things that were so temporal and of no value to me any longer. My former prayer life consisted of "give me" style conversation, which now seemed so incredibly shallow.

I do know that there was absolutely no way I was going to chant faith-based sayings over and over. I didn't dismiss that practice at all; meditation and confession are biblically sound doctrines, and I attributed them in large part to have kept my mind sound up to then. However, I simply wanted to "be" and remain quiet in my devotion. I felt as though it was not about a special formula; it was about quiet intimacy and wonderment of all He was in my life.

The daily chore of trying to pray the pain away was a pointless exercise to say the least. Embracing my past and feeling the hurt was a part of this journey. I knew this stage wouldn't last forever, but it couldn't be rushed either. That didn't mean that I felt absent in my relationship with God or that He was absent for me. Quite the contrary, I had never felt so in tune to His heartbeat. His presence had sustained me since day one of this wild ride.

Even though I had been quiet, He had not. I had a notebook full of teachings and outlines that I had penned along the way. He was no longer my distant relative; He was my precious Father who I had grown to love.

Another huge area that was rocked the first months was my relationship with Jerry. We had gone from combative to peaceable in eight short weeks. Jerry had completely blown my mind with his love and support for me. One area that he had managed well was allowing me time to separate sexually while I worked through my issues. He did not push or rush me. Obviously, seeing the night frights and body tremors brought home the reality how horrifying it was to deal with. He took the time in making his own appointment with Dr. Storm to get advice on what to do. In my book, any husband who was willing to admit that he didn't have all the answers concerning his wife becomes wildly attractive in a New York minute.

My effort to decontaminate the act of sex was extremely difficult. It didn't help to know that the only way I was successfully intimate with my husband the past twenty-three years was my ability to "splinter." Knowing that I would actually be "me" during our sexual union was a huge mountain for me to climb. I wanted to be in the present, but it scared the living daylights out of me.

Thankfully, Jerry understood that he was powerless to decontaminate my view on sex. Understandably, I would have resented him for trying, since he had much to gain if he was successful. His motivation for my help would be thought of as a selfish one and not that of wanting my best interest.

Having dealt with various different molestation memories, there were certain acts that I was unwilling to do, at least at the moment. When I had explained this to Jerry, rather than telling me not to equate him with the perpetrator, he told me he would respect my need to regain my comfort level in whatever area I had discussed with him. Miraculously, he knew that it was not a personal reflection on him; it was a painful reflection of what evil was done to me.

I had heard that this is an incredibly rough area for most couples to work through, and it's no small surprise. Often it's hard for the partner to understand that the one who was violated may never be able to do the same act or have the same words spoken during intimacy. When I told Jerry this, for some reason he totally got it. If Jerry didn't respect my request, how would I possibly be able to trust or feel safe with him? I didn't want him to be linked to something that once caused me great pain. I felt that I was not only protecting me; I saw it as protecting us.

What made the progression of decontamination exceptionally difficult was that the same act when done by one person was a sickening violation and by another person, it was an expression of love. To differentiate between the two was not for the faint of heart. It was astonishing to have one act carry so much emotional weight. How is it possible that when it is done with love and respect, it can bond two souls together, but when it is done as a violation it can cause immeasurable damage to the soul of the one desecrated? To have both pain and pleasure linked to the same act is so grossly evil no one can do the cleansing and healing process alone. Although I didn't feel as though Jerry could be a part of the sanitation process, that didn't mean I could master it without help.

Sessions with Dr. Storm, books, teaching CDs and much prayer had given me the ability to have the "want to." That was my starting point. I didn't want to make love, but I wanted to "want to." Honestly, that was a huge step for me.

Out of the blue, we had been given on overnight stay at a hotel in the beautiful city of La Jolla. It is only a forty-five minute drive from our home, but we always felt as though we were hundreds of miles away when we visited. It has fine dining, striking ocean views, and some of the most beautiful flowerbeds to adorn city streets. I had inwardly determined that this would be the perfect opportunity for us to reconnect as a couple. I was not going to tell Jerry about my decision. Just in case I chickened out at the last minute, I didn't want to feel as though I had let him down too.

Still obsessing over learning as much as I could, on the drive down to the hotel instead of listening to our favorite music station, we listened to the teaching CDs Dr. Storm loaned me. I had found the information fascinating and wanted Jerry to hear it too. You wouldn't necessarily think that it would be the best set up for a romantic getaway, but what the instructor was saying actually helped me in overcoming my fears in the area of intimacy.

We pulled into the hotel's parking structure and walked into the lobby. It was expansive and had a rather large pond that was laid out to look like a stream. Koi fish were swimming, poking their mouths to the top, eating the food morsels left for them. The fish were white and splotched in various colors of oranges, blacks, and yellows. Tables and chairs surrounded the indoor pond, with a large quiet bar in the center. Off to one side of the grand lobby were two large glass elevators that were in constant motion delivering guests to their desired floors.

You could see parents chasing after their children who appeared excited to be on vacation. They would frantically grab the younger ones as they reached into the pond attempting to catch the fish. Executives gathered around the tables, engrossed in conversations, with laptops spread out to document their business dealings. There were men and women dressed casually, talking and laughing while enjoying a drink from the bar. The atmosphere was electrifyingly jubilant. You could tell summer was well on its way.

We went to the front desk, checked-in, and rode the elevator up to our room. After freshening up, we left for a leisurely walk. We came across a quaint little restaurant and decided to go in for dessert. Our conversation revolved around the events of the last two months as well as the teaching series we listened to on the drive down. We stayed long enough to close the place, and the server had been so gracious to apologize for having to clean-up around us. We paid the bill and left a generous tip for her impeccable service and hospitality.

As we walked back to the hotel, I began to get nervous realizing what the night had in store. You would have thought I was a virgin bride on her wedding night and not a woman who has been married to the same man for twenty-three years. Butterflies were flying at such an obnoxious speed inside me, it felt as though they were the size of hawks. Jerry was clueless to both my plan and my reluctance to go through with the plan. All he knew was that we were enjoying a wonderful evening out, just the two of us.

While getting ready for bed a thought occurred to me. Dr. Storm said that sex was a holy thing. At the time, I thought that was a laughable claim but I had come to realize that truer words were never spoken. If I wanted to overcome my fear of intimacy, I needed to do something I never dreamed would be connected to sex—I prayed with my husband. Dressed and ready for bed I approached Jerry with my thoughts and concerns about being sexually intimate with him that evening. He listened with immense care and concern, which actually gave me great boldness and courage. Then I asked him to pray for me and ask the Lord to bless our time together. If anyone had ever told me that I would have done such a thing, I would have laughed in their face for being so utterly ridiculous. Believe it or not, that moment of prayer together was so precious, the memory will remain with me forever.

After our prayer, I warned Jerry that I was scared out of my mind. He understood my reluctance and told me that, at anytime if I became uncomfortable, he was willing to stop. I did not intend to stop that night. My memories had tormented me and had taken me captive. The very thought that my violators owned this piece of me was much of my motivation to reclaim it. I wanted the sexual intimacy back under my control and not the control of predators from long ago. I was determined to be present for the encounter and not splinter off. I would be Jerry's wife while making love tonight; this would be a first for me.

While being sexually intimate with Jerry, my emotions

ran the gamut from wonderfully sweet to being completely terrified. The toxic images from my past tried to pollute my mind, but I refused to entertain them. That moment with Jerry was such a close and wonderful encounter, I would not let anything destroy that. I chose to believe that making love with my husband was a sacred and holy bond. I was safe and free with the man that I love; it doesn't get much better than that.

Afterward, feeling totally secure, I laid safe and protected in his arms. In some ways, my sexual union with Jerry was totally magical and new. My encounters with him used to be purely physical and emotionally detached. That night I had crossed the threshold to having them be an emotional and spiritual experience that required me to be in the present and fully alive. God not only paid back what was taken from me, He gave so much more than what I originally had. He replaced what He never wanted stolen, what a generous act of love and mercy on His part.

To have rescued that area of my life and even reclaiming my body was like conquering the biggest giant in the land. Jerry and I both recognized that, although that night was special, it would probably continue to be challenging for a while. Time and patience would be required to get to the place of my total comfort in our sexual intimacy. I never knew I could trust God in this area of my life. Only He can deliver in that powerful way, and I had found that it is His holy desire to do so.

I also conceded the fact that God would have been unable to help if I wasn't first willing to allow myself to be vulnerable and make love to Jerry. He was willing to match my act of surrender with His powerful presence of peace to calm my fear. God brought hope to a hopeless situation, as only He can do. That night was no less of a miracle to me than walking on the water was to His disciple. Stepping out when you feel unsafe is scary, no matter what the situation is. Whether in a tumultuous ocean or in a turbulent soul, God can provide peace in the storms of our lives.

The next morning, Jerry and I enjoyed a quiet break-fast together before returning home to life as usual. I began wondering where my counseling would lead and how I would know when I was totally freed from the chains of my past. My answer to the question concerning my free-dom would soon be making its way to me. With a mysti-cal mistaken phone call, I would encounter a family member with whom I had not talked to in over two years. Everything was going to take a spectacular turn; God was not only going to show up in my life; to my great amaze-ment, He was going to take the opportunity to completely show off.

CHAPTER SIXTEEN

Unexplainable

School was out, and summer was in full swing. That meant trips to the beach and endless hours out by the pool watching the kids swim and play with their friends. Normally, I was a little worried about the children being home and having to fill the time with various activities. This year was so much different from any other previous summers. We had several trips planned, but, other than that, I pretty much just wanted to relax and let them play and figure it out for themselves. I officially stepped down from my role of activity director.

The only commitment I was involved in at that time was a teaching position at church. Sandra continued to be the leader of the program. She was hosting a teacher's meeting in her home. I stepped down from much of my duties about four months before to focus on my relationships at home. I was feeling like I could recommit to my teaching and was looking forward to what lies ahead.

I had met Sandra about two years earlier when the moms' group was forming at our church. The group had grown to around 250 women that met on a weekly basis. I had never really had a leader like Sandra before. She was probably one of the strongest women I knew and wonderfully authentic. Her personal relationship with the Lord was something I greatly admired. She was the only leader that I had worked with who celebrated the uniqueness of each teacher and let her flourish with her own style.

She was actually one of the people who encouraged me to get counseling several months ago. I met with her about four months back and filled her in on all the torrid details of my crumbling marriage and family. She said I should step down from leadership for a while so I could focus on getting my life back on track. Although I knew I would miss teaching, I also knew I had nothing to give.

I had let her in on the facets of what had come out during my counseling sessions, and she had been so faithful to stand by me. If I had to use one word to describe her, it would be "safe." You can totally be yourself around her without feeling as though you run the risk of being judged.

Professionally, Sandra was an interior decorator who lives in one of the neighboring beach communities. Going to her home was not just a visit; it was an experience. From her kitchen and family room, you could look out the windows, over her backyard, to enjoy an unobstructed view of the Pacific Ocean. Her taste was exquisite, and her home was full of all the richness of color and style that graces the covers of magazines. Her gift of design was only matched by her gift of hospitality. Sandra was incredibly generous and loved to entertain and make people feel like her home was their home during the stay.

There were several calls I needed to make before arriving at the gathering in Sandra's home. Always having been one for multitasking, I saved the phone calls for the forty-minute drive down to her house. While zipping down the toll road, I dialed one of the numbers on my list.

After a few rings, a man answered.

"Hello?"

"Hi, is Susan there?"

"Who?"

"Susan; is Susan available?"

"What?"

"I was wondering if Susan is home."

After a momentary pause, the voice said, "Veronica, it's me, Dad. You dialed the wrong number."

My mind went reeling trying to figure out what just happened. My parents lived out of state, so, in order for me to contact them, I would have had to dial the number one, followed by the area code and then their phone number, for a total of eleven numbers. I called someone within my area code, so I only pushed seven numbers. It wasn't as if I was in my address book and mistakenly contacted my father; Susan wasn't in my address book. My dad wasn't in my speed dial, so there was no way for me to have pushed a single number to have reached him either.

Trying to collect my thoughts, I began jabbering away. I really wasn't so much talking to my dad as much as I was thinking out loud at how this could have happened. "Wait, how did I get you? I don't understand how I did this. This is impossible! Your phone number isn't even close to the same numbers as hers."

"Well, you did."

Still frazzled, I continued. "Yes, I guess I did. I just don't understand how that happened."

"OK, but it happened, how are you?" My dad asked not having talked to me in two years.

Pausing, then with an authentic reply, I responded, "I'm actually doing really good, Dad. How are you?"

"Oh, pretty well, I suppose"

"That's good. Is work going well?"

"Yes, it's going pretty good."

"Great, I'm really glad to hear that."

There was an awkward silence. It seemed like an eternity before it was broken.

My dad, not knowing what else to do, responded, "Well, I guess that's all there is to say."

"Yeah, I gotta go. It was really nice hearing your voice, Dad. *I love you.*"

Yet another silence. I waited, hoping for a returned sentiment, but I would be greatly disappointed. After what seemed like another eternity, it was my turn to break the silence.

"Ok, bye Dad."

"Bye."

We both hung up.

Immediately, I burst into laughter. Talking aloud, although no one was there to listen, I said, "He actually didn't say he loved me in return. Wow! He was the one I was holding on to all these years, and he doesn't even tell me he loves me?"

Frantically, I dialed Jerry's phone number to let him in on what I just did. Eagerly, still driving, I waited for Jerry to pick up the phone. Ugh, voice mail. Waiting for the prompt, still laughing, I began my lengthy message regarding the mistaken phone call.

Almost to Sandra's house now, I had no intention of trying to get a hold of Susan again. My phone, or perhaps God, was playing tricks on me. As I drove up to the gates of her housing development, my phone rang, and I saw that Jerry was returning my call. I told the guard at the gate my name, and he allowed me to enter. While driving the streets to her house, I picked up the phone. Unlike me, he didn't see the humor in it at all. He was devastated that my dad did not return the "I love you" sentiment.

Still giggling at how wild the whole phone call transpired, I responded, "For some reason it doesn't really bother me too much. I'm still trying to grasp how he was on the other end of the line. Jerry, it was impossible for me to call him. I'm not being overly dramatic here; there really was no way of me getting him on the phone. I know I only dialed seven numbers."

Jerry, still saddened at what happened, tried to make sense of it all. "What do you think it means? Why do you think you were supposed to get a hold of him? I'm with you—this was no coincidence or accident. Is the phone call going to hit you later on?"

"I am somewhat concerned that it might affect me later. Right now, I'm still in a little bit of shock, but, after the dust settles, it could be very hurtful once I let it sink in. I'll call Dr. Storm and see if I can get in later today. Even if I'm not hurt by my dad's lack of response, I most certainly don't know how to handle my family anymore. I'll call you when I'm done with the meeting. I'm here, so I have to go. Love you Honey, bye."

241

Before going to Sandra's door, I made a quick phone call to Dr. Storm. He rearranged his schedule and could fit me in later on that afternoon. That being taken care of, I would be able to concentrate better at the meeting. No one there but Sandra even knew about my situation. I still felt a need for privacy and really didn't care to let others in on the complicated mess of my family. How do you work incest and satanic covens into a conversation anyway? Yep, best to keep it to myself.

The meeting was still going, but I slipped away at 3:15 to make it down the street to Dr. Storm's office. My heart was a little sad at the way my dad had responded to my mistaken call. I began mentally to make excuses for him, which was my normal method of operation. I thought to myself, *Maybe he was just too stunned by my call, so he didn't know how to respond. He is probably kicking himself for not saying "I love you" in return. I'm sure if he had to do it all over again, he would say it in a heartbeat.*

Then reason would kick in. *Even if he was too stunned to say it, he could have immediately called back. He could have said, "I know we agreed not to talk to each other, but I can't help but call to apologize for not saying, 'I love you.' Please know that I do, and I'm glad you mistakenly called me." That seemed like the normal response to a botched conversation. Like Jerry said, he would have been all over it if he were in the same situation.*

Walking across the street to go to his office, I began contemplating how I was going to tell Dr. Storm about the call. Would he believe it was some kind of divine connection too? There was no other way to explain it. But, if it was a divine connection, why did it happen?

Sitting in the waiting room once more, I started to inwardly chuckle at how many times I had been here the past couple of months. Dr. Storm kept telling me that I had made tremendous progress in the past ten weeks. He assured me that it would normally take a person several years to plow through what I had. All I knew was that mental and emotional health was an expensive proposition. I had spent money on homes, clothes and various other things in my life, but never mental healthcare. Our marriage had been saved, and now my mental and emotional freedom was the next thing to achieve. Overall, it was money well spent.

Dr. Storm was ready and willing to help. Wanting to make the most of our time, I immediately started telling him about my mistaken phone call to my dad. Trying not to sound too "ooky spooky," I tried my best to convey to him how impossible it was for me to have phoned my dad that morning. He was also unable to explain such a coincidence. However, right then, he was more concerned with how the conversation went.

"So your dad didn't say he loved you when you told him that you loved him? What was your reaction?"

"I didn't know how to react. I mean, I let the dead air on the phone line last long enough for him to have said it, but he never did. I just told him 'goodbye' for the most part. What else could I do?"

"How are you doing with that? Did it crush you? You seem to be handling it all pretty well."

"Yeah, that's the thing. I thought I would be totally crushed, but I'm not. I was laughing hysterically after I hung up. I just kept thinking, 'I have my dad on the phone, and I don't even recognize his voice.'"

"Veronica, we have spent a lot of sessions regarding your father, so you have had a chance to see the relationship for what it really is and not the imaginary relationship you wanted it to be. The phone call couldn't have happened at a better time. You see him for who he really is and not what you always dreamed he was. Now, what do you plan on doing?"

"That's sort of why I'm here. I want out! I can't do this anymore. Two years ago, I told my parents that I wanted to be in relationship with them as long as they were nice to me. I truly don't think that's too high of an expectation, do you? They actually were unable to do that. Now I talk to my father, and he won't even tell me he loves me? With all of this counseling and seeing my family for what it really is, I really want to be free from all of it. I can't take the rejection anymore. And for the first time in my life, I think I actually deserve better too."

"OK, that's a pretty big step Veronica. How are you going to handle it? There are so many factors involved."

"The first thing you need to know is that my brother and sister are going to have a meltdown. They always try to guilt me back into relationship with my folks. They are going to be furious, but what else can I do? You said our goal is my freedom. I think that is what I want. I just want to be free from the painful people in my life who think it's their God-given duty to make me feel like I am worthless."

"OK, but remember what I said a few weeks back. You have to deal with a generation at a time. First, you have to confront your brother before you can deal with your parents. You have to do this in proper order. After that, no matter what your brother's reaction is, then you can confront your parents."

"Are you kidding me? You have totally misunderstood; I'm not confronting my parents! My mom scares the crap out of me. I just want to walk away and fall off the radar, that's all. I'm not too sure how to do it though. I've tried going unnoticed, and then, here I go and mistakenly call my dad. I don't know how to break the family ties, but this I do know—it can't be in a confrontation. I can never be in the same room with my mom. I know you think I'm ridiculous for being a forty-three-year old woman who is frightened of her mom, but I don't care. You have never met her and you don't know what she is capable of.

Continuing with my plan, I said, "As far as confronting my brother goes, I think I am ready to do that. I'm a little in the dark about how it works. I don't know the first thing about confronting someone who molested you. I can imagine it will be one of the most terrifying things I can ever do."

Dr. Storm was busy writing in my file. The warrior had once again emerged and was sitting across from him in his office. Not even a little timid about my brother any longer, I was finally willing to start taking on the issues or, as it were, family. Helping me to chart out the course, he began.

"First you have to decide when and where it will take place. I highly recommend that you are not alone. You should choose a place where you feel safe, and both of you could talk freely about your childhood. You also have to be prepared for a whole host of reactions. I can help you get ready so you won't be caught off guard. After you are done dealing with your brother, then we can address the issues you have with your parents."

We talked the remainder of the session about where I would go from there. My chest began to tighten with the plan of action that we were discussing. It was actually going to happen—I was going to confront my brother. How would I ever get the courage to actually go through with it? I would have to muster it up somehow, because business as usual no longer worked with me. I was changing; now the world around me needed to change too.

Leaving his office, I got another appointment on the calendar to begin working out the details. Jerry was going to be so surprised that I had decided to confront my brother. He knew it would ultimately happen; he just didn't know it would be this soon.

On the drive back home, I was once again zipping on the toll road making record time. Wanting to fill Jerry in on all the details of the session, I phoned him. Trying to carry on an uninterrupted conversation was a chore. My phone kept cutting out due to the lack of reception on the toll road. In between my disconnected calls, the revelation hit me. *My phone carrier doesn't have reception on the toll road.* How on earth was I able to talk to my dad this morning? I should have never been able to carry on a conversation with him; it simply wasn't possible! I realized it was more of a divine connection than I had previously thought.

I arrived home with the sense of amazement about what had happened that morning. I was also alarmed at the decision I made in Dr. Storm's office to confront my brother.

The wheels of the plan were in full motion. No one was going to stop it from getting to its final destination—my freedom.

CHAPTER SEVENTEEN

Eye of the Storm

Pulling into the garage of my home, I was greeted by my kids. I loved coming home and having the warm reception that often awaited me. Jerry arrived home from work just in time for the whole family to enjoy dinner together. Our conversation revolved around our family vacation, only a few short days away. The children told us their desired itinerary and what they wanted to pack for the various activities we had planned. More than ever, I was looking forward to our getaway. I welcomed a short-term reprieve from all of the drama.

Finishing with dinner and the dishes, I stopped by the computer to retrieve my email. My heart momentarily stopped when I saw an email from my father. I had that immediate burst of adrenaline that actually felt as though a knife had pierced my heart. With apprehension, I sat down and began reading.

Veronica,

It was great to hear your voice this morning. I think your misdial was of the Lord. Mom and I spent considerable time this last weekend discussing what we could do to begin the process of

248

solving or at least exploring the issues that have come between us.

Then I had a dream Saturday night involving us. As usual, I don't remember any details, just that it was a positive one. Seems to me as if the Lord is prompting me to see about getting in touch with you and see what you think.

We are willing to fly down and stay at a hotel or motel near the airport and meet with you, or if you prefer to meet with a neutral third party present.

We will be looking forward to hearing your answer.

Love,
Dad

Disappointed that my dad didn't mention any regrets for not saying "I love you," I immediately called Jerry to come and read the email. Shaken, I told him, "They want to fly down here to meet with me. I can't meet them, Jerry; it will be awful. This is another set-up; I just know it. Being in the same room with my mom isn't even an option. She is so mean; I can't do it again."

Jerry's first response was, "He didn't mention that he neglected to say, 'I love you.' How could he not backtrack and say that it has been haunting him all day? Another thing: he said they were talking this past weekend on exploring the issues, what's to explore? You outlined your mom's singling you out over the years and all the other many offenses they have done. The only conclusion they came to was you were a bad daughter. Why would they expect you to be willing to explore those issues again? You should probably run this by Dr. Storm before you make any decisions."

"I know, I totally agree. For now, I'll go ahead and email my dad and tell him I'll give them my answer in a couple of days."

Jerry stopped me. "Why do you think you need to respond right away? It took your dad two years to contact you and that was only because you accidentally called him today. You are allowed to wait a few days until you have had a chance to talk this over with Dr. Storm. You shouldn't rush this. Time is on your side."

I knew Jerry was right. I immediately fell back into being the obedient five-year old when I heard from them. While getting ready for bed, I was anxious as I thought about my dad's email. Was I allowed to say no to their offer of coming down? When my brother and sister found out, they would definitely tell me I had to do it. Mom and Dad would look like they were doing everything possible to mend the fences, so how could I say I didn't want them to? Again, I would be the divisive one, and my parents would be the ones who look like they were rejected. Seemed to me that no matter what I did, I was screwed.

I began to pray and ask the Lord for guidance. As far as I was concerned, He was the One who got me into the mess. I knew I didn't dial my dad's phone number this morning, so what was God up to? While I was praying, a thought came to me. *Handle them like Joseph handled his brothers.* What a brilliant idea. I ran downstairs and grabbed my Bible. I quickly turned to the story of Joseph found in Genesis, chapters 42 through 45. Although I was pretty well acquainted with the story, I had never looked at it from a strategic point of view. I began to take notes on what I was reading.

The story was quite lengthy about Joseph being sold by his brothers into slavery because they were jealous of his relationship with their father. A lot transpires in the story; however, the part I paid close attention to was when Joseph was promoted to work directly under Pharaoh. That meant he was in charge of the food distribution while Egypt was in famine.

After several years, Joseph's brothers traveled down to Egypt to buy food. When they came into Joseph's presence, his brothers didn't even recognize him because he was only a teenager when they had sold him. Now he was a man in authority. Joseph immediately recognized his brothers but did not make them aware of who he was.

Through a series of events, Joseph set his brothers up to look as though they had stolen from the Pharaoh. The brother's were falsely accused of this crime and would be thrown into prison. Joseph's strategy was to see if his brothers had changed or if they were sorry for what they had done to him. They had concluded that they were in prison because of God judging them for the betrayal of their brother many years earlier. After many years of testing his brothers' character, Joseph was convinced they were truly repentant for what they had done to him.

He told his brothers his identity and began weeping so loudly that everyone in the palace could hear. From the beginning of the story, where the brothers go to Egypt to buy food, to the conclusion, where they discover Joseph, their brother, is still alive, many years pass. This is no overnight journey; it was the test of time.

After reading the story, I was captivated at how Joseph

was willing to use even deception to test his brothers' character to see if the years had changed them. He clearly demonstrated that testing the ones who had betrayed him in the past was not only acceptable but also wise. In other words, he wanted to make sure they were safe before allowing reconciliation to occur.

I told Jerry about how I thought the Lord was directing me to handle my family like Joseph handled his. He supported the approach whole heartedly. I didn't really know what this would look like in the case of my family; however, I did know that I needed to be careful and proceed with caution with managing the relationships.

Happily retreating to the bedroom for the night, I fell fast asleep, still a little restless from both my meeting with Dr. Storm and the email from my father. Quite unexpectedly, I woke up in a fright in the middle of the night. I began to shake and quiver once more as I had in the early part of my counseling. The very thought of having to be in the same room with my parents was enough to send me over the edge.

I began to doubt Dr. Storm's ability to see past the deception of appearances and feared he might get lured into my mom's web of lies. What if he didn't know how to properly read my dad's email? I knew how to read between the lines, but would he? I also knew that my mom helped write the email; it was totally unlike him to act alone. She was behind the scenes planning and plotting, I just knew it.

My heart seemed to clench, and my body was trembling. I hated it when I had to wake Jerry up from a sound sleep so he could help quiet my nerves. I rolled over and tapped him on the arm to try and gently wake him. He rolled over and saw my tear-marked cheeks and my body shaking. He, of course, assumed that I was having my flash-backs again. I told him this had nothing to do with my brother; I was terrified that I might have to face my parents again.

Wide-awake now, he assured me that there was no need to fear such a confrontation. "Veronica, you are the decision maker here, not them. You never have to be in their presence again if that is what you decide. They are not emo-tionally safe to you. You have tried to mend the fences but are always left emotionally bloodied at the end of the at-tempt. You have every right to tell them you decline their offer and simply don't trust them."

I countered with my concerns that my family would all have proof that I was being divisive if I was not willing to at least try to reconcile. I also expounded on my unease of having Dr. Storm thrown into the mix. I never allowed my family to be involved with any other people in my life. That only gave them the opportunity to convey how highly spir-itual they were and how wayward I was. My mom would probably go to great lengths to make her case with Dr. Storm at how crazy she thought I was.

Not the least bit swayed by my argument, he re-sponded, "Again Veronica, you are the decision maker. Why are you afraid of appearances? You know what is real and what is the illusion. What Dr. Storm, your brother, or sister think is totally irrelevant. Besides, you know Dr. Storm will see through it. He has become pretty acquainted with your family's dealings and can help you answer your dad's email effectively. Don't forget that the Lord told you to handle them like Joseph handled his brothers. Testing them and making sure they are safe is mandatory."

Jerry's argument was successful. I began to realize that I was in the position of control. "I will turn down their offer and tell them I want to be free from the family once and for all. I don't care what my brother and sister think of me anymore. I am so tired of psychological warfare and trying to figure out what is going on behind the scenes. As I told Dr. Storm in his office today, I want out. I don't want any part of this drama anymore."

"Good for you! They are your family; they are supposed to be your support system, not your cause of pain. I hope that when this is all over you can pick up the pieces and know that the kids and I are your family. We will be here for you."

Our conversation started at 3:00 am and ended at 6:00 am. Not having to get up for another hour and a half, we tried to make up for yet another night's lack of rest.

It had been two days since I received the email from my father, and I couldn't be happier that Jerry was going to Dr. Storm's office with me for my appointment. I was concerned that Dr. Storm would think that I had a moral and spiritual obligation to accept my parents' offer. For years now, so many of my Christian friends had told me to pray for the reconciliation of my family. They advised me to "turn the other cheek" and do whatever it took to make the relationships work. I knew Dr. Storm well enough by now that he never encouraged toxic relationships, so that's not why I was concerned. My fear was he would be fooled by the appearance of the email my dad sent not knowing the underlying motivation of what was actually being offered.

Jerry and I sat together in the waiting room of Dr. Storm's office. We talked and giggled, waiting for Dr. Storm to arrive. Right on time, smiling in his usual way, he said, "Jerry, I'm glad you are able to join us today. How is it going with you?"

"Great, how are things with you?"

"Very well, thank you."

The two of them have always gotten along famously. They took a few minutes to catch up with each other and then the session began.

"So, Veronica, how are you doing? Have you been thinking about how you are going to confront your brother?"

"Yes, that has been on the forefront of my mind for the better part of two days. But before we address that, I wanted to read you an email my dad sent me after I left your office a couple of days ago."

Dr. Storm was visibly surprised at hearing my dad had contacted me after the phone call.

I began reading it to him, and, after I finished, I began to doubt my interpretation of the email. How will Dr. Storm see it? I looked across to study his face. That was my usual method of deciphering what was going on in his head. I wondered if he knew I was constantly reading him to track his mental thought process. It was not just his words I wanted; it was how he came to those words. I needed to begin to start thinking like a normal, healthy, and clear-headed person, so I tried to learn as much as possible to gain insight into how this works. At this juncture, I didn't consider myself as a patient, but rather a student. I wanted freedom, which included being free from my old way of thinking that had held me captive for so many years.

This was a critical point in my relationship with Dr. Storm. If he sided with my dad and did not see it from my perspective, we would have a problem. I did trust Dr. Storm, but only to the degree that I was able. I was still a little skittish around anyone who seemed to be in my court, fearing they would cross over at a moment's notice. I had my mom and sister to thank for that!

"Hmm, that was interesting. What do you make of it?" Dr. Storm asked, offering no opinion of his own.

"Well, first let me clarify this for you. I hardly think my dad is the author of this email; I believe my mom is behind it. He probably did want to email me; however, it did not leave his computer and get to mine without her approval and influence. Another thing, if you noticed, he didn't mention the lack of response to my 'I love you.' That was a screaming omission in my book."

"My dad also said there could be a third party mediator. Yeah, they must know I'm in counseling. Remember after I met with my sister and she said she was glad to hear I was in counseling, so I could see the error of my ways? Well, rest assured my parents are ecstatic! I'm pretty certain they think you feel as though I am a jacked-up mess of a woman and you will side with their holy selves."

"Then the part he wrote about the two of them discussing what they could do to begin the process of solving, or at least exploring the issues that have come between us—

that doesn't even make sense. What is there to explore? He did not say that they have had a change of heart or that they see they have treated me unfairly. As far as I can tell, all they want to do is open dialogue so they can continue to make their case against me. I don't mean to sound paranoid; that's just how it is."

"Wow, you really do know how to read your family. Like I said before, that must be terribly exhausting for you. Always having to be on your guard and to read in-between the lines to know what the real motivation is, is a full-time job. I'll defer to you on this one—you know so much more about them than I do. What is your answer to your father going to be?"

Relieved that he didn't say I needed to take my parents up on their offer, I decided I could still trust Dr. Storm. I continued, "I'm not exactly sure yet, but, when I prayed about it, the Lord told me to handle them like Joseph handled his brothers."

Laughing, Dr. Storm said, "That's great! What does that mean to you? How do you translate how Joseph handled his brothers to your situation?"

"I think it means that I need to be careful and that I don't have to trust them until they prove themselves to be trustworthy. I also noticed that, on several occasions, Joseph was so hurt by the past betrayal of his brothers that he would go off by himself to cry. At one time, his cries could be heard throughout the palace. I'm pretty sure this is going to be an emotionally painful experience for me."

Jerry, who had remained relatively quiet, entered the conversation. "I told her it was within her rights to turn down the offer altogether. When I first read the email, I couldn't believe her dad didn't even comment on not saying 'I love you.' I told Veronica that not only should he have immediately called her back after they hung up, but, at the very minimum, he should have opened his email with his apology."

I interjected. "Yeah, the night I received my dad's email, I was pretty shaken. I woke up in the middle of the night terrified that I had to have them come down for a confrontation. I woke Jerry up so he could help talk me through the situation. We stayed up three hours discussing what I should do and how to proceed. By the time we were finished, I decided that I was going to email my father and let him know I want to end all communication."

A little shocked, Dr. Storm replied, "You do? Veronica, they have no power over you. Facing them and holding them accountable might be a very liberating experience for you. You have a voice: you are allowed to speak up and be heard. When we started this process, I said your freedom is the ultimate goal. I want you to be free from the terror you feel when you are with them. Are you sure you don't want to face them and hold them accountable?"

"I have spoken up in the past with them, and, trust me, I am not heard. I know it sounds extreme that I want to end communication, but it isn't. They are the scariest people I know, and I don't want to subject myself to their plans anymore. You have to trust me on this one: it is a set up. I will email him and ask him to please, just let me go. That will accomplish two things: it will temporarily get my parents off my back, and it will open conversation with my brother and

258

sister. Besides, they are hardly ones who take orders from their child. I will still get emails from them, just you wait and see."

"Now, about my brother, I have been going over how I should confront him. I'll tell him that I have made a decision regarding my relationship with our parents. That always gets his attention. When he agrees to meet with me, instead of talking about our parents, I'll confront him about our childhood. It's a little deceptive, but it's the only way I can think of to actually get him to meet with me. I just don't know where the confrontation should take place."

Jerry, concerned for my safety, spoke up. "I don't want you to do it where you are alone with him. It has to be in a public place."

"I know. I was thinking a restaurant. Then I thought about when we are in the middle of the conversation, can you imagine the server coming over and offering us dessert? I can't think of anything worse than that. I also don't want to be concerned about having people at the tables next to us over hearing what we are talking about. Maybe a park or some place like that."

Jerry, not liking the direction I was going, interrupted again. "I don't feel comfortable with you meeting your brother at a park. I know it wouldn't be right for me to be there, but I don't want you to be alone or vulnerable."

"Well, I hardly think doing it in one of our houses is a good idea. We can't risk any of my brother's kids or our children walking in on the conversation."

Dr. Storm offered his assistance. "You can meet in my office if you would like. I would be happy to be a third party mediator. Would you feel more comfortable with that?"

Excited, I answered, "Would you do that? That would be fantastic! Thank you so much for offering to have it here. Boy, I bet you had no idea what you were getting into when you took us on for marriage counseling did you!"

"No, I really didn't, but I'm happy to help. We're going to see this through just like I promised."

The stage was set and the plan was in full swing. I would confront my brother in Dr. Storm's office with him there as the mediator. Now, how would I get my brother to come down? I would think like Joseph and devise a way. Putting our heads together, the three of us came up with the perfect plan on how to proceed with the much-anticipated confrontation.

CHAPTER EIGHTEEN

Action Plan

While continuing with our session, I once again visited my storage room. Taking quick inventory, I still saw the ominous box on the top shelf that was never to be opened. I hadn't asked much of God through this process. I only asked that He respect my wishes never to have me open that package.

While Dr. Storm and Jerry continued their dialogue, I inwardly smiled at how organized the beautifully wrapped packages were on the shelves of my mind. No cross contamination had occurred, and all was well. Then I saw it again, that shadowy container that I saw the last time I was surveying my inventory. What is it and why is it here? There was a certain familiarity about it; however, I couldn't quite remember placing it in here. I did know that there was a certain dread linked to it. My mind had chronicled all the events of my life with meticulous detail. I had the ability to know where each event was housed and in what container it had been placed. To have a box that I didn't recall placing here was terribly disturbing. Not to mention, it wasn't in plain view like the others.

Dismayed, I began to walk towards it. As I approached, Dr. Storm interrupted with the conversation already in place. I exited my closet and was mentally re-engaged in the session. "When are you calling your brother Veronica?" Dr. Storm asked.

"We leave tomorrow for our family vacation, so I guess I will make the phone calls to my brother and sister when I get back. They are a package deal. I can't contact only my brother; I have to bring my sister into this. I'll email my father and let him know that I am not interested in having a "face to face" and that all communication needs to stop. After I send it, I will make the calls to my brother and sister to notify them why I decided to sever ties with our parents. I think this will open the door for further dialogue with my brother, and I will approach him on coming into your office to help discuss it."

Taking a moment to collect my thoughts, I reiterated a concern of mine. "I have no intention of coming out swinging at my brother when I confront him. I am very concerned that he was a victim too and that he was acting out from his pain. I cannot bear the responsibility that this will send him over the top. I plan on being factual, not combative, if you know what I mean."

Dr. Storm joined me with my train of thought. "I know, Veronica. He was a victim and that most certainly helps to explain his actions. But in no way does it excuse them. I'm sure you'll do a great job of being careful how you approach him."

Jerry, visibly upset, interjected. "I take strong issue with that. Yes, he was a victim many, many years ago, but what about now? He is a grown man with children of his own. His daughter is older than the age Veronica was when he began molesting her. That alone should have been his wake up call. He has done nothing to make up for what he did. No apology, no acknowledgement of wrong doing, just same old, same old. I don't think Veronica should walk softly in this confrontation at all. He should be strongly held accountable for what he did and even for not being the one who took the initiative. There should be no compassion for someone who chooses to sexually violate someone and makes no attempt for atonement."

Dr. Storm and I listened attentively to Jerry's objections. No way would either of us interrupt. Jerry was usually mild mannered and un-opinionated during our sessions. He had stated many times that this was my journey and that he was here for my support. For him to speak up so authoritatively left me a little speechless. Jerry, on a roll, continued.

"Veronica, you have told me about how even in the adult years he has made references to your teen years as though you were the deviant one. I have no problem with you coming out hard and strong. I know you think God would want you to handle this thing gingerly, but I absolutely disagree. Your brother was in his early twenties the last time he came into your room. He was an adult! It's time for him to know what he did and how it affected you. Don't let him off the hook and pussy foot around it. You deserve better."

Being very careful to choose my words, I began. "Jerry, I know this is difficult for you to understand, really I do. I do not intend to let him off the hook. When I confront him, I will be very direct and clear about what he did and how it charted a destructive course for me. However, you weren't there to witness his sexual assault. You have no idea what he went through. I also think he should have taken the initiative to apologize. I'm sure he would have if he knew how badly it hurt me. I think it is only fair that I give him the benefit of the doubt. I can't bring myself to feel the same way about him that you do. I don't blame you in the slightest. I just cannot do it."

Silence filled the office like a cold winter's mist. Dr. Storm waited to see if there would be any more words exchanged between Jerry and me. We all silently looked at each other waiting for someone to pick up the ball dropped by the two players in the game. Jerry and I were standing at opposite ends of the court and yet still remained on the same team. He loved me and felt the need to protect me. How could I not love him for that?

Dr Storm didn't touch this one with a ten-foot pole. Only I could decide this issue. Confronting my brother was hard enough; being told how to feel while I did it couldn't be anyone's directive. There was no further exploration of this topic. In Dr. Storm's magical way, he redirected the conversation to a topic both Jerry and I were united on.

"The way you are going to approach your brother through the phone call sounds like a good plan. We can discuss it in greater detail at your next session. Now, I want you to promise me something, you two," Dr. Storm said looking at both Jerry and me. "Take this vacation to totally enjoy each other and your children. We can tackle this stuff when you get back. Can you do that?"

"Absolutely!" I said with total confidence. "This is

going to get pretty hairy. I need to come into it rested and prayed up."

Jerry agreed and we set up another time on the calendar for our next session. Walking to our car, Jerry and I decided where we would go for dinner. He told me there was this quaint little Italian restaurant in Dana Point, which was a neighboring beach city. They always booked great jazz bands and the menu was expansive with extraordinary dishes to choose from. It had become our custom to sneak in a mid-week date night after a session with Dr. Storm. We were never at a loss for conversation.

This time was different though. My heart was heavy with the reality that I was coming out with one of the family's secrets. To look my brother in the eye and actually say out loud the things that he did to me was starting to set in. My emotions were running all over the map. I felt anger, mixed with disgust, extreme sorrow, immeasurable anxiety, and, oddly enough, love laced with compassion. He was my brother, and he had often been so good to me. Our unspoken contract, the partnership birthed in hell was coming full circle and now I wanted out. As painful as it was, I knew of no other way to continue to be in relationship with him without letting our secret out.

We pulled into the restaurant parking lot and chose a table out on the patio. The summer air continued to be warm and inviting. For a Thursday night, the little restaurant was running a full load. With the live jazz music playing in the background, Jerry and I poured over the menu deciding which entrées to choose.

I sat quietly looking out over the beautiful hanging

flower baskets that encompassed the restaurant's covered patio. They were packed full of colorful petunias, impatiens, and daisies that had vivid blue and purple lobelias draping down the sides. Trailing ivy in various shades of green was intertwined in the floral arrangements. I watched as the baskets swayed in the gentle wind that was bounding off the ocean. The scene was picturesque. The fragrance from the kitchen filled the air with delectable aromas that caused my stomach to growl in eager anticipation. I was glad one of the servers had brought us a basket of fresh-baked bread to help take the edge off before our dinners arrived. I was either starving or had a total loss of appetite when I left a session. There seemed to be no middle ground with me. While pouring olive oil and Balsamic vinegar onto our bread plate, Jerry caught my eye, and I offered a slight smile to offset the silence.

"You're thinking about your brother aren't you?" Jerry asked in a hushed tone.

"Yes, I can't believe I'm actually going to do it. I never thought this day would come. So much has happened in such a short time."

"It has been fast, Veronica. When a seasoned professional, who has been in practice for over twenty-five years, says that he has never seen anything like this before, you know your head should spin. You've done an amazing job, staying focused and unwavering in the counseling process. I'm really proud of you. I don't know how you have managed to sludge your way through it, but you have."

Jerry reached across the table, and I firmly gripped his hand. "I know it's been hard on you too. I don't think most husbands could have handled it the way you have. I'm pretty sure if their wife had come to them with these kinds of issues to talk through, their response would have been 'That's what girlfriends are for.' Thank you for never shutting me down or turning me away."

The server approached our table with two large plates of pasta. Mine was bow tie pasta mixed with vegetables and olive oil, and Jerry's pasta was covered in a red marina sauce with Italian sausage. The flavors blended beautifully as we sat and listened to the band in the background. More needed to be said; however, I was too tired. At that moment, simple silence would have to do.

With our stomachs full and the evening spent, we left the restaurant for the drive home. Tomorrow we would go on vacation, and I planned to do exactly what Dr. Storm recommended: forget my family for the next several days. Arriving home, we found the kids were totally amped up when we pulled in, with suitcases packed and the energy level tangible. We were all in need of the much anticipated get-away, and I planned on making the most of it.

While on vacation, the time flew by quickly and we returned home to begin business as usual. We had scheduled our next appointment for Dr. Storm to be the next evening, knowing that we must move ahead before I lose my nerve. I was not looking forward to what I had to do, but I knew it must be done.

Since it was our last night, we all stayed up ridiculously late to make the most of the time. Alarm clocks buzzed early the next morning, waking us up from our sound sleep. The vacation was wonderful; we were all a little sad to leave.

When we returned home, I compiled the response to my dad's email so I could run it by Dr. Storm that evening. The words began flowing, with little to no effort. That was all the confirmation I needed. I was ready to begin the process. I looked at what I had written.

Dear Dad,

I gave myself some time to contemplate your email so I could think and pray about what my response would be. I too think the mistaken phone call was of the Lord. I don't however think it was for the same reason you apparently do.

Confronting the both of you two years ago was one of the hardest things I have ever done. It was an effort to help heal and hopefully begin a new and healthy relationship with my parents. But instead of reconciliation and apologies I was met with accusations and blame.

After our phone call on Thursday, I was shocked and awestruck at how I could have mistakenly dialed your phone number. I was also amazed at how I could be on the phone with my dad and not even recognize his voice. But the final shock to me was when I said "I love you Dad" and I was met with silence. Of course at first I gave you the benefit of the doubt at being totally taken off guard that you were unable to speak. I thought for awhile that maybe you were regretting having left me with dead air and were kicking yourself for not returning the sentiment. But then I came to myself and realized that if you were sorry for not saying I love you, you would have quickly returned the call and said that although we are not on speaking terms right now I don't want you to ever think that I don't love you.

I gave serious thought to your offer of having a sit down talk with a third party mediator. My heart raced with fear thinking that I would have to be in the same room with the two people who have been the cause of so much pain and hurt in my life. The very thought of seeing mom and hearing all her painful accusations sent me into a tailspin. Having to listen once more how her hurtful actions were justified due to the kind of daughter she says I am would be more than I could handle. Then I thought of how you would respond if I answered back or said something you thought was inappropriate to your wife. I would have to have you correct me and tell me that it was your turn to talk and how I would sit there feeling powerless to defend myself as I have on so many other occasions.

My going to bed thinking of a face to face confrontation with you both actually made me wake up in the middle of the night terrified that it might actually happen. I am embarrassed to admit that I didn't think I had the right to turn down such an offer. I was literally horrified about what I would be subjected to. Based on past history I realized that it wasn't reconciliation you seek but another chance to let me know where I have missed it and how I am the cause of a family divided. I would assume that you thought your prayers were answered and that the Lord has shown me the errors of my ways and that I am now open to your rebuke. I realized that you would never come to the enlightenment that your choices and behavior have ripped a family apart and I am only the one holding you accountable. It has occurred to me that you would never let me hold you accountable for your actions but instead need to place blame the on me to alleviate your own guilt. I have no other conclusion to draw based on the past discussions.

It is because of this that I have come to the conclusion that I have. The past two years being free from our relationship has unfortunately been the most peaceful and free years I have ever experienced as an adult. I haven't been subjected to ridicule and conditional love. I don't have to worry about being rejected and trying to figure out what I did to deserve such treatment.

See I too think the call was of the Lord. It confirmed my decision two years ago not to be in relationship with two people who only want to love me on their terms. You not saying I love you back helped me know that the decision I made was justified and healthy. It also made me face the harsh reality that nothing has changed over the past two years. Your email saying that you two talked last weekend of maybe starting to explore the issues that have come between us again also confirmed my decision. What possible exploration is necessary? I clearly outlined my grievances in our email exchanges. One for instance is Mom coming to my house and talking bad about my past to my children all the while singing the praises of the two of you for having prayed me through my rebellion. Not telling them why I would have chosen to self medicate from such a painful teen experience with a mom suffering from depression and taking it out on me. Not to mention going to kiss mom goodbye on another visit only for her to turn her head letting me know that she does not think me worthy of such affections. Taking time to visit you at my brother's house for Father's day and having her walk past me and my kids to give her son and his kids kisses goodnight knowing that we were leaving but again making sure I felt the pain of her rejection. These are of course only a few of the offensive behaviors and were reiterated to help jar your memories.

You only need to refer back to all my emails to explore the issues. You see, there is no process that could undo what has been done. The only thing that was ever necessary was the both of you telling me that you love me unconditionally and want to learn how to create a safe and healthy relationship. It is clear that pride would not allow you to do such things.

Mom said in one of her emails that she hopes that none of my kids will do to me what I have done to her. Regrettably, the pattern of manipulation and conditional love did not end with her but it has with me. I know this pattern all too well as I watched it as a girl as grandma caused her so much pain. I remember telling mom over and over that she didn't need to be in relationship with her mom when she is always so mean and left her feeling worthless. I also remember telling her that "honor your father and mother" does not mean that you have to be in relationship with them and allow them to continue to hurt you.

I am taking my own advice and walking away from the same destructive relationship that I have with the two of you. But she is not to worry, the pattern of conditional love and lack of acceptance has stopped with my generation. My kids never have to earn an "I love you" it is given freely and with much affection and not based on their behavior at the time. They won't have to wonder, as I have on so many visits, why I would pay for lunch with one their siblings but insist that they pay for my lunch. Can you imagine wondering why you weren't even worth the price of a hamburger? That is a question they will never have to contemplate. Favoritism is not a factor in this home. With God's grace I will never let pride come between me and my children and I would never use my money as a measurement of their worth or value. They will always enjoy a safe haven with me.

I can honestly say before God that I am at peace with my decision and I know that it is the right and healthy thing to do. I also know that I have exhausted all my resources for reconciliation and have found it not possible. You had an amazing God given opportunity to tell me you love me and you chose not to. I respect your decision to leave it unsaid now please respect my decision to end all communication and go on with my life. The price I have to pay to hear those words are too great, I have earned the right to be free. Also you should know that Jerry not only supports my choice but insists on it.

-Veronica

After reading it, I was left with a multitude of emotions. The first of the emotions was a sense of liberty and well-being. I actually stood up for myself and had clearly outlined why I had to walk away. The other layers of emotions weren't nearly as rewarding. They were the pain of the true caliber of my worth to them and the fear of retribution. I knew that, although I had asked for all communication to cease, that would hardly be the case. I didn't write the email for my father; it was a direct communication to my mother.

This was her beckoning. My dad had become the pawn in my exit plan to freedom. He was a willing player, who would allow himself to be used as the go-between for a daughter and mother.

After I emailed it to my father, I sat at the computer and began gently massaging my temples with my index and middle fingers. I closed my eyes and took deep breaths as though I was an athlete preparing for a championship game. I wanted to prepare myself mentally and emotionally for what the next several days would bring. Now, I would make the calls to my siblings. That should launch my plan into motion. My sister would immediately notify my mom about my phone call to her regarding my dad's email. No doubt, the two of them would begin working out details of their own. It would only be a matter of time before my mom stuck her head up. Historically, she was not one to remain silent while I was on the offence. I needed her to come out to play. When she did, she would do what she did best, put me in my rightful place in the family. I had to have her show her true colors so I could display them for my brother and sister.

Not only a warrior was emerging from within, Joseph the ruler was coming out. I chose no longer to be at my family's mercy; I much preferred God's. My family had no idea what lay ahead and that I was launching into a plan of my own.

CHAPTER NINETEEN:

The Strategy

Jerry and I kissed the children good-bye as we made our way out the door. I had already had Jerry proofread the letter to my dad, and he was completely on board with the message. This had been long in coming for Jerry. When we were first married, my mom and Jerry had a slight run-in. It was only a mere difference of opinion, but that was huge in my family. Jerry openly disagreed with her about something and although he handled it respectfully, it totally threw me for a loop.

I told him that he is NEVER to disagree with her; it simply wasn't worth it. Then I asked him to leave all communication with my family to me. He knew that I had a rough relationship with my parents, in particular my mom, but he had no idea the magnitude of the problem. Out of respect for me, he had remained in the background, not interfering with my family dynamic. Now, he was no longer my silent partner; he was my champion.

Our sessions with Dr. Storm had taken on a completely new tone. At one of our earlier sessions, Dr. Storm had expressed that he felt a certain affinity with Jerry and me. "Once in a while, a couple comes along that I feel a strong connection with; you two are that couple." He then informed us that he had planned on going into semi-retirement at the beginning of the year. He said he and his wife prayed about it, and they just didn't feel it was the year for him to do it. "If I had retired, I wouldn't have taken you two on as new clients. I really think you are one of the reasons I was not to have retired this year. God is moving in such a way; I wouldn't have wanted to have missed this. It is such a privilege to be a part of this journey with you."

Always professional, a friendly kind of relationship had nonetheless developed. We were all on a mission together, the collective efforts for my freedom. Whenever I thanked Dr. Storm for all he had done to contribute to my progression, he would tell me that he didn't think he had done much. Nevertheless, whether he wanted credit or not, he had been a valued expert on my journey.

Jerry and I waited in Dr. Storm's office for our scheduled appointment time to arrive. In the earlier part of my counseling, I used to get so nervous while I sat waiting, not anymore. I had a new feeling of peace that I had never experienced before. Along with the new serenity, I didn't have the usual sense of being emotionally paralyzed that I once had. I knew I had the ability to make choices and be proactive, not just be a helpless bystander in my life. Jerry and I joked around killing time. Dr. Storm approached.

"Hello, you two. How was vacation?"

"We had a great time," I said with a huge smile. "The weather was perfect for all the activities and we were able to get some relaxation in as well."

"Super, I was hoping you guys were having a good time. Why don't you come on back so we can begin?"

Sitting in our usual places, I quickly reached into my purse to retrieve the letter to my father.

"I wrote my dad the response to his email. It's a little long; however, I wanted to make sure to cover all the bases. Can I read it to you?"

"Sure, go right ahead." Dr. Storm looked intent while sitting back in his chair.

I read the two-page letter with Dr. Storm fully engaged in my reading. After completed, I asked, "Well, what do you think? Is it too harsh? I wanted to be perfectly clear but not cruel."

Thoughtfully, he answered, "That was well written, Veronica. It touches on every aspect that we have been talking about over the past several months. You articulated your thoughts and emotions, very well. Do you write often? You seem to be good at it."

Laughing, I said, "Heck no! I can't write; I'd be lousy at it. So you don't think it was over the top? I mean I want to be factual, not accusatory."

"Yes, that's what I got out of it. You outlined a clear pattern of behavior and made a case for why you need to be free. It was a little heartbreaking to listen to. Are you certain you want all communication to cease?"

"Oh brother! I only said that to get the wheels in motion. Trust me, I will hear back from him. Of course, it won't only be just him; my mom will be smack dab in the middle of it. She has to rise up, that's the only way this will work. It's all just a matter of time."

We spent the next hour going over the confrontation with my brother. That was what this was about, after all. I needed to have a reason to contact him. Being on the other end of a plan seemed so counterintuitive to me. For the first time in my life, I actually didn't feel like I was in survival mode. I was in the driver's seat.

Wrapping up, Dr. Storm checked on my confidence level. "Do you think you will be able to go through with this?"

"I am going to be scared out of my mind, but I'm not going to back down. Do you know what managing my family feels like to me? All the toxic relationships, secrets and psychological warfare, I feel like I am the manager of a dump. I work hard at making sure toxins aren't released, maintain careful watch on the trash being thrown my way, and, above all, ensure there is never any kind of cross-contamination. At the end of the day, I am looking around at how well I am managing my life, and then it hits me. I didn't manage a life; I managed a dump. This is my official two-week notice; I don't want to be a dump manager anymore."

"Wow, that was well said. Are you sure you don't like to write? You definitely have a way with words."

"Nah, even if I wanted to, I wouldn't have a clue at what I would write about."

Before we left, we chose a couple of session dates for me to be able to give my brother. That would allow for one less phone call and reduce the possibility of him backing out once committed.

"OK, I'll send the email to my dad tonight and call my brother and sister tomorrow. I really don't have a plan 'B' if this doesn't work."

Dr. Storm confidently assured me. "God has gotten you this far. He'll take care of the rest."

Jerry and I left his office and went on our usual mid-week date. We didn't feel like going to a restaurant so we grabbed a bite to eat from a fast food place. We wound up in Laguna Beach and strolled along the shoreline, right before sunset. Seagulls were busy picking up food scraps left by the beachgoers, and kids were still frolicking in the water, while parents relaxed on the sand. After our walk, we plopped on a bench and snuggled close while watching the sunset over the ocean. In a matter of minutes, the palm trees and cliffs became darkened silhouettes against the dusk sky. It was a breathtaking sight and a relaxing way to end the evening.

When we arrived home, I ran upstairs to email my father. My courage was compounded once my plan was in motion. Most assuredly, I would get a reply from him in the next couple of days. Tomorrow I would call my brother and sister to inform them of my severed ties with our parents. I had to get myself emotionally ready for the next step. I kept reminding myself that I was to think and act like Joseph in the Bible: Be alert, pro-active and one step ahead of them.

After a good night's rest, I was eager to make my phone calls. The first call would be to my sister. She probably already knew about the mistaken phone call to my dad and his email to me. My mom and she are close, and my mom would have already informed her. There hadn't been enough time for her to know about the email I sent to my dad last night. It was imperative that I get to her before my mom did.

I tried calling her but was unsuccessful at reaching her. I left a message to get back to me as soon as possible. My next call was to my brother. This was much harder than I thought it would be. My heart pumped so fast, it actually hurt. I dialed each number slowly making sure to dial correctly. I half-hoped that I would be switched to voicemail. That didn't happen. My brother answered.

"Hi Ron, what's up?"

My old nickname is Ronnie, but he always shortened it to Ron. This was somewhat a term of endearment to me, which made this call even harder. Bucking up, I responded, "I wanted to talk to you about something. Do you have a minute?"

"Actually, I have a meeting that I have to go to in around five minutes. What is this about?"

"Oh, I just wanted to update you on something that has gone on between Dad and me. Last time you were upset that I didn't tell you, so this time I'm letting you in the loop."

"Can I call you tonight after work? I'm taking the boys to a ballgame, but I can call you before then. How would around 5:00 be? I should have at least an hour to talk before I have to head out. Is that OK?"

"Sure, that would be fine. I'll talk to you later on this evening. Bye."

"Bye, Ron."

My mind was in complete contradiction to my heart. I knew this had to be done, but I didn't want to hurt him or shame him. It was such a dark twisted lot to feel the need to protect your molester. It would have been so much easier if he were unkind to me. The underlying comments and in-nuendos were so easily excused when he was usually nice and familiar.

I wrestled the rest of the day with what I would say when they returned my phone calls. Finally, later on that afternoon, my sister called. Trying not to sputter, I began to tell her about how I mistakenly called Dad and how I had said "I love you" at the end and was only met with silence.

Before I could get too far into the conversation she said, "Let me stop you before you go any further. In the interest of fairness, I want you to know that mom has told me about the phone call. I have heard their side of the story, but I do want to hear yours."

Any fear that I had when the conversation started had quickly diminished. Immediately I could picture the two females on the phone talking about how God was finally getting my attention and how this was the perfect time for our family to be reunited. I also knew that my counseling was discussed at great length and that was why my dad of-fered to have a "third party" present. I already assumed that was true, but now she just confirmed it.

I went on for about ten minutes filling her in on the de-tails of the mistaken phone call and then my dad's email later that evening. I told her that he never even acknowl-edged not saying "I love you" in return to my sentiment. I began my exaggeration by moaning how wounded I was and how it had pained me deeply.

Then I went with my surprise attack. I told her that I sent Dad a return email last night and that I would no longer have any communication between the three of us.

The words had barely escaped my mouth, when she snapped in her reply.

"What? I can honestly say that is not what I was expecting you to say. You're not taking them up on their offer to come down and meet with you? I really don't understand why you wouldn't. They were kind enough to allow you to choose the time, place, and person who would be the mediator, and you refuse?"

I could almost see her face on the other end of my phone line. Scrambling, trying to figure out how to convince me to fall into their plan of having our parents come down for a face-to-face confrontation. Not letting on that I had a finger on the pulse of what went on behind the scenes, I continued.

"There simply is no need for them to come down. We have tried to work this out for the past two years and all I receive from them is accusations and disgust. Then, when Dad emailed me, he didn't say he felt bad about how they treated me or that they need to apologize. He said he thinks the phone call was of the Lord, and yet he didn't even acknowledge his gross lack of affection."

Trying not to come undone, she objected. "I can't believe you are doing this! They said you could choose the mediator. I would assume you would have jumped at the chance. I mean, you could have chosen Dr. Storm. You would feel like you could trust him. I really think you're missing it. You have a God-given opportunity to make amends, and you're refusing it."

The conversation went exactly as predicted. Mom and she both thought I was the crazy one. I was sure my mom was totally convinced of her ability to swoon the doctor and have him see all my family's problems are a direct result of me. My refusing to agree to the face-to-face confrontation was completely unexpected and had thrown her into a tail-spin. Apparently, they didn't have a "Plan B" either. The heated debate continued for roughly an hour. Her accusing me of being out of God's will and me telling her to stop thinking she is my spiritual advisor.

The conversation turned explosive on both ends. She continued to outline for me how I was in direct defiance of God's will, and I blasted her for thinking she knew better than I did. She further told me how I could choose to have it in Dr. Storm's office, which would mean I would be in control. Yeah, like that would ever happen. I was never in control as long as my mom was present. She also brought up how I have destroyed any chance of her ever having a happy Christmas again. By not making amends, the family would not be able to be under one roof. Apparently, God wanted us all to celebrate together. I must have missed that memo.

Finally, I told her I was finished trying to explain myself. She then told me she didn't agree with my decision; however she would respect it, which provided little to no comfort.

I knew my sister would call Mom after we hung up. When she told my mom that I had informed her about Dad's lack of apology, that would definitely get my parents busy writing an apology email to me. At the end of this, my mom needed to make sure that they appeared to have done everything in their power to reconcile and I was the one who drove an arrow through their hearts.

Hanging up the phone, I realized I needed to handle this differently with my brother. God was so gracious by allowing me to talk to my sister first. It helped me to see that I needed to revise my plan. There was no way I was going to give him any information on the phone. Instead, I would use the information as the bait to get him to Dr. Storm's. If I went into all the details about what happened, he would surely respond in the same fashion and there would be no need for him to come into Dr. Storm's office. He would disagree with my decision, but respect my right to make it. And by respect, I mean continuously tell me I was wrong and God was disapproving, but disobedience was my right. I had to come up with another plan.

My brother called right on time: it was 5:00. Instead of answering, I let him go to my voicemail. Knowing this was going to cause his curiosity to pique, I allowed time for him to be left without answers. This would truly be one of the longest nights of my life. I had to be patient, not return his phone call, so I could make him hungry for information.

Night had fallen and everyone but me was in bed fast asleep. I was reading a book; however, my mind wouldn't stay on the written page. I couldn't help but go over the short phone call with my brother that afternoon. "Hi Ron, what's up?" played repeatedly on my mental tape player. He had no idea what I was up to, and it was taking its toll on me. I really couldn't stand the thought of hurting him and catching him off guard. He was going to feel so betrayed when he found out the true reason why I had him come into Dr. Storm's office.

I began to cry, and it welled up from my innermost

being. This would change everything. I already didn't have relationships with my parents; when this was over, I might not have a relationship with my brother either. Is it possible to feel like an orphan even when you're forty-three? It was as though I had been informed of a sudden death of a loved one. I felt the loss as though it had already happened. Even with that, I was not going to back down. I had to get it out in the open and try to rebuild on a healthier level, if possible.

I tried to come up with another plan. I knew I would have to deceive him. I would exaggerate and tell him that I cried for hours and was terribly hurt when I got off the phone with our sister. I'd explain that the only way I would be able to handle telling him would be with my therapist present. I'd try to make it sound like I was on the brink of a nervous breakdown so he would feel compelled to help. Hopefully, this would cause his brotherly protective mode to kick in. I was not ever given to drama with my family, so I hoped I would be able to convince him. I really wasn't too sure if he would buy it.

Sleep was scarce. Tossing and turning, I caught only about two hours worth of rest. I didn't feel too tired; I was too skittish about the phone call I had to make. I hoped my sister hadn't beaten me to the call. I needed him to want the information and not have it freely given by her.

Finally, it was time to make the call. With my heart practically jumping out of my chest, I dialed and waited for him to answer. Waiting, waiting, finally he picked up.

"Hi Ron, I called you last night, but I got your voicemail."

Going for an Oscar-worthy performance, I began. "I

284

know. I'm sorry I didn't pick up. I was still so upset from talking to our sister. I told her about what went on between Dad and I, and she totally freaked out. I really can't handle this anymore. I want to tell you everything, but I actually cried three hours after I hung up with her, and I don't want that to happen again."

"I'm sorry you're so upset Ronnie. You don't have to tell me if you don't want too."

That was not the response I was looking for. Unrelenting, I continued. "Oh no, I want to tell you, I think you should know. It will have an adverse effect on our family dynamic. However, I was wondering if you would come to a counseling session with me so I could tell you there. That way, if I begin to struggle with the information, my doctor can help me. He could also help us figure out where we go from here and answer any questions you have concerning my decision."

"Go to a counseling session? I don't know, I don't think that is necessary. You can just wait and tell me in a month or so when you're feeling better. I think I get the gist of it anyway. I don't want to be the cause of any more pain for you. Don't worry about me. I can find out when you are more comfortable."

This was going to be much harder than I thought. Now it was time to pull out all the stops and act like I was on the brink of a breakdown. With tremendous frenzied emotion, I pleaded. "I couldn't possibly wait another month! I want this over. I can't take it anymore! I'm not sleeping; I'm not eating; I'm a complete wreck. I really need you to come in the office with me so I can get this over with. Please, please won't you do this for me? It can be in the early evening so you won't have to miss much work. I'm begging you."

OK, it was official: I was completely humiliated! A part of me hoped he was not buying it. How could he possibly believe I could be this much of a basket case? I wasn't too sure if I would be relieved that he believed my mock hysterics, or insulted. He had better take the bait; then the sacrifice of my dignity would be worth it.

"I don't know if I would feel comfortable going to a therapist's office. I want to help you but I feel somewhat uneasy about it. If I decide to go, can my wife come too?"

Wow, that question was not in my mental rehearsal. "Umm, I don't think I would be comfortable with her there. I mean she hasn't been involved in any of the family issues up till now. I would really hate to drag her in on it in the middle."

"Yeah, I guess you're right. She probably wouldn't want to come anyways. How about I sleep on it and call you with my answer tomorrow? I'm kind of leaning towards a 'no' but I will think about it overnight."

"Sure, that would be fine, I guess. I really hope you will do it. It would mean the world to me."

With that said, we gave our goodbyes and then.....dial tone.

CHAPTER TWENTY

Unknown

Throwing the phone down and flopping backwards onto my bed, I began to replay the conversation in my mind. The phone call was relatively short, but it packed a powerful punch. "He's leaning towards 'no'?" I prayed. "Lord, if this is how it is supposed to happen, then I trust You to take care of it. Dr. Storm was right; You have been so faithful up till now.'"

Before getting ready for bed, I checked my email one more time. Just like clockwork, I received an email from my father. My heart dropped as I clicked to open and read it.

Veronica,

I received your email. I did realize after we hung up that I had not said "I Love You" at the end. I was surprised by the call and trying to process several things at once I guess. At the end I was trying to decide if bringing up getting together would be "blind siding" you. Apparently that was the "dead air" time. I apologize for the omission Veronica from the bottom of my heart. I do love you Veronica and I cannot even conceive of time when I would not. We are surly having a very hard time in our relationship but the thought of not loving you has never ever crossed my mind. I did consider calling you and believe me it was not pride that kept me from it, it was the fear of making you angry about calling you after being explicitly told not to call you. I thought it would just add additional hurt to our relationship. Obviously it was a bad decision as it caused more hurt than ever. I don't know what else to say, but I'm sorry and ask you for your forgiveness. I will keep praying for a healing in our relationship and believing that God will make it happen. Love, Dad

Ugh, seriously, my life sucked. I absolutely knew I would receive an explanation email from my dad, but I wasn't prepared for it to be so heartfelt. Maybe now Dr. Storm would realize why it was hard for me to be mad at my dad and my brother. I had my sister screaming at me the other day and accusing me of being out of God's will. I'm pretty certain my mom was busy praying that I would see the error of my ways. Then, I had my brother and dad saying such gracious things to me.

This was where the lines always became blurred for me. Good and evil weren't so clearly noticeable in a family like mine. Now, with this email from my father, I could be easily sucked back in. However, I had to face the reality that he was blaming me for not saying 'I love you." For him to say he was afraid of me was laughable at best.

Just the same old excuses: as always, I was the reason for the division. He would have called immediately back if it weren't for the fact that I am an angry person? Why should I not be insulted at that? Accountability was lost on him. I would have to wait to respond to this until after I knew if my brother would come to Dr. Storm's with me.

The next day Jerry was taking our son away for a "Guy's Weekend." That left me and my daughters with a "Girl's Weekend" of our own. We would spend the day shopping, only stopping for dinner. After the day of girl fun, we would return home for the evening, watching endless hours of "chick flicks."

The morning sun pierced through our window with its standard promise of a new beginning. Jerry was eager to get up and out with our son. Looking at the clock, I jumped out of bed to see if my brother had left a message or text before I woke up—nope, no messages. Quickly, I ran downstairs to see if the boys needed any help with their packing. I was too late to be of any assistance. The car was packed, and they were excited to head down to San Diego. Jerry planned on renting a speed boat and having the two of them go for long rides on the water, whipping the boat around for kicks. Not my idea of a good time, that's for sure. The two of them could have their male bonding time, while the four of us girls were safe and secure on dry land – shopping!

Jerry kissed me goodbye and made me promise to call him as soon as I heard back from my brother. Almost an hour had passed and my three daughters were slowly waking up and coming downstairs. They were all excited about our weekend. As the four of us busied ourselves with the planning, it was hard to stay even remotely focused. Taking on family issues was definitely not for the faint of heart. Keeping them from your children was tantamount to living a double life.

The weather was warm, so we decided on a large outdoor mall that was about twenty minutes away. The day dragged on with no contact from my brother. My sister, however, had not remained silent. I had received a couple of phone calls from her. I didn't have the stomach to talk to her again. Always one for drama, she left the dreariest messages that she needed to talk to me right away. Yeah, that wasn't going to happen. I already felt like I was juggling too many plates up in the air as it was. Pretending that everything was normal with my daughters and like I was having a mental break down with my brother. I seriously didn't need to throw my sister into this elaborate mix.

While buying some candy for our movie night, I heard my phone ring. Quickly I grabbed it and saw my brother's name pop up. Still in the check stand, I was unable to pick up. It seemed to take forever for him to go into voicemail. By that time, the girls were busy loading the car with our bags full of candy and other goodies for our junk food feast. I, on the other hand, jumped into the driver's seat to retrieve my message. Waiting, it began.

"Hi Ron. So yeah, I would be happy to help you and come down to your doctor's office for a session. I think you said one of the timeslots was Tuesday, the later the better. You can call me this weekend to let me know the time and place. I really hope this will help you through this tough time." My fingers were shaking as I texted him back thanking him for agreeing to come.

My mind began to race in every imaginable direction. I had spent all my time and energy plotting on how to get him into the office. I hadn't spent a minute of my time planning on what to say when he got there. Immediately, I texted Jerry to let him know that my brother had agreed to the meeting. I didn't know whether to laugh, cry, or throw up! The session was scheduled for Tuesday, which meant the meeting was only four days away. I was climbing the walls knowing that I wouldn't be able to talk to Jerry the entire night. I thought it would surely be my undoing.

I hastily texted my friend Michele to let her know my brother's response. She had been a bedrock of support to me during that time. We had laughed until we cried, and cried until we laughed, while talking about my family. She was one of the best friends you could ever ask for. After texting her, I realized that I needed to fly under the radar the next few days with my sister as well. She couldn't be allowed to know about the session. I really didn't want to have to explain or come up with a fictitious explanation as to why I was meeting with him in Dr. Storm's office. I had made an art out of avoiding contact with both my mom and my sister. This was the easiest of my tasks that weekend.

The next call I placed was to Dr. Storm. We set the appointment date for Tuesday and another session date for Monday to help me prepare for the confrontation. We both wanted to make sure that I was geared up for whatever response I might receive from my brother.

After leaving the voicemail on Dr. Storm's phone regarding next week's sessions, I emailed my friends to let them know that my brother had agreed to the session. I'm pretty convinced no one could do this without a wealth of support and love surrounding them.

The weekend passed ever so slowly, but Sunday was finally here; all the while butterflies had taken up permanent residence in my stomach. I had to call my brother to tell him our session was scheduled for Tuesday at 4:00. Although I was a little afraid to call him because he might tell me he has changed his mind, I dialed his number. To my complete surprise, my sister-in-law answered my brother's cell phone.

"Hi Ronnie, how's it going?"

Trying not to choke out my answer, I said, "Fine, how about you?"

"Pretty good, I guess. We are in the car right now, so I had to pick up the phone. Hey, we were talking and we thought it would be fun to have our two families go on a small vacation together. We need to be in Vegas in August and wanted to know if you guys could join us."

Yet another curve ball I hadn't seen coming. Fortunately, the only date that worked with them was the one week we would be out of state visiting my husband's family. She was disappointed and told me she hoped we could do it next year. Somehow, I thought she might feel differently after Tuesday!

After giving her the directions, I was somewhat relieved that I didn't have to talk to my brother again. Hanging up the phone, the reality of what I was doing hit me like a ton of bricks. Until then, I never understood how inadequate of a word "difficult" was. This was not just difficult—it was gut wrenching. Whole hosts of questions swirled around my brain with no answers to be found. What should I say exactly and how should I say it? Unbelievably, I was actually shallow enough to wonder what a person was supposed to wear to such an event as this.

Not able to calm my restless stomach, for the third night in a row, I skimped on my dinner. All that day, I was retrieving emails from my friends. They were all completely shocked that I was going through with this. As my biggest cheerleaders, they told me of my bravery and that they would continue to pray for strength and wisdom on what to say. Stacie, a friend, had offered to meet me at a coffee house tomorrow morning before my session with Dr. Storm. I was thrilled I would be able to talk with her about my prep session with Dr. Storm and the Tuesday confrontation with my brother.

I had known Stacie for around fifteen years. We met at the same moms' group where Michele and I had met. It hadn't been until this past year that Stacie and I became close. I guess I could say that about almost everyone in my life. Dr. Storm once said, "You are only as close as your secrets." Truer words were never spoken. I was relishing the new intimacy I now had with so many of the women in my circle of friends. This had to be one of the biggest rewards of my counseling: the ability to differentiate between the toxic relationships and the healthy ones. When I was in survival mode, I saw all relationships as potentially threatening.

Monday morning arrived, and the countdown to Tuesday had begun. I hastily got ready to meet Stacie for coffee. When I arrived, she was already there saving two seats for us. Waving as I entered, I got in line to purchase my coffee. Medium drip coffee, black, no sugar or cream, just the way I liked it.

The coffee house was dimly lit, with sunlight trailing in

through the large picture windows. The walls were painted in rich earth tones of browns, tans and muted greens. There were large cushioned chairs inviting customers to stay and enjoy long visits. A sound track of old standards was softly playing, while friendly chatter drowned out the words of the songs from the nineteen-forties. It was the perfect place for us to catch up.

Two things that I loved about Stacie: she was seriously one of the funniest people I know, and, like Michele, you can't shock her. No matter what I said about my past or what took place in that house, I never get a stunned response from her. She remarked, "All the stuff you have told me should be shocking, but it never is. I'm either a great listener or seriously disturbed; I really don't know which one. Either way, I'm glad you are able to confide in me."

Another thing I loved about her was that she was never afraid to ask the tough questions. There was something so comfortable when you are with a friend who doesn't consider your life a taboo subject. Many people were uneasy talking to me about what was going on and thought that it would be prying. When they were uncomfortable, I was uncomfortable. That was never the case with Stacie.

As a true friend, she too applauded my willingness to confront my brother and said she didn't know if she would be courageous enough to do it. She then made me a very generous offer.

"If you need me to be there waiting for you when you come out of your session with your brother, I would be happy to come and support you."

"Oh, that is so nice of you. Actually, Jerry is going to be

waiting in the car for me. I'm sure he is going to want to know everything that went on during the confrontation."

"OK, but if he is unable to be there, or if you need additional support, you call me, and I'll drop everything to be there."

"Thanks, Stacie! I will definitely call you if I need you, I promise."

It was time to go. We hugged and I headed out the door. My life seemed like a whirlwind to me. It was as though I was going through the motions of the most unimaginable movie plot there was. Everything in my family was in a complete upheaval, and yet I was seemingly in control. Details were not being dictated to me; it was as if God was the one writing this story line; a surreal experience to say the least.

Arriving at Dr. Storm's office for my 1:00 appointment, I walked across the street to enter the lobby of the large corporate building. The security guard at the desk smiled and waved as I waited for the elevator door to open. Life is funny. He was just sitting there doing his job, and I was on my way up to meet with my doctor about facing my molester. You really never know what goes on in the life of others around you.

Dr. Storm did not make me wait this time for my appointment. As soon as he heard the office door open, he came out of his private office to greet me. Before I could even sit down, I heard, "Hello Veronica, why don't you come on back?"

Sitting down in our usual spots, we dove into the session.

"So tomorrow's the day, Veronica. How are you doing?"

"I feel like I'm on autopilot. I'm just going through the motions of what I know needs to be done. Everything is going to change in my life; it's most unsettling."

"Yes, but you have taken the proper time to think about it. Now you realize it is what needs to be done. So let's rehearse what will happen tomorrow. Do you know what you're going to say to him?"

"Yeah, pretty much. I have been going over it in my mind. I'll write a few things down but I know I will probably not even refer to my notes. I really don't plan on going over it today; I won't be sure exactly what I'll say until the time comes."

"Sure, that's fine. Then why don't I give you some possible reactions that you might receive from your brother and then how you might deal with them. You ready?"

"As ready as I'll ever be." "OK, first one. What if after you finish confronting him, you can tell he remembers but he denies it? What if he gets angry and starts to verbally lash out at you?"

"Umm, that's not his style. There is no possible way he will start yelling, but, if he does, I'll just let him rant until he is done. When he has finished, I'll tell him I don't believe him. He knows the truth. I have no intention on letting him off the hook. If he continues, I'll tell him we're finished here. What he does after that is entirely up to him."

Nodding in agreement and writing in my file, Dr. Storm continued. "If that happens, he will probably start the negotiations. He will tell you not to tell anyone else in the family because it isn't true. What would you do then?"

"I'd tell him I am not bound to silence simply because he says I am. He has the right to his side of the story and I have the right to speak my side. If I want to tell our parents and sister for the greater good, I will do it. What he wants to do after I have told them, again, is completely up to him."

"Good, here's another one. What if he admits to everything and then starts to cry and pleads with you to keep quiet? Maybe he throws himself at your feet and apologizes profusely but begs you not to tell anyone, what then?"

"I would accept his apology and tell him that I am free to tell whoever I want. I have done him the favor of keeping his ugly secret for decades, and it was just about my undoing. Then I guess I would say to him that I think he needs at least to tell his wife; she has a right to know. As far as not telling our parents and sister, I really don't know what my answer would be. I probably would tell him that we should let them know and then hold them accountable for not getting him help after he was assaulted by the babysitter."

"Very good. Here's another possible reaction. What if he is sincerely apologetic and tells you he has not gone a day without thinking about what he did to you? That he has been haunted by this and he is so sorry that you had to be the one to bring it up? What would your response be to that?"

"Again, I would accept his apology and tell him that I understand. I would reiterate that I have no hard feelings; I just wanted to get it out in the open. I guess I would tell him that I think it should have been him to approach me on it and not the other way around. I would like him to answer the question of why he didn't."

"OK, now the hardest one for you. What if you can tell he really has no recollection of it? He denies the babysitter incident and also vehemently denies having ever touched you. How will you handle that?"

I could feel all the blood drain from my face. That was my worst nightmare, the reason I had remained silent. The confrontation tomorrow was extremely risky for me. If my brother really didn't remember, I didn't know if I would be able to return for more sessions. I really wouldn't be able to look Dr. Storm in the eye after that. Feeling a little woozy, I answered the worst of all the questions.

"My heart just stopped beating for a few seconds, by the way. Yes, that is the most difficult of the possible responses. I really don't know what I would do. I mean, I would try to jar his memory, but if he has suppressed it for his own survival then I don't suppose I would be successful in reminding him. How would my brother and I ever be able to be in the same room again if that happens?"

"It's one of the possibilities, you know."

"I know. It's definitely my least favorite."

"OK, let's say he does everything just right. He remembers what he did; he remembers the babysitter; he apologizes, and he wants the secret out so the family can start new—would that make everything all right for you?"

"No, that wouldn't make it all better. His response is irrelevant actually. There is nothing my brother could do or say to turn back the hands of time. What is done, is done. I'm not looking for anything on his end."

"I feel the reason for the meeting is to get the secret out and no longer have it as my cross to bear. It would be wonderful if he did apologize, but really, what would that help? Being able to look him in the eye and tell him how badly it hurt me and affected my life is the bottom line of the meeting; everything else is almost a moot point. As we discussed earlier, this is about my children, his children and future generations. I want the pattern to stop."

Smiling, he said, "Good, Veronica. You're ready."

There was one last topic for me to discuss. "I am starting to feel bad about confronting him tomorrow. This whole thing is going to totally blindside him. He thinks I'm going to talk about my relationship with our parents, when I am actually going to smack him in the gut with our history. He is going to feel awful; just you wait and see."

Dr. Storm didn't appear to like the direction my mind was going. His face was a cross between concern and stern all wrapped up into one. "You have no reason to feel guilty. What you are doing is the healthiest thing, not only for you, but also for him. There is guilt involved in this situation, but it does not lie with you."

The allotted time was up, and I reached into my purse for my wallet. While standing up, I looked at Dr. Storm and asked one more question before I left.

Half scared out of my mind, I asked, "Is it normal to doubt your memories?"

With a serious expression, he answered, "Yes, very normal."

"What if I made all of this stuff up? What if I really am crazy, and none of it happened?"

With complete confidence, he replied, "You didn't make anything up. I know it really did happen."

"You do?"

Looking somewhat past me and out the window, as if remembering our past sessions, he then returned his eyes to me. "Yes, I believe everything you have told me. I know it is true."

With that vote of confidence, I walked out of his office ready to return tomorrow for the dreaded confrontation.

The rest of my day was a complete blur. All I could think about was what was going to happen tomorrow. Sleeping would not come easy, that much I knew. Jerry was angry, but I knew it was not with me. The brother-in-law that he loved and thought he knew was the one accused of molesting his wife. Oh, how he would enjoy having only two minutes alone in the room with him. Instead, he would be agonizing in the car outside of Dr. Storm's office waiting for the session to be over. He was doing what was right, but not natural. Fighting all normal male urges to protect the wife he loves, he deferred to me knowing that this was my journey.

That night, it was hard not to obsess over the details of my childhood. As if my mind were a blank canvas, the pictures of the events that occurred continued to paint themselves, bidding for my attention. No matter what I did to erase the involuntary artistry, the imaginary paintings reappeared, unwilling to go away. With one stroke of the paintbrush, I saw myself as an eleven-year-old girl with my brother—naked and on top of me. I heard his advice on how to please him and what a compliment it was that he had chosen me.

The paint splashed up against my mental canvas, images of

him telling me he had purposefully exposed himself to me on several occasions. How he said that he was delighted to wait for me to walk past his room, with him unclothed—aroused so I could see him. He explained to my eleven-year-old intellect what it meant for him to have an erection and how I should be flattered by such a response. I heard his laughter and saw how we played games, unclothed, asking me to touch him and then he would touch me.

With vengeance, the artist swished the brush with sadistic vibrant colors to portray my brother's smile as he looked on my little body, taking in its childishness and then asking to see it again after it had matured into womanhood. In a heated rage, the artist pressed the brush on the canvas, crushing its fragile bristles, as he had the gruesome task of painting my brother's look of disappointment and my brother's dissatisfaction with me for not having developed breasts yet. In consolation, my brother affirmed me, telling me he still liked what he saw, but asked for promises of access to me in future years. He detailed my brother telling me he anxiously awaited being able to look at my developed body and being able to touch it upon request. He expressed how I should allow this as a token of my loyalty. The mural was not complete until the artist rendered my brother taking pleasure in offering his body in return as payment.

The artist was repulsed while portraying my brother positioning me in various ways and instructing me on the sexual terms of what he was doing. All the while, my brother was smiling and coaxing, convincing me that it was natural, not a big deal at all. The ghost-like portrayal of his touches and kisses on my young body were a burning recollection like acid on my soul.

The painter's hand grew weary as he stroked out my brother making the most of the six hours alone he would have with me. His paint supply began to diminish as he tried in vain to portray that seemingly endless summer of day—after day—after day—after...

The imaginary paintbrush relentlessly continued to create pictures of my brother's sexual deviance in my teen years. I saw him masturbating as I innocently walked into the bathroom. I didn't know he was in there before I entered. Instead of closing the door upon my arrival, he flung it open so I could see him do his deed. My imaginary artist finished this portrait of my brother, paying close attention to drawing his eyes that were fastened in my direction.

In another mural, I saw myself as a young woman, around seventeen to eighteen years old. I was depicted, sleeping in the safety of my own bed, relieved to have a night's rest. Then, with almost a violent stroke of the brush, the painting showed how I was awakened, shocked to have my brother's touch once more. The canvas of my mind illustrated me frantically grabbing for covers, but having the covers quickly removed by his hands. With various bright yellows, the illusionary artist angrily painted the beams of light shining from the flashlight, held by my brother's hand, illuminating my naked body.

Taking great care, the brush smoothed and blended the paint to portray my face in soft pinks and reds as embarrassment colored my skin, while my brother peered down on my naked flesh. Although the picture rendered my room in midnight hues from the darkness of the night, the paintbrush sorrowfully stroked out my private areas that were highlighted with the aid of my brother's flashlight.

The artisan painted my facial expression of shock and sadness at having to fight off the unwanted sexual touches of my brother.

The artist's tool masterfully sketched for me to see the sheer hor-
ror of that moment when I was being violated by the one I loved.
I heard my heart-rending pleas that he leave. In unrestrained fury,
the brush drew, in explicit detail, my brother's longing face, his
craving eyes, his touch, his begging to remain with me, to lie with
me. I recalled my threatening him with screaming if he didn't
leave and the look of disappointment on his face that I would not
satisfy his sexual desires.

How would I speak of such things the next day in the
presence of my brother? I was tormented with the reality
that he might not remember or that he might deny his
crimes against me. Worse yet, what if he thought I owed
him when I was seventeen to do what he wanted—when
he wanted? Is it possible that I was to blame for my
brother's actions because of the childish responses I had
when I was eleven? For the better part of the night, I prayed
for the courage to speak the unthinkable the next day in Dr.
Storm's office. After many vexing hours, sleep finally made
its way to me.

****

Even as I slumbered, my mind was busy rehearsing
what I would say to my brother. I only managed to get
about four hours of sleep and as expected, I woke up ab-
surdly early. Before getting out of bed, I had a very important task to do. It was imperative for me to do mental
inventory. There would be many boxes that I would need
to have access to. Rearranging my containers so the proper
ones would be in front and ready to be retrieved, I saw the
ominous box on the top shelf once more. Thankfully, that

horrifying box had nothing to do with that day.

Dismissing the box on the top shelf once more, I began the meticulous process of untying ribbons and opening lids as to have the contents ready and available for me. I began to look at all the articles that represented the memories needed to confront my brother. The list was vast, so I was careful to make a mental note of where each one was and at what time in the session I would need it. Placing all boxes in chronological order was crucial so I would be able to speak without doubt or regret.

There, the inventory was complete, and all the necessary containers were set to pop open at my beckoning. Ready to leave my mental storage room, I stood back and looked at the shelves holding my precious memories, some torrid, some wonderful, and then I saw it again—the shadowy container that I couldn't quite remember placing on the shelf. I knew it did not need to be opened for the session. All those boxes were present and accounted for. It caused more fear in me than the ominous box on the top shelf. I really didn't have time or energy to figure it out that day; I already had enough on my plate.

To kill some time, I ran a few errands to keep busy. When I returned home, all the kids were downstairs lounging and watching TV in their pajamas. It was late morning, and, with no plans today, they were relaxing, enjoying one of their favorite parts of summer, doing totally nothing. Continuing with my act at home, I pretended that today was just another ordinary day. I greeted them all with a wide smile.

They asked me to watch one of their favorite TV programs and I reluctantly joined them. While sitting there, my mind started racing and my heart began violently beating. I was about to have a panic attack. Quickly, I got up off the sofa and began to head upstairs, out of view from my children. Climbing the stairs, I feared this wasn't a panic attack; I seriously thought I was having a heart attack. While on the stair landing, totally out of breath, I stopped and clutched my chest to help ease the pain. My eyes began to blur and then I knew; I was going to pass out. Grabbing the railing for support, I couldn't stop the inevitable.

My world went completely black.

****

I woke up lying on the stair landing to the sound of laughter coming from my children who were still watching TV. Fortunately, they didn't see me lying on our stairs. With my heart still beating entirely too fast, I slowly continued the flight of stairs and entered my bedroom. I plopped down onto my bed half thinking I could look down and see the beat of my heart through my shirt. I couldn't seem to calm myself down. Lying there, I told the Lord that the past might not have killed me but my present sure was giving it a good old college try.

Then a thought came to me. I had checked my email earlier that morning, and my friend Jennifer had sent me an encouraging note. She included a scripture – I needed that scripture. Slowly, so I wouldn't black out again, I got up and went to the computer to print Jennifer's email. The scripture was Deuteronomy 31:8 (King James Version):

And the LORD, he it is that doth go before thee; he will be with thee, he will not fail thee, neither forsake thee: fear not, neither be dismayed.

I printed out several copies of the scripture, and I taped them on the same pages of the notes I was bringing to Dr. Storm's office. I meditated on that scripture as I got ready and dressed for the session. Dark colors seemed appropriate for such an occasion, so I chose denim capris with a white and dark green tank top and finished the ensemble with a matching short sleeve sweater. Yes, even on a day like this I was still concerned about my wardrobe.

****

Driving to the office, I was only thinking about Deuteronomy 31:8. I said it aloud while zipping down the corridor. I pulled into my usual parking space and took a deep breath before leaving my car. I placed my notebook into my purse, and I began to walk across the street to Dr. Storm's office. I rushed so my brother wouldn't see me in case he decided to arrive early. Running to catch the open elevator, I entered and went all the way to the back. Leaning against the wall, I experienced the longest ten-story climb of my life. Arriving on the tenth floor, the elevator door opened, and I was half-tempted to remain in there riding it up and down for the next hour. Knowing that was not really an option, I pushed myself to stand upright, walked out the door and down the corridor to Dr. Storm's office. As promised, he heard the door open and immediately came out to greet me.

"Well, here we are. How are you doing? Is there any-thing you need me to do before your brother arrives?"

"Other than completely taking my place, I can't think of a thing."

With compassion he conceded, "Yeah, I can see where that would be nice for you. So do you have it all planned out and know what you are going to say?"

"Yes, I'm pretty sure. I have rehearsed it in my mind all day long. I think I will cover everything that needs to be covered."

Talking a few more minutes, we both locked eyes and were immediately quiet as we heard the office door open. As my pulse raced, Dr. Storm softy asked if I was ready to begin. Without saying a word, I nodded my head in ap-proval and watched him walk out the door to greet my brother. I listened attentively to the two men exchange names and pleasantries. Then I heard Dr. Storm inviting him back to the office. This was it; I took a deep breath and watched the door open.

Seeing my brother enter the room, I jumped up to greet him with a smile, and we exchanged a quick hug. I pointed to the couch for him to take a seat and make himself com-fortable while I sat on the smaller sofa opposite him. With my heart in my throat, Dr. Storm launched the session just as we had planned.

With a calm controlled tone, he began. "Thank you so much for coming down today to help Veronica. I know it means a lot to her that you were willing to make the drive and take some time off work."

"I'm going to start us out today by laying a few ground

rules so we can make the most of the meeting. Because this is Veronica's session, let's have her start us out by saying what she needs to say. I would ask that you not interrupt, knowing that you will have plenty of time to state your opinion and make any comments you would like after she is through. Veronica, I ask that when it is his turn to talk that you also not interrupt and allow him to talk. Do you both agree to the conditions?"

We both nodded our heads in agreement. My brother looked my way with a slight smile and friendly nod. He was sitting on the opposite corner of the couch where I usually sat. He was relaxed, leaning back with one leg crossed over the other. His right arm was stretched out on the top back of the couch with his other arm resting in his lap. He appeared totally at ease.

Dr. Storm continued. "Good. Then why don't you begin Veronica?"

With both men looking my direction, I turned my attention to my brother, swallowed hard, and began.

"First, I also want to thank you for coming down today. It really does mean a lot to me that you would take time away from work and your family to come here because I asked you to. With that said, I'll go ahead and start.

As you may or may not know, Jerry and I came here three months ago for marriage counseling. While in one of our earlier sessions, Dr. Storm asked each of us to tell about our family dynamics and our family history. Instead of telling our own stories, he had us share each other's stories. When Jerry started telling Dr. Storm about our family history, he told him about how Mom has treated me over the years and how badly it has hurt me. He also told Dr. Storm at how inequitable the treatment is between our sister and me in the family."

"After Jerry was through with his opinion of our family, Dr. Storm asked me if that was how I saw it too. I told him that it was accurate. Then he apologized to me at how I was treated and asked me if I thought anyone in the family was safe. Without hesitation, I said, 'Yes, my brother was safe.'"

Upon hearing this, my brother dipped his head and smiled at me knowingly. The gesture pierced my heart. I couldn't believe I was actually going to do this. I figured it was now or never. This was why I came here, so I go for the surprise disclosure.

"Dr. Storm was thrilled to hear that you were safe to me. But then I thought, I hope he understands that you were safe, except for when you weren't safe."

With that said, I looked at my brother to see if he comprehended what I had just revealed. He didn't even flinch. He just kept eye contact and maintained his relaxed position on the sofa. Did he not get where I was going with this? Plowing on, I continued.

"I told Dr. Storm about what happened between us starting when I was eleven, but then I informed him I knew why you would do it. I mean after what the babysitter did to you. I can't remember the exact ages we were, do you?"

This was it, the moment of truth. Would he remember or did he block it out for his own emotional survival? Waiting for a response, I tried to mirror his relaxed state and waited for his reply. Finally, he casually answered.

"No, I don't really remember how old I was either."

He remembered! After three decades of waiting, I finally had my answer. With this knowledge, I knew how to proceed with the confrontation. What happened next would alter my emotional universe. Unbeknownst to me, with my brother in the lead, Dr. Storm and I were about to be escorted into the dark side.

CHAPTER TWENTY-ONE

Unthinkable

I felt incredibly torn by my brother's recollection. One was exhilaration that he remembered, and the other was complete sorrow that he had lived with the memory of the assault. I was immediately struck by his facial expression. With his continued relaxed posture and out stretched hand on the sofa, I felt a chill go up my spine—He was smiling at me.

Rattled by that, but trying not to skip a beat, I pressed on with our discussion.

"Yeah, it's been kind of bugging me that I couldn't quite remember our ages. I think I was around age six to seven years old."

His face was still so relaxed and peaceful, one would have thought I was talking about a day at the beach and not his sexual assault. I was going to go deeper than I originally planned. I wanted to get the reaction that was befitting the crime.

"I remember that day as if it were only yesterday. When the babysitter took you into your room, we were right outside the door listening to everything take place. I felt so awful and completely powerless to help you. I remember seeing you cowering and crying in the corner. When the babysitter threatened to kill us if we told, I didn't know what to do. Thankfully, our sister finally told Mom, but that wasn't until after the third time."

OK, still no reaction. His lack of emotion was of great concern. Instead of treading lightly with confronting him about our history, I was going in for the kill. I absolutely insisted on having the proper response.

"When our sister told Mom, all Mom said was that she was going to take care of it. I know for a fact that the police weren't called, and no charges were ever filed against her. I assume Mom told Dad; she told him everything, but Dad never talked to us girls about it or asked if we needed help. Did either Mom or Dad ever talk to you?"

With a smile and what appeared to be a thoughtful, peaceful expression, he replied, "No, they never did. None of us talked about it after it happened."

Still not the reaction I was going for. Now it was time for our history. Feeling way more empowered than I did when I first started, I continued.

"I assume it must have affected you, I mean because of what you did to me the summer I was eleven. I can't remember how long it went on, but it seemed as though it was for quite some time. Do you remember how long it lasted?"

With my heart in my toenails, I hadn't unlocked my eyes from his. Waiting, waiting, not willing to go forward until he reacted, I almost quivered with what I was met with. It occurred to me that I was getting a reaction, it just didn't compute right away. He was smiling while I spoke of the past events at age eleven. He was actually smiling. Oh dear God, were they pleasant memories to him?

Again, just as agreeable as if I asked him what he had for lunch, he grinned and remarked, "No, I don't remember how long it lasted either. It does seem like it was for a while though."

This reply had caught me off guard. Dr. Storm and I had practiced a whole host of possible reactions, none of which was this one. How could my brother be so calm about this subject, how could he still be smiling? Holding nothing back, I continued outlining the effects his behavior had on me in my teen years.

I told him about my hair pulling and near drug overdose when I was thirteen and Mom's ambivalence to it. How I was the only one placed on restrictions for months at a time, when I was never told of my offense. Dating men while still a young teen girl and plotting my own suicide. Telling him that I started drinking and taking drugs to self-medicate to help ease the pain.

While I spoke, he continued to look relaxed and at times concerned that I seemed to have had a bad go of it during my teen years. He nodded and smiled as I told of the horrifying events of my youth. Now he was beginning to freak me out, if not totally ticking me off. He just sat there acting as if this was just another normal conversation that happened to be taking place in a therapist's office. How dare he not be at least uncomfortable with talking about our history? No squirming, no loss of eye contact, no looking at the doctor in complete humiliation, just having an ordinary conversation with his sister. I, on the other hand, felt as though I was standing in the middle of a toxic waste spill that would pollute my mind forever.

This would not do! I demanded a reaction. Not the least bit timid, the warrior was coming out to play. Showing no shame, I said, "You were the only one who was really nice to me in my late teen years. Actually, you were one of my best friends. I used to love it when you would come home late from work and come into my bedroom to see if I was awake to ask me how my day was. Sometimes we would talk for two minutes and other times for an hour. I always counted on you to be concerned about me especially because no one else in the family seemed particularly interested."

"Then it happened, I heard you sneak in my bedroom when you thought I was asleep. You scared me half to death. I would stir and pretend like I was waking up. That would be enough to make you leave my room. I knew what you were up to, but I never confronted you on it. I had enough to deal with, with our mom on the prowl. I trained myself to be a light sleeper, so I could hear my door open and scare you away. It worked for so long. However, one night I didn't wake up in time. There you were, undressing me. I was so terrified. You were my brother, how could you? When I asked you to leave, you begged me to stay. I asked you again, and you wouldn't budge. The only reason you left was that I threatened to scream. That night crushed me. I couldn't believe you would do it to me again. We were so close. I trusted you."

"The next day, when I saw you, even though it was

awkward, I pretended it never happened. You were my only ally in the family; I couldn't have you turn against me too. To be perfectly honest, I would have never screamed if you didn't leave. They would have never believed me if I told them what you did. Even if they did believe me that night, somehow they would have ultimately concluded it was my fault."

"Do you remember when people would meet us for the first time, and they would assume that we were married? All we were doing was hanging out together, going to a movie, or grabbing a bite to eat, yet they seemed to sense something was diffcrent from just a brother and sister relationship. That was rather odd to me back then, and I never understood it until these past few months. Even complete outsiders seemed to detect something wasn't right. The thought of it makes me sick."

"That is why I asked you to come here today. I wanted to get it out and no longer have it be the untold secret. It really did affect me. Did it affect you? Did it affect the way you parented?"

There, I said it! I only left a few instances out concerning his deviant behavior towards me in the in-between years of ages eleven thru seventeen. After all, this should have been plenty to rock his world. But there I sat, looking at my brother who was completely tranquil, without any negative emotion radiating from him.

Dr. Storm and I rehearsed all kinds of scenarios that I might be finding myself in while I confronted by brother, even he didn't come up with that one. And who could blame him? How were we to know that my brother would not be horrified or ashamed? What kind of healthy person could have allowed their mind to conjure up this reaction? My brother appeared as though I was talking about our cherished memories, not instances of incest. Refusing to speak to fill the dead air, I looked at him waiting for him to answer my last question.

Now admittedly, I am a spaz. I think fast; therefore, I talk fast, I always have. Conversely, my brother is like a hill-billy bear compared to me. He has a sharp mind but he talks at the speed of a snail. He is careful to choose his words and is relaxed in his demeanor. Today would not be the exception. He slowly and casually began to answer the questions that were floating in the air like some kind of poisonous gas.

"Did it affect me? Hmm, I don't think so. You talk about what the babysitter did to me and I really don't remember it being as upsetting as you do. You say I was devastated; I can't say that I recall it that way. I mean, I didn't like it, but it wasn't as terrifying to me as you tell it. I guess I was cry-ing. I can't say I remember. I'll admit I was scared at the time, but it didn't last long, at least I don't think it did. But I am sorry that it seemed to have affected you. I suppose it would have been uncomfortable for you to have been lis-tening on the outside, but again, it wasn't that bad."

"You also say that she came back a couple of times. Again, I only remember her doing it one time. Not that it re-ally matters I suppose. It all happened so long ago. I can as-sure you, I wasn't that upset by it."

Drawing breath and still just as composed, he contin-ued. "As far as Mom or Dad talking to me, no, they never did. You say they should have, but I don't know, maybe they should have, maybe they shouldn't have. It really didn't matter. I can't say that I would have wanted to talk about it anyway. Either way, it was no big deal."

"Did it affect the way I parented? As you can imagine, we are careful with whom we have chosen over the years to babysit our kids. We usually have one of my wife's family members do it. I wouldn't want a total stranger, you know, for all the obvious reasons."

"You also brought up what happened between us that one summer. Yes, of course I remember," he said effortlessly, looking at me with a smile.

The depravity of that moment was sucking the air right out of my lungs. My brother's lack of appreciation of those evil events was beyond startling to me. I might have placed the molestation in the "normal" category, but I knew what happened wasn't right. I just assumed all older brothers did those things to their younger sisters. It was everyone's dirty little secret. But make no mistake: I always thought it was a dirty, filthy secret. He clearly didn't see it that way.

When I was having my turn to speak, my brother obeyed Dr. Storm's rules and did not interrupt. I, too, had agreed to those conditions, and I would abide by them. I would resist the urge to speak and quite honestly the urge to choke the very life right out of him.

As he sat comfortable on the sofa, he continued.

"You seem to think that what happened between us was because of what the babysitter did, I don't think so. I don't remember exactly how it all began that summer, but you didn't seem to mind. I never forced you; I would have to say it was pretty consensual."

I was pretty certain that I was standing at the gates of hell right now. I thought it would look different from this air-conditioned executive office and would be much, much hotter. Nevertheless, this had to be it. Evil had never been so real to me than it was at that moment. And coming from me, and all I have been exposed to, that was saying something. Consensual, did he actually have the nerve to say I consented? He could have stabbed me with a knife and it would have hurt less. If demons were applauding his performance three decades ago, they were giving him a standing ovation that day.

I felt a little limp and wanted to slide down into my shoes. I was looking across the room at the brother who I thought escaped all the madness. The brother who I defended to Dr. Storm and would insist that I shouldn't confront him because it would mortify him. Yes, it was this brother who I saw before me, smiling, relaxed, and clear in his own conscience. After all, as he mentioned, he didn't have a gun to my head or knife at my throat while he was on top of me. God, I could hardly breathe, he actually had more to say.

"I am a little surprised at all the other things you told me. I had no idea you almost overdosed when you were thirteen. I suppose there was no way any of us could know that you were pulling your hair out. As far as the whole suicide thing, wow, that is a surprise. I knew about the drinking and drugs; I just figured you were a little on the wild side. You and Mom have always had your spats; I never thought they were too serious. It's all a little shocking to me that I didn't know you as well as I thought I did."

With a friendly warm expression, he recalled, "Like you said, we were so close. I too considered you one of my best friends. How weird that we could have both been in that house at the same time and see life so differently."

Did he just reiterate that we were close back then, as though it was a good thing? What a freak! When I commented on the fact that we were so close, it wasn't a compliment; it was an indictment! I was pointing out that now I see it was all a set up. That's what predators do—they make you feel safe, so you let your guard down. We weren't the close brother and sister as I once supposed; we were the clueless prey and maniacal hunter. How could he totally miss the fact that he not only violated my body, more importantly, he violated my soul? He dared to continue with his rationalizations.

"Now the part about me coming into your room when you were around seventeen to eighteen; I don't remember it happening that way. You weren't in your room—that would have been wrong for me to go in there. How I remember it was, we were having a slumber party of sorts in the front room and were both in sleeping bags." Then, smiling he said, "I did start undressing you, but, after all, I just assumed you wouldn't mind."

With a slight pause and smirking, he said, "Remember, you were a willing participant years earlier, so I thought you would be up for it again. But, when you asked me to stop, I did. Well, I didn't at first, but I really didn't think you were serious. I just kept going because I truly thought you wouldn't mind. I honestly thought you would want to - *you know*…. I couldn't believe it when you threatened to scream.

As soon as I could tell that you weren't joking, I left. I never bothered you after that. And if you can remember correctly, I did say I was sorry as I was leaving."

Holy crud, did he think we were sharing a "nod, nod, wink, wink" moment? As if this couldn't get any more absurd, he actually was telling me it would have been wrong for him to come into my room. What the hell was he talking about? Coming into my room was wrong; undressing and fondling me, on the other hand, totally fine. And who in their right mind has a freaking sleepover at the ages of eighteen and twenty-one? Is this how he has justified it all these years? He makes up an imaginary slumber party for two!

OK, I needed to get this straight in my own mind. Going into a room is wrong; undressing a sister and preparing to have sex with her is OK, but only at a sleepover. All this, of course, can only be done if you have molested the sister previously when she was eleven, and she didn't scratch your eyes out. That way you know you have permission to have total access to her at any given perverse moment of your choosing. I'm so glad I got the ground rules clear. I don't think I could have come up with them on my own. I do wish I had those rules earlier; it would have saved me a whole lot of mental anguish and time.

Man, oh man, how could I have never seen this before today? My brother didn't have some momentary lack of judgments. He was a sick, twisted, calculating pervert who was nice in the daytime hours and on the perverse prowl at night while being protected by the cloak of darkness.

I was half wondering what in the world Dr. Storm was

thinking right about now. This was clearly not turning out as either of us planned. He was out of my scope of view, sitting kind of behind me. I envisioned him with his eyes the size of quarters and his mouth hanging open. At that point, it was every man for himself. He would have to scoop his own chin up off the floor; I was too busy picking up the shattered pieces of my heart. It was still my brother's turn to talk, so I waited patiently for my molester to finish his rebuttal.

As leisurely as ever, in his drawled way, he continued.

"Because you brought it up, I would assume that it still bothers you. Even though I apologized back then, I would be happy to tell you I'm sorry again."

Grinning he added, "Although it is hard to apologize for something that should just be blamed on male teen hormones, I will say that I am sorry for *my part* and that it still apparently upsets you."

It was time for me to do something that I was fearfully great at: emotionally disconnecting. I learned to do that many years ago, and it was necessary to call on that skill right now. I had faced my biggest fear; I had done what I said I could never do. I looked my brother in his eyes and told him his unwanted sexual misdeeds hurt me in ways that were immeasurable. What was my reward? A brother who smiled and said that it was no big deal, that it was actually consensual. As I continued to sit there in my silent state, I tried to diagram the architecture of his mind. I then realized his mind was not in need of mapping. It was his soul that was in need of examination. Was he an empty shell or does something else takeover when one has been so badly wounded and left to fend for themselves? Gosh, I wanted to shake him and yell, "Wake up!" "Please wake up."

Seemingly out of touch with reality, a husband, a father, a soccer coach, a leader in the church, a pillar of the community, and a much-loved friend couldn't see wanting sex with his sister while he was an adult as wrong. How could he be so nonchalant when recalling the events of that summer when I was eleven and then when I was eighteen and his other evil acts in the in-between years? The warrior in me had much to say. It was my turn to speak.

"I didn't know if you would remember everything. I am relieved that you do. I thought Mom hired the babysitter several more times, but, as you said, it really doesn't matter. Even if it was only one time, once was more than enough. I do remember you being terribly traumatized when she left your room. Your face in that moment will forever be etched in my mind."

"As far as that summer is concerned, you said you didn't remember how it all started, well I do. You would call me back to the bathroom and I would not know that it was a set up. When I would get there, you would be standing there with only a towel wrapped around you and then you would drop it so I could see you. I would immediately cover my eyes and of all things apologize to you for being there. That happened many times in the bathroom and your bedroom when I would be innocently walking past, not knowing you were there, waiting for me."

This seemed to resonate with his recollection, and my

brother actually chuckled while staring at me. Not a condescending laugh, more like an "Oh, that's right" snicker. It appeared as though he found this amusing. As one can imagine, I was void of any humor at that juncture, so I would have to make do with my disgust.

"Then, when they left you in charge to take care of me that summer, you started the sexual advances and lessons. That's how it all started. I do hope that clears it up for you. As far as it being consensual, I'm not too sure how an eleven-year-old girl can consent to something she didn't even know existed. I'll let you answer that question and wrestle those demons in your own nighttime hours."

"Now, that part about us having a sleepover in the front room when I was eighteen, I really can't figure that one out. What in the world would we be doing in sleeping bags at that age? That places you at around twenty-one years old—really, a slumber party? I can assure you, you came into my room. I remember that night well. Dear God, you wouldn't leave. I couldn't believe it; you wouldn't leave until I threatened you."

"What I really can't wrap my mind around though is you said 'opening my door and coming into my room would have been wrong.' You don't seem to think that undressing and trying to seduce me and then when I wake and tell you to leave, but you beg to stay, is the offense. You think opening a door is the transgression, really? You might have that a little backward and trust me, that wasn't the first time you came into my room; it was the first time I didn't wake up in time."

Just as calm and polite as ever, he waited for his turn to

refute the allegations. He saw that I was finished, so he continued to enlighten me.

"No, I'm sure it was in the front room, and, like I said, when I could tell that you really weren't interested, I stopped."

Well, that settles it. When my brother found out I wasn't interested in having sex with him, after several of my terrified protests, he ultimately did stop. That absolutely makes him the recipient of the "Brother of the Year" award. Oh, how I wish I had bought him a trophy or made him a plaque! It was the very least I could have done for such a wonderful sibling. I think he is waiting for me to thank him for stopping when I threatened to scream and expose him, pun intended; after all, he was being so considerate. Hmm, I think I'll pass on that one. Instead, I'm gonna wrap this up.

"Yes, I remember you begging me not to tell Mom or Dad as you were leaving and then, to your credit, you said sorry while shutting my door."

After no response from my brother, Dr. Storm spoke for the first time.

"Veronica, is there anything else you would like to ask or say?

Smugly, I said, "Nope, I'm good."

Looking at my brother, he asked, "Is there anything else you would like to comment on?"

My brother responded, looking at me. "Yes, actually, I would like to know if you plan on ever getting back in touch with Mom and Dad?"

Talk about conversation whiplash! I thought I was good at switching gears; apparently, I had met my match. From incest to parents—that's the logical transition topic. I was making an official proclamation; this was no longer a confrontation, it was a freak fest. What the heck, I'm game. With still a little time left on the clock, I would answer that question quite confidently.

"No, absolutely not. I have had enough pain thrown my way over the years; it's time for me to duck out. All I have asked was for them to acknowledge there is a screwed-up dynamic going on and their response—it was me. I am through trying to make something work that causes me so much hurt."

My brother, looking at the doctor for moral support, said, "Now, that's what I have a problem with. Being Christians, I don't think we can ever use the word 'never' in our vocabulary. God can do anything, and I want her to be open to Him mending the relationship with our parents. I don't want it for anyone's benefit but hers. I think it's in her best interest to come back into relationship with them. I hate to see her hurting like this. As a Christian, I just can't believe that it is right to shut God out like this, and say she will 'never' be in contact with our parents again."

Oakie dokie – my brother just reiterated the fact that we were Christians and actually brought God into his defensive plan against me. One minute justifying undressing and wanting sex with me, the next telling me I was blocking God from having His way in our family.

My older brother seemed to be taking his role very seriously. He was willing to be a spiritual advisor to his younger, theologically incorrect sister. Huh. He seemed to think, and by his estimation God did too, his wicked perverseness was but a minor infraction compared to my unwillingness to call our folks. Obviously, he was of the opinion that Christians were not supposed to have the word "never" in their vocabulary. He couldn't seem to say, *'I should have "never" molested my sister.'* Really? As a Christian, I was not allowed to have the word "never" in my vocabulary? Hmmm, somehow, I couldn't embrace his theology on that one.

At that point, I wanted to hold up a mirror to see if he actually had a reflection. No time for that; I just wanted this over with.

My brother might have been addressing the doctor, but clearly he was talking to me. So I retorted accordingly. "Why would I sign up for that mess? Dad doesn't even tell me he loves me after not talking to me in two years? We're parents; we both know that's not right!"

Bemused, he replied, "I have to admit, I don't have a category for that. I don't know what he was thinking. I just think at some point that you should give them another chance. I truly mean it when I say that it would be for your own good. This is not about our sister or me, and how your unwillingness to come back affects us. I'm genuinely concerned for your own well being."

"What I want for you is to be able to be in the same room with Mom, have her do what she always does, and not have it affect you. That you will know she is just doing what comes natural to her and you shouldn't be bothered by it"

Stunned, I remarked, "OK, let me get this straight. You want me to be in relationship with our mom, permit her to say or do whatever she wants to do to me, but I get a thicker skin and not allow it to hurt me?"

Smiling as if we are finally on the same page, he laughed, threw one hand up in the air, and said, "Yes, that's exactly what I mean."

Cackling, I threw my head back in laughter and declared, "Umm, I vote NO!"

Dr. Storm enthusiastically joined the conversation, which caught both my brother and I off guard. Looking at my brother, he almost burst.

"YES, and isn't that what we want for her! She knows she has choices and that she is allowed to make healthy ones. She never knew that before, and now she is making a healthy relational choice. She doesn't want to be in relationship with people who inflict pain."

My brother, somewhat stammering, replied, "Well, of course, that's what I want for her. I think that is a good decision for now, just not forever. You never know what God can do. It is our responsibility as Christians to allow God to work."

Still resolved and not backing down, Dr. Storm continued. "When Veronica came into my office several months ago, it was as if she was a caged, wounded animal. She was agitated and circling her cage not knowing there could possibly be a way out. A few weeks ago, she discovered there was a door in her cage. She realized that just maybe she is allowed to make some choices to allow her to have an emotionally safe and healthy future."

Now changing his gaze from my brother and onto me, almost jubilant, he affirmed, "However, today, Veronica has found the key. Not only does she know there is a door, but she is unlocking it to her freedom."

Smiling at Dr. Storm, acknowledging his affirmation, I knew that was the closing statement, our time was up. Suddenly, it occurred to me that Dr. Storm and I didn't rehearse the exit plan. My brother would insist on walking me to my car and that in no way could happen. Trying not to show my panic, quickly I devised an exit strategy of my own. Dr. Storm did me a favor by squeezing us into his schedule that day. He had another appointment waiting, and he needed us to leave his office. Not having the luxury of running the departure plan by Dr. Storm, I prayed to God that he would follow my lead. Going for it, I threw caution to the wind and could only hope that Dr. Storm would know what I was doing and join me in my scheme.

CHAPTER TWENTY-TWO

The Warrior

My mind was jumbled, and my emotional meter was on overload. The disconnect I had achieved earlier in the session was no longer in effect. I wasn't too sure how much longer I could keep it together.

Looking at my brother, politely I said, "I really do want to thank you again for coming down here today. I was so concerned I would upset you. I know it must have been mortifying for you to sit here and rehash this terrible stuff."

Smiling, he lightly assured me, "It wasn't mortifying at all. I'm happy to talk to you about it. If you need to talk about it further, we could grab a bite to eat or something and continue."

Repulsed, I stuttered, "No, I'm good. I don't need any further discussions."

I stood up, and my brother followed my lead. Dr. Storm thanked him once more for coming and started with the goodbyes. He began escorting both of us to the door, but, before he could get too far, I interrupted him hoping he would figure out what I was doing.

Turning to my brother, "OK, well I am staying here for a little longer to continue with Dr. Storm. I will call you in about a week or so to see where we go from here."

I turned my gaze to Dr. Storm hoping he knew what I was doing. My eyes were pleading with him to allow me to stay just a few minutes longer so my brother would leave. Feeling as though an Uzi was firing off inside me, to my relief, Dr. Storm followed the plan to perfection.

Looking at my brother, he said, "Thanks again for coming, I'll escort you out."

The clock was ticking, I knew the scheduled time for his other appointment was a little past due, so I was grateful he understood my plight.

My brother did not give up easily.

"Are you sure you don't want to go get some dinner? I'm happy to wait for you while you finish your session with Dr. Storm. It seems like we are not through here yet." *Oh mercy, would someone please help me!* It just kept getting better and better. I needed him out of the office and I needed it immediately!

"No, like I said, I need some time to work through what we have talked about. I will call you in a week. I ask that you give me that time and don't contact me before then, OK?"

Tentatively he replied, "Sure, I understand. If you change your mind, feel free to call sooner. Like I said, I'm happy to continue the dialogue with you."

Dr. Storm walked my brother to the door and then closed it behind him. Turning with bright eyes and arms outstretched for a hug, he exclaimed, "Congratulations, you did it! You said you never could confront him and you did. You were incredible! At first, I thought that maybe you were backing out. When you started about being in marriage counseling, I wasn't too sure where you were going with that thought. But then, when you began telling him about having to talk about your past, I couldn't believe how well you approached the subject. You couldn't have done a better job." Still beaming, he said, "I'm so proud of you, I really am. Aren't you?"

I couldn't quite feel the excitement he did. I gladly accepted the hug; maybe he could keep me from collapsing. I was trying to make sense of what had taken place the last hour. My family seldom denied my memories. They simply say I am inflating and blowing them out of proportion. *Overly sensitive* is the label I had been trying to tear off my forehead for years.

"Umm, yeah, I guess I'm proud of myself. I really can't believe I had the nerve to say everything that I did."

A little hesitant, I asked, "Did it appear to you that he talked about them as fond memories? He wasn't upset at all, was he? I thought I would throw him a bone and tell him I knew it had to be mortifying. He actually said it wasn't mortifying. It was fine and that he was happy to talk about it."

Thoughtfully he replied, "Yes Veronica, you're right. He wasn't upset by the recollections. He appeared as though he saw nothing wrong with what he did. I'm so glad you did confront him so you know the truth."

Trying to get me to focus on the upside, he continued, "But you did it! You did what you said you could never do. I want you to be happy for yourself right now."

Embarrassed, looking down, I murmured, "Yeah, but he said it was consensual."

"But you handled that perfectly. Telling him that you didn't know how an eleven-year old girl could consent and that you will let him wrestle those demons in the nighttime hours was perfect. I was thrilled when you responded to him and didn't let him get away with it. Now, let the fact that you were brave enough to have this moment sink in. We will deal with everything else next time you come in, OK?

With one more quick hug, I exited. Walking to the elevator I was frantically texting Jerry and a couple of friends. Not wanting to go into the details in a text message, I simply wrote in all caps "HE REMEMBERED." The elevator door opened while my phone began its buzzing with everyone's replies. Once again, I walked to the back and stared straight ahead, while others were busy talking on the ride down.

This was all too much for me to comprehend. The betrayal of my brother was starting to penetrate my awareness. A tsunami-sized wave of emotion was beginning to rise up within me. The emotional house of cards I so carefully constructed as my place of refuge was swept away as mere broken rubble. In an elevator, with strangers along for the ride, a solitary tear graced my cheek as I recalled the image of my brother's smiling face. I thought *he escaped, I never considered him one of them*. He was different to me somehow. The illusion was being ripped away from the false reality I masterfully created in my youth.

In a daze like state, I began to walk to the car, knowing Jerry was waiting my arrival. My phone rang once more and I looked to see which of my friends was trying to contact me. Alarmed, I saw that it was not a friend; it was my

332

brother. A flash of anger mixed with grief hit. I went to hit the reject button. Then a thought: there was something that I had wished I had asked my brother, but forgot to. I answered.

"Hello"

"Hi Ron, I wanted to let you know that I am still here, in the parking lot, in case you wanted to go out to dinner or something so we could continue to talk. Do you want to grab a bite to eat?"

Exasperated at having to answer that question again, I said, "No I don't want to go out to dinner; however, there is something I wanted to ask you."

"Sure, what?"

Knowing there is about the same age difference between his son and daughter, that there is with us, I projected the offense onto them in hopes of making it clear. I wished to wake him up from his three-decade evil slumber.

"If your son did to your daughter what you did to me, would that be OK with you?"

Taken back with such a question, he stammered, "Well, umm, uh, well, all I can say is, you asked me if what happened affected how I parented and I guess it did in a way. We have an 'open door' policy."

"I don't know what that is. What do you mean?"

"We don't allow our kids to have their doors closed when they are in their bedrooms. That way they know that anyone can see into their room at anytime. It's just a kind of safety measure we came up with."

Trying to infuse logic into the conversation, speaking slowly, I concluded, "Because if your son did something to your daughter, that would be wrong with you, is that what you're saying? It would actually be devastating to her, right? That's why you want their doors to remain open. You don't want anything horrible to happen to your daughter because that would cause her harm."

"Well, umm, like I said, I'm happy to go out to dinner and discuss this. We could go over to the shopping area and you could choose the restaurant."

Completely unnerved with his gross lack of response and in an angrier tone, I demanded, "I would assume that if your son did to your daughter what you did to me, you would kick the shit out of him. Am I right?"

Hearing a slight gasp on the other end of the line, I knew that last sentence seemed to have struck a cord with him. I'm sure he was shocked that I, as a Christian, would use such foul language. In true religious hypocrisy, he seemed to have landed on the wrong offense once more.

He began to stutter for a reply. Then regaining his composure, calmly he said, "Yeah, well, umm, like I said, if you want to talk about this further, I'm still here in the parking structure and I would be happy to go to a restaurant to continue this conversation. It seems like you are still upset about what happened."

"No, I don't want dinner! I can't talk to you anymore. I need time. I told you in Dr. Storm's office that I needed a week to know what I am going to do. However, now I need two weeks. I mean it this time. Do not contact me for at least two weeks. Actually, don't contact me at all. When I'm ready, which might be a little more than two weeks, I will call you, OK?"

"OK, if you're sure."

"I'm definitely sure, bye."

Without waiting for a goodbye, I hung up.

I picked up my pace, half running, to get to my car. Jerry saw me approach and opened my door. Quickly I entered with mascara-stained cheeks and slouched down on the seat exhausted.

When Jerry entered the car, he reached over to hold my hand. "Your brother remembered; that had to be such a relief for you. Are you OK?"

I began the long dissertation about what just took place in Dr. Storm's office. Jerry's face went from shocked to sympathetic and everything in between. When I got to the part about my brother saying it was consensual, Jerry's impulses took over.

In a flash, his face turned to rage, his fist was clinched, and he turned from me to looking out the window. He scanned the street to see if he was able to locate his adversary. Still a little jittery from the confrontation, I flinched with this reaction. Jerry's attention immediately diverted back to me. Unclenching his fist, he reached out again to take hold of my hand and apologized profusely for making me jump.

Sorrowfully acknowledging him, I countered, "You have no need to apologize to me. You are allowed to be angry with him. This affects you as much as it affects me."

Calming down, he replied, "This is not about me; it is about you. I'll have time to work through my emotions later; right now I just want to focus on how to help you."

With this having been said, I buried my face into his

chest and began to wail. My world was crumbling; everything I believed in about my family was a total falsehood. In my vain imagination, I believed him to be repentant of all his misdeeds. The utter humiliation and deceit broke me to the core. The counterfeit blueprint of my childhood and adolescence was exposed for the lie that it was. I never knew such betrayal and heartache existed.

Jerry tried to console me, but that was an impossible task. We began to drive down the coast in an effort to escape the place of my rejection. It was way past dinnertime, so we pulled into a quaint exclusive shopping area off Pacific Coast Highway for dinner. There was absolutely no way that I could go into a restaurant, so Jerry went in and placed an order to go.

While in the car alone, I started to cry uncontrollably. My brother actually looked me dead in the eye and said, "I just assumed you wouldn't mind" while talking about him coming into my room. I have been horrified on his behalf all these years, and, in his wild twisted mind, he seemingly had no regrets. He actually thought I was an accomplice in his deviant sexual game. For him to have thrust his lustful inclination on me went beyond the realm of reason and cuts deeper than when the sexual violations occurred.

Again, I asked God, "Why now, why do I have to face all the contents of my boxes?" I looked out the window to all the shoppers coming and going. I felt an urge I had not felt since the beginning stages of my counseling: I wanted to shop!

I wanted to spend all the money we had and then

spend money we didn't. I wanted to purchase designer outfits with shoes and purses. I then wanted to buy accessories to go with my new wardrobe and hear the chime of the cash register that would act as a healing ointment for my anguish. I desired to have all the bags fill every square inch of my trunk space. More than life, I wanted store clerks tripping over themselves in hopes of a high commission from a woman in desperate need of feeling worthy of their attention. A void inside of me longed to be filled with newly acquired items that shouted my value on this planet.

I watched an elegant woman dressed exquisitely walking to her car, arms laden with her new-found treasures. I might not know her, yet I wanted to be her. I coveted her trim, surgically enhanced body, her black convertible Jaguar, and her impeccable sense of style. I was convinced that no one had ever used her and then disposed of her as some unworthy, insignificant female. Every voice inside of me screamed that I deserved to shop, shop, and then shop some more.

Jerry walked across the parking lot to our car with our Italian dinner in a paper sack. I told him that staying there for me was a little like an alcoholic parking outside of a bar. He read me loud and clear, and we began to drive down PCH once more. The air was warm, and the ocean was crystal clear with the waves crashing white on the sand. Birds flew overhead in a cloudless sky, while palm trees swayed in the breeze; it was another beautiful California day. We chose a place to park with an amazing unobstructed view of the ocean. Not being able to stomach my dinner, I sat looking out over the green grass and down a rocky cliff to the striking sea below.

Quietly pondering, I reflected back on the events of the past few months. The overwhelming emotion had died down, and a certain calm resolve had taken its place. I saw the ocean and imagined all the intricate creatures that swam below the surface. Knowing every creature had a purpose, I imagined pods of dolphins, schools of fish, and the various crawling creatures at the depth of the ocean's floor. The majestic colors of the plant life and soft, flowing jellyfish that gave themselves to the imposing current. With the delicate balance of nature so clearly displayed, I sat in awe of my Creator.

While admiring the visual beauty of that moment, a thought came to me. Looking at Jerry, I said, "If God could create something as powerful and majestic as the ocean and all the creatures that swim in its waters, He can take care of me. I know I didn't expect the response that I got from my brother, but the most important thing is he remembered. God knew that he remembered, and He wanted me to face him and get the truth. He even arranged it so my brother would come down to the office for the session. God gave me the strength and courage to actually look him in the eye and confront him. I did it! Oh my gosh, this is huge. I'm not afraid anymore. If I can do that, I think I can do anything."

You know what else? My brother calling me back was actually a miracle too. When he first called, I was furious, but it ended up being the best part of the confrontation. I know I would have been kicking myself for not bringing his children into the perverseness. I was hoping to shock him into the reality of what he did. Even though it didn't work, at least I was able to say it. I would have forever been beating myself up for not saying it, and God gave me a second chance."

"Of course there is the mistaken phone call to my dad. There was no possible way I accidentally dialed his number that day. Even if I had, I was on a road that doesn't have cell reception. Every member of my family is exposing themselves to me in such a clear way; I am starting to see that none of this is coincidental at all."

I momentarily stopped talking, and I looked Jerry square in his eyes. In an instant, I was aware of God's hand in my life. The feeling of adulation completely enveloped me. Suddenly a smiled streaked across my face, and I declared, "Wait a minute, God isn't doing this *to* me: He is doing this *for* me! God wants me well; He really wants me whole! Oh my gosh, God loves me, He really loves me! He has been behind the scenes orchestrating all of this from the very beginning. He is actually on my side. My family has always told me I am outside of God's will and that I am in need of instruction from them. I have always had a hard time knowing who to believe, me or them. Holy crud, God is actually conspiring with me!"

I began to cry once more, but they were not tears of sorrow: they were tears of joy. The knowledge that the God of the universe not only tolerated me but also actually loved me, overpowered all the negative emotions that had consumed me only moments earlier.

With this new revelation, a feeling of empowerment started to take hold. Not only did I want out of my family,

I had complete confidence God wanted me out too. Nothing was as it seemed. The battle lines were drawn; there was a new war raging. I had originally only thought—I needed to be free from my parents—but it became painfully clear that I needed to be freed from my entire family's clutches.

With the knowledge that God was on my side, I knew I could do the impossible. The conspiracy had begun. All hell was about to break loose. Releasing control of my life into His hands, in less than two weeks, together we would do the impossible. My freedom would be a reality.

CHAPTER TWENTY-THREE

Masks Removed

Unable to return home yet, I called Stacie and asked if she could meet me. I needed time for my eyes to clear up so my kids wouldn't know I had been crying. We met at a restaurant after Jerry dropped me off to pick up my car. It proved to be another failed attempt to eat. Stacie was riveted to each word, while adding humor as only she can do. Talking about it seemed to help; it made it more real somehow. It also helped to see it through someone else's eyes. I could easily downplay events in my family. I was taught by the best. We talked for a couple of hours while I began to recompose myself.

As I left the restaurant, I noticed that I had missed numerous phone calls, which at least four were from Michele. She was out of town on business and eagerly wanted a returned phone call to know that I was OK. I might have been losing my family, but my friends were coming out in full force.

I drove slowly home to what had become my life. My brother's words passed through the recesses of my mind and pierced my heart with the recollection of the session. I wished I could have been consumed into the flaming truth of what happened only hours earlier. Instead, it was a slow merciless burn, taking its time to leave its cruel mark. Repulsion and sorrow each took their turn in my mind, as I replayed the events of the evening.

Restlessly I walked upstairs wanting to bid farewell to that excruciating day. Unable to sleep, I decided to continue to test my parents to see if there was any hope of reconciliation. Much to my surprise, after facing my brother, I no longer feared facing my parents. This time, like the biblical example of Joseph, I pulled out all the stops. I desperately tried to see if my mother would show her true colors and be the mom to me I knew she was. Or maybe, just maybe, she had changed and would do whatever it took to make amends. Up until then, my dad had been her puppet. With this email, I predicted she would come out with full vengeance. I began writing….

Dear Dad,

You broke my heart two years ago and just when I thought I was immune to your pain, you did it again. I just don't understand how a person who says that they love me so much can cause me such emotional trauma.

I have spent my life thinking I simply wasn't worth the effort. I have spent the last two years with the knowledge that this must be true.

The underlying blame placed on me for you not saying I love you, didn't go unnoticed. You afraid, I don't think so. The father I was raised with and who two years ago told me to be quiet so he could speak, didn't have any trouble being authoritative and putting me in my place. You seem fearless when you answered my heart wrenching email two years ago with a demand for an apology. After I poured my heart out to you and asked you what was going on, all you could land on were two words I used when referring to mom as, "that woman". Accountability and truth scare you, not me. You also show no cowardice while telling me the errors of my ways. So now you want me to accept the fact that a man who raised me with such authority is not proud, but scared to return affection, I hardly think so.

Your biggest obstacle right now is that I no longer listen to the definition you have given me as to what a good father does, but I now listen to a husband telling me what a good father should do. I actually did think you might be right. I so readily accept whatever label you want to place on me: scary, disruptive, divisive and so on. But fortunately, I have a loving husband who will not allow you to shame me in such ways.

You see, Jerry is a wonderful father. So when he read your explanation he quickly helped me read through the madness. Once again, he told me how a father who really did love me would have handled the situation. Jerry has been completely shocked and overwhelmed at how you guys have treated me, especially the past two years. He continually reminds me that if one of our daughters would have come to him and told him that he was a cause of hurt and pain in their life, his world would have stood still. He said that he would listen attentively and acknowledged any wrong doing, and then begged for forgiveness. He would have been much more concerned about relationship than being right.

343

When I told him about the phone call and the unreturned 'I love you", he was mortified for my sake. But then when he read your explanation he was astonished that a father would blame his daughter for his own short comings. Jerry once again reminded me of how a father who truly loves his daughter would have handled the call. No amount of fear or intimidation would have come between him and his love for his girl. A simple returned phone call and quick 'I love you' would have been the least action any father should do. But to not even acknowledge the absence of the sentiment in the first email goes without excuse. When Jerry read the first email he immediately asked, "Where is the apology for not saying 'I love you'? He didn't even acknowledge he did that to you!" Jerry simply couldn't believe you would withhold such a simple sentiment from your daughter two times in a row. To add further insult and follow up the lack of response with a statement of fear of that daughter and blame her is totally unacceptable. You never have any trouble or fear saying things that you think will prove your point, but now I am to believe that you are afraid to say 'I love you', that is not going to happen. You had no fear stating over and over that you were the priest of the household in God's eyes and I was to obey you without question. I don't know of this powerless father that you claim to be.

I believe you when you said you were afraid alright, but not about what you stated. You were busy trying to figure out if I deserved such sentiment and would my mother, your wife, approve. I am not the scary one in this dynamic. I know you have someone to fear, but it isn't me. Never have you taken the position of coward when dealing with one of your kids.

Dad, I do think your apology was heartfelt and sincere, but I just don't know how to accept an apology that is laced with me being scary and somehow responsible for your behavior. I will however extend my forgiveness to you for not being able to love me as you are called to do. I also forgive you for choosing pride over relationship. I had already chosen to forgive you of these offenses a long time ago."

I love my dad but allowing him to be a silent partner to my mother's schemes wasn't doing either one of us a favor. I was guessing my mom would read the email and hit the roof! I was certain this would do what it was sent to do—have my mom come out to play. While saying the old line from the game hide-and-seek, "Olly Olly Oxen Free," I pressed "send" and away it went. Satisfied, yet still heart-broken, I went off to bed.

The morning came, and I decided to take my kids to the beach. My mind was a flurry of thoughts as I watched my children ride the ocean waves so carefree. As I reclined in my beach chair, the session replayed in my heart acting as a clandestine poison, leaving anguish in its wake. I was finding small comfort in the fact that Dr. Storm had witnessed my brother's unnatural response. If not, I would have no doubtingly begun wavering in my recollection. It seemed too absurd to be true.

After about four hours, we packed up to leave. I checked my phone, and I seemed to have missed some calls and texts. While the kids finished drying off, to my utter surprise, I didn't just miss some texts from my friends; two were from my brother. I didn't even know if I wanted to read them. But, as usual, curiosity got the better of me, so I opened my phone and read the first message. *"Will you please call me at noon? I have something I need to talk to you about."* I guess when I didn't return the first message, he thought he had better elaborate on the second one. *"I really want to talk to you, but not about what you think. It is good, I promise. Please call me today."* OK, that settles it. My brother is completely insane!

If the two text messages weren't enough, he had called and left me a voice message: *"Hey Ron, I really want to talk to you about something. You didn't call me today at noon, so I am going to call you tonight after I get home from work. I promise it is good. If you don't pick up the phone, I'll just leave you a detailed voice message. I really hope you will let me talk to you, I think it will make you feel better. Talk to you later, bye."* I was repulsed as I listened to his trite message. In anger, I flipped my phone shut and flung it into my purse.

The clock slowly ticked away until it was past the dinner hour. Right on schedule, my brother called as promised. I refused to pick up. I kept to my demands that I would not talk to him for at least two weeks. I went back and forth in my mind as to whether I should listen to it. I swear, curiosity is like the devil himself—it just keeps bugging you like the nuisance it is! Not able to handle it anymore, I retrieved the message.

"Hi Ronnie, I know you said to wait a couple of weeks, but I thought I should call and touch base. I got to thinking about what we talked about yesterday, and I really do think it is in your best interest to get back together with our parents. I know they have

hurt you, but you are only hurting yourself by cutting them off. I'm not saying you should do it right away, but after some time has passed. Again, this isn't about me and how it affects my family; I only want what is best for you. I really hate to see you hurting this way and I feel that when you let the past stay in the past, you will be better off. And ummm, about the other thing we discussed, like I said, I am happy to talk about that again if you need to. I am here to help in any way I can. Call me back. If you still want to wait for two weeks, I guess that would be fine. I just think the sooner you forgive mom and dad, the easier it would be for you. Feel free to call anytime. Love you, bye."

Wow, I talked to him about incest only twenty-four hours earlier, and he landed on the last five minutes of the session regarding our parents. What in the freak kind of family do I belong to? I just lay on our bed and relayed the bizarre message to Jerry. Jerry was speechless with this one. We both thought he was calling to beg me not to tell the other family members about what took place the day before in Dr. Storm's office. Or, better yet, to apologize for being such a clueless idiot on how it all went down. But no, he only wanted what's best for me, which in his twisted mind was for me to call our parents and make nice. Of course, being the sweet protective brother that he was, he did remind me that this was for me and not for him.

Within a few hours, the inevitable finally happened. I got the email response from my mother. Boy, I knew she was going to be angry, and she most certainly did not disappoint! While I was checking my emails, my mom's came blazing through the screen reeking with lethal contempt.

My heart momentarily stopped, and my eyes were transfixed on the screen. She typed her words in large, bold print so she could accurately relay her tone.

No matter what you say or do, we will not stop loving you nor stop praying for reconciliation. We have honored your boundaries of not seeing our face or hearing our voice. Because of the nature of your e-mails, which are cruel and mean spirited, we are requesting for you to stop all e-mails. If you want to say something, you pick up the phone and make arrangements to speak to us face to face. No longer are you to hide behind this electronic verbal assault. I expect you to read into this e-mail as another attack on you, "the victim," but you are doing to us what you accuse us of doing to you, mental emotional abuse. If you choose to answer this e-mail with an e-mail, it will be deleted before being read. All future e-mails from you will be deleted before we read them. We will no longer be your beating board. Please know this, if you ever want to work this out, we will meet with you at anytime or anyplace. We love you.

I could actually hear her voice and see her face while reading it. It felt like fire flamed from her typed words. This was the exact response from her that I was expecting and even wanted, so why did it hurt so badly? Unfortunately, there was always a part of me that longed for and dreamed that she would be nice to me. That she would give anything to make it right. That was my exhausting mental course—

from hope to harsh reality and back again in some vicious cycle. The email hit with the powerful blunt force of a deadly emotional weapon she intended it to be. I asked for it and I got it—my mom came out to play! Oh, I loathed it when she brought God into her bitter, sick plots. I didn't know which I hated worse: when she was being malicious and then said she was praying for me or ending with "we love you." Both were equally wicked.

Everything was happening so fast. I knew God was doing something miraculous; I felt as though I was merely along for the ride. Having my entire family rise up at once was unprecedented. I wanted to have some time to myself. I didn't know what my next move should be.

Jerry agreed that I should go away Friday night to gather my thoughts. He too saw the speed at which all of this was coming together. He wanted to make sure I was confident when I came up with a plan. Friday came, and I checked into a nearby beach hotel. Michele came to meet me for lunch. The sun was shining brightly as some billowy clouds scattered across the sky. The restaurant offered outdoor dining which overlooked the pool several floors below. We could hear the laughter of children playing in the water, while mothers were busy taking pictures to capture the gleeful expressions on their children's faces.

We chose a table that was somewhat removed from the other tables so we could enjoy some privacy. The heat of the sun on our skin was welcoming; however, the cold front from my mom's email would soon kill the beauty of our surroundings. After we both placed our orders, I handed the email to Michele. Quietly, I sat waiting to hear her thoughts. She read it and then looked at me over her glasses with shock and sympathy.

We talked about the blaring email and my brother calling me the day after the confrontation.

"I don't know how to be in relationship with them anymore."

Sadly, Michele replied, "You can't be in relationship with your brother, that's pretty clear. As far as your mom is concerned, I don't get it at all. A friend of mine confronted her mom about her own childhood. Her dad was an alcoholic, and her mom drank most of the time, too. She confronted her mom about how hard it was, that even though she was a child, she had to be the adult. She had to take care of her younger sisters, and it robbed her of any childhood. The mom, hearing her adult daughter, recount her childhood memories began to weep uncontrollably and get down on her hands and knees to beg her for forgiveness. That is how a good mother responds, Veronica. I can't even imagine ever writing something like this to my daughter if she came to me in her adult years and let me know that I had hurt her."

For the next several hours, we sat under the shade of the umbrella drinking ice tea and talking about what I should do next. Michele knew I was terrified of my mother and felt unsafe while in her presence. I wanted to email a response to my mother's email, but I knew that wasn't the way it should be handled. The fact that my mother said she would delete all future emails was of little consequence. There would be no way she would delete anything I sent her. She would read it, fume, tell my father, and then not reply so I would think it went unopened.

However, that would not give me the finality I wanted. I really didn't know how to have closure without a face-to-face confrontation.

Michele asked me about the relationship with my sister. "Are you going to remain in contact with her? She is the only one you seem to be close to in your family."

I began to explain to her that I felt my sister had changed over the years. Or perhaps she hadn't changed—I had. Although I always was of the opinion that my sister wasn't concerned about my well-being, it did seem the behavior had escalated over the past several years. I couldn't take being set up for emotional let downs anymore or having her constantly putting me in my place. I expressed that I felt a certain sense of obligation towards her, but that I didn't get anything out of the relationship and hadn't for years. It was out of family loyalty that I allowed her to remain in my life. I didn't trust my sister, that much I knew. However, I was still unclear how I was going to handle her.

After many hours of discussion and countless refills of ice tea, the afternoon passed, so it was time we said our goodbyes. Nothing was decided, but it felt good to have had the opportunity to discuss it exhaustively.

Early that evening, Jerry arrived, and we enjoyed dinner together while talking about the events over the last couple of weeks. The heaviness in my heart continued to weigh on me like the power of a two-ton elephant. My decision was made. I looked across the table and said, "I'm finished with my family. I need out. I don't know how exactly it will come together, but I will somehow exit. I just need some time to figure it out."

I knew Jerry was greatly relieved that I came to that conclusion. We paid our check and left for a summer's evening drive along the coast.

The air was unusually warm, so we decided to drive with the top down on our convertible. While riding, I gazed up to the heavens to look at the numerous stars illuminating the sky. Although a sight of beauty, there was also a certain wonder to the great complexities of life. The enormity to the heavens above was only equaled to the emptiness I felt in my heart. I cannot comprehend loving people who have caused me so much pain, yet I did. I hoped against hope that they would think I was worth fighting for. I didn't want them to confirm my biggest fear: that I was worthless to them and could be effortlessly discarded.

Then unexpectedly, the air turned cold, almost as though there was urgency to it. I grabbed a sweatshirt from the backseat and wrapped it around my bare arms. I rested my head on the seat and fixed my eyes back to the sky that was freckled with stars. I couldn't help but be impressed at its beauty. In awe I thought, *"Well God, You did it again. You painted another magnificent masterpiece!"*

The overnight stay at the hotel was just what I needed. I was resolute with my decision to leave the family, however conflicted on what to do about my sister. It appeared to me that she had followed the path of my mother. My emotional well-being didn't seem to be of great concern to her. Even with that, I still felt a sense of duty to keep her in my life. She continuously reminded me that the kids and I are the only family she has. She had never felt close to my brother and his family. That was a fact she would continuously remind me of. Even with that, I almost needed a clean break. Because of her close relationship with my mom, whatever I did and said from that point on would be relayed to my parents. That would mean that my brother and parents would still have an inlet to my children and me if I remained in contact with her. My sister would unwittingly answer my daunting question regarding our relationship the next day.

****

Sunday came, and I received a call from my sister. I ignored it. She was the last one I wanted to talk to. As I predicted, her voice was dramatic with contrived distress that she was concerned about me and wanted to come down to bring me a present. I was pretty sure the real reason she wanted to come over was she knew I had a session with our brother and was dying to find out what happened, mostly of course, to see if he was able to sway me into a change of heart regarding my relationship with them. I disregarded her request for a returned phone call. Within a matter of two hours, there were no less than three more messages requesting a visit that day. More determined than ever, on the last message, she informed me that she was coming down to drop off a care package.

OK, I guessed there was no avoiding her. An hour later, there was the anticipated knock on the door. I opened it to see my sister, solemn faced, looking as though she was just diagnosed with some terminal disease. All I could think was *Oh brother, here we go again....*

She entered dreary as ever, gave me a tight hug and told me her heart was just breaking for me. "I am so sad that dad didn't tell you he loved you. You sounded so awful the last time we spoke. I just wanted to come and give you a little something." She held out a gift bag for me to unpack. In it was some chocolate, Mr. Bubble – bubble bath, a few other odds and ends, and a card. Now mind you, I wasn't expecting much, but who in their right mind would drive over an hour to give a grown woman Mr. Bubble? I had to chuckle at the contents of the alleged care package. My sister knows I'm not a huge fan of chocolate and I HATE taking baths. My guess would be she grabbed some stuff out of her house and threw it into a gift bag and "voila" you have a present! When I was finished unpacking it, she said, "I know you don't really like baths or chocolate, I just thought it was cute."

While taking a seat, she continued. "I know you are busy, and I can't stay long, but how are you doing?" For someone who couldn't stay long, she sure was making herself comfortable.

"Well, I'm not doing that good actually. This has been a long, hard process for me. I am trying to make the right healthy decisions and that's not always the most obvious choice."

She moved closer with tears in her eyes and replied, "I'm sorry it hurts so badly for you, I'm terribly hurt by this too."

OK, here we go. This had to be some kind of record for

her. This was my tragedy for about five minutes and then magically it quickly became hers. Normally I would relent and give her the condolences she required. Normal was no longer normal for me, so I remarked, "Really, Dad not telling me he loves me is harder on you than me? I know Mom must have told you about her scathing email to me. So, her email to me cuts you also?"

Her tears were quickly replaced with anger. "Veronica, why do you always think everything is about you? This affects me; it affects everyone in the family. You are not the only one hurt here you know. Your decision not to talk to Mom and Dad is painful to all of us! I dread Christmas coming around; it isn't the same with our family divided. It used to be so fun, now it's ruined for me."

"Wait a minute," I exclaimed. "Our parents and brother spend Christmas with you and your husband. I am the one who doesn't have extended family on Christmas, not you, and you're the victim?"

Now incensed, she barked, "I don't even know how to act around you. I feel like I have to watch every word I say. You know Mom and I are close, but I don't feel free to talk about our closeness to you because it will somehow hurt you. Even when we are with our friends, I guard what I say because I'm afraid if I say something about Mom or Dad you will be hurt. It's not fair to me. I should be able to talk about whatever I want to and not be concerned that it will hurt you. Mom is nice to me and is an important part of my life. If I want to talk about them, I should be able to."

"Oh, for heaven's sake! I have never told you not to talk about Mom. And, by the way, you do talk about her, all of the time. You are always informing me of how close the two of you are, so get off your high horse!"

"I do not talk about her all of the time. The last time we were out with our friends, I wanted to tell them Mom got a new puppy. Here I am, with my closest friends, and I can't even share with them that my mom got a new puppy because you are there."

Geeze! I truly think if I were to take a bullet in the heart and my blood splattered on her blouse, she would blame me for damaging her shirt. She would get all upset at how everyone seemed to think I was the one in need of comfort when clearly she was the only one who has suffered the loss of a beloved article of clothing. I realized then that she was way too high maintenance for me. Angrier than ever, I countered, "If you wanted them to know Mom got a puppy so badly, why didn't you pick up the phone to call them or send them an email! There are twenty-four hours in a day. You can talk to them any time you want! Better yet, what would possess you to wait until I am there to tell them anyway? You know what? It doesn't matter. Tell them whatever you want whenever you want. Don't be concerned about me. I'm over it!"

This didn't seem to be going in the direction she wanted it to. She coolly added, "See, you are angry. I don't want you to be upset or hurt. I'm afraid of losing you and my nieces and nephew. I love you."

Love? I'm not thoroughly convinced anyone in my family knew the meaning of that word. Desperately wanting her out of my house, I looked directly into her eyes and said, "I got to thinking the other day that it feels as though I am living in a dump. I am surrounded by toxic relationships everywhere I turn. You know what? I don't want to be the manager of a dump anymore. I need to have healthy people in my life and nurture healthy relationships, not manage toxic ones. That's all I'm doing."

Seeing a stunned expression on her face, I stood, thanked her for coming and for the so-called present, and then escorted her to the door. My question was answered; I needed to cut ties from all of them. In an instant, a plan came to my mind. When I was finished, there would be no mistaking that they were to leave me alone. Dr. Storm was very much a part of the whole orchestration. The next day in our session, I would see if I could get him on board with the way I wanted to exit.

CHAPTER TWENTY-FOUR

Curtain Call

Morning arrived, and I was eager about my appointment with Dr. Storm. I told Jerry my plan, and he agreed with the way I wanted to handle my family. He was, however, skeptical on whether or not I would be able pull it off. My session wasn't scheduled until four o'clock later that day. That gave me much time to pray and go over the plans in my head.

Jerry was excited about joining me for the session. On the way down to Dr. Storm's office, I felt an unusual sense of calm. In my heart of hearts, I knew this was all going to work out. Jerry and I sat once more in the waiting room killing time before the appointment. I had so much to catch him up on. Almost a week had passed and I hadn't seen Dr. Storm since the confrontation with my brother. My family had given me much to talk about!

Dr. Storm walked out with his usual bright smile. He greeted both Jerry and me, and we all took our usual places. We wasted no time and dove right into the topic of my brother. Even though the conversation was grotesque, we couldn't help but laugh at the outlandish way it all happened. Dr. Storm confirmed for Jerry everything I had told him about my brother's behavior in the last session. He relayed how he went up to Oregon on some business, and, instead of flying, he rented a car so he could contemplate what he witnessed the day before.

"Veronica and I went over all the potential reactions that she could be faced with when confronting her brother. With all the possible scenarios, it didn't occur to me to prepare her that her brother might actually remember the past events of incest with such affection. It was really an unsettling thing to see. I needed to take a few days to listen to some Christian teaching CDs and pray. In my twenty-five years of practice, I have never seen anything like that. I don't think either one of us was prepared to be part of something so disturbing."

I began to tell Dr. Storm about my brother contacting me the very next day. Then I had him read the email I sent to my father. He supported the communication but was surprised that I had escalated the contact with my parents. Grabbing my purse, I pulled out the email from my mother.

Reaching across the room, Dr. Storm took the paper and began to read.

I added, "Well, she took the bait. You'll notice the email was sent to my dad, but my mom was the one who replied."

When finished, he looked up in bewilderment. "Wow, you can almost feel the venom leaping off the page. She is furious with you. You nailed it! You said she would come out fighting and she did. You always seem to be able to predict what they are going to do."

"I have lived in the line of fire for most of my life. The only way I have managed is to study their behavior and try to remain one step ahead. I always wish for a different outcome, but I never get one." I told him about my sister's visit and that I had finally decided I needed to sever ties with my entire family. With all that said, he affirmed my decision. He then asked how I planned on doing it.

"Well, I have been thinking about that, and I do have a plan. I was wondering if I could ask your help to make it happen."

"Sure, what do you need me to do?" Dr. Storm was leaning forward and listening attentively.

"I am going to call my mom and tell her I got her email. To throw her off guard, I'll say she was right and I agree to a face-to-face meeting. I'll make it sound like I am scared and totally repentant for having sent my dad the email. This will be enough incentive for them to both fly down. She would give anything to have me cower in her presence and apologize for being such an ungrateful daughter. After she agrees to the meeting, I'll ask her if they could come down on Thursday for an appointment in your office with you as the mediator. She will conclude that I am asking them to come down for you to help with reconciliation. After I get off the phone with her, I'll call my sister and tell her that I would like for her to join us in the session. I'm telling you right now, she will be praising Jesus that her prayers have been answered and that I have finally seen the errors of my ways. Next call will, of course, be to my brother. I'll tell him that I considered his messages and he is right: it is time for the whole family to be together. So, would you mind having it take place in your office?"

Dr. Storm found himself having to catch up with the

speed at which this process was going. "You sure do work fast Veronica. One minute you sit here telling me you will never be in the same room with your parents and just two weeks later you want them to fly down. Yes, I told you from the start that it is my goal to have you free from the bondage of your family. So you mentioned Thursday is the day you are looking at." Grabbing his appointment book, he started flipping the pages on his calendar a couple of weeks ahead to see what was available. "Which week were you thinking of?"

Laughing, I replied, "This Thursday, you know, three days from now."

"What? Do you really think you can pull it off that fast?"

"Yes I do. All I know is, when I was praying about how to make this happen, I really felt like it was supposed to be on Thursday. Maybe I'm wrong, but I don't think I am. Do you have availability on Thursday afternoon?"

Still a little amazed, he looked down at his planner and told me he could arrange it so we have from four o'clock to six o'clock.

The next order of business was preparing for the confrontation. "OK Veronica, let's go over all the possible reactions you might encounter with your family. You seem to know what they will do and when they will do it. So this time, you prepare me with what you think will happen. First, how is your mom going to react?"

"Oh, that's easy. She is going to go ballistic! The reason she will so readily agree to coming to your office is she thinks she will be able to conspire with you. Somehow, she will find a way to get you alone and then she will tell you I am the evil crazy one. My mom is small in size but make no mistake: she is a firecracker. She will come in warm and ingratiating, ready for me to repent. When she sees what I am doing, she will come completely unglued. She doesn't like to spend money on me, so the fact that they bought plane tickets will send her over the top." Grinning, I said sarcastically, "I am only complying with the demands in her email that the next time we speak it is to be in person."

Dr. Storm was confused about one thing. "Your mom won't be able to get me alone. I would never agree to that."

"Oh, you won't have a choice. She will blindside you. I'm just telling you to be prepared, that's all."

He furrowed his brow, looking perplexed. Dr. Storm cautiously replied, "OK, well, you've been right about everything up till now, so I'm sure you're right about this. I just don't know how she could do it."

"She'll find a way, trust me on this one. Next is my dad. He can go one of two ways. He might act authoritative and tell me that, as the priest of the family, I am not to talk to him and mom that way. He has a way of keeping me in line. If he doesn't take that approach, then he will be the obedient, silent observer. That would mean my mom has mapped out everything that they are to say and do. He will be following her direction."

Dr. Storm was busy writing all of this down in my file. With the speed he was writing, I thought he was writing it down verbatim.

"Next you have my brother. You have already met the hillbilly bear. You know how he will react. That only leaves my sister. She is the loose cannon of the bunch. She's a little harder to predict. She can either sit here looking down trodden as though she is the ultimate-victim in this pandemonium or she can come out fighting. If she chooses fighting, we all need to duck and cover. She can get as mad as a hornet and sting like one too. I think that pretty much covers it. So are you still up for it?"

"Yes, I'm up for it. My question to you, are you up for it? Are you certain you want to exit your family and end all communication forever? I don't want you to have any regrets. It will mean that you are dead to them. Are you prepared for the finality of it all?"

The word "dead" rang in my ear like a piercing siren. In my trite way, I only concluded that they would be dead to me, not I as the casualty. He was wise in his estimation; I would be dead to them. They would still have each other. They would still be a family, minus one. Would any one of them mourn over the loss of me or in their fury would they dance on my emotional grave? I was also painfully aware of how this decision would affect my children. In an instant, without their knowledge or approval, they would be cut off from their cousins, aunts, uncles, and grandparents. Would they think of me as a protective mother or a vindictive manipulator?

This seemed terribly unfair. A flash forward to all holidays and my children's graduation ceremonies and weddings came to my mind's eye. There would be no representation from my family there. It would be as though I had no heritage, no linking bloodline. Are these my only two choices? To remain connected to a family who caused me pain and turmoil or be detached with no relatives of my own. With a lump in my throat, I said, "I am ready for this. I feel that I need to protect my children from this insanity. I simply cannot manage my old life anymore. I have come too far and know too much."

"Good, I think you're ready too. So, Jerry, do you plan on being here for the confrontation?"

"Yes, I absolutely will. I know this isn't about me; this is something Veronica needs to do. I will be here for her support and to make sure they don't cross any lines. There is one more thing we need to tell you. Veronica's mom will be livid with you after she finds out what the meeting is really about. It's in your best interest if you act as though you had no idea what she was up to."

Adding to this, I implored, "We are serious about this. My mom might try to come after your medical license and file complaints with whatever department she can find. She does not take being crossed lightly. If she thinks you were a part of my scheme, she may try to bring you down. So, you are to act just as perplexed as they do with the meeting. If you are questioned, you are to say you thought I was going to reconcile with them too. She is one scary lady; you don't want to mess with her."

Looking a little concerned, he said, "OK, if asked, I will tell them I didn't know in advance what you were up to. I have to say, though, you're not doing anything wrong. You are allowed to confront people. This could be in their best interest if they allow it to be."

Nodding my head, "Yeah, that won't happen. You need to prepare yourself for a total blow out!"

We spent the rest of the session charting out the strategic part of getting my family in his office. We decided that Jerry and I would arrive at four o'clock. I would tell the family members to arrive at four-thirty. That would give us a thirty-minute lead-time so our paths wouldn't cross in the parking lot or lobby.

Then I asked, "Is this pretty common? I mean deciding to confront family members because of what was uncovered in counseling?"

Dr. Storm was thoughtful in his reply. "Yes, often a confrontation is necessary, especially when there is abuse involved. What makes your particular case rare: normally the whole family will confront one individual. Or, perhaps one family member will confront another family member. Never have I seen a case where one member has reason to confront all the other members of their family. Your history is most certainly unique. This is definitely a first for me."

Wrapping up the session, I told Dr. Storm that I would notify him immediately when I found out if my family would come. Jerry and I left his office ready to go out on our usual "end of session" date. The car ride was silent as we drove to one of our favorite Mexican restaurants for dinner. Butterflies were doing spirals in my stomach at the sheer thought of what I must do next. I had to make the phone calls that night. The emotional rollercoaster was getting on my last nerve. One minute I was almost giddy with excitement that my freedom would soon be a reality, the next minute I was grieving over the impending loss of my family. One could get motion sickness riding on such a track. I had relented to the fact the emotional wavering was all part of the process.

We pulled up to a parking spot on Pacific Coast Highway and had to put money in the parking meter. Jerry ran to a store to get some change. I remained in the car and decided there was no time like the present; I would make my first call. I hadn't dialed this phone number in over two years; I was calling my mom.

The phone rang several times, and I prayed I wouldn't get the answering machine. By the third ring, I heard, "Hello?" It was my mother. Here I go.

"Hello, Mom."

Mistaking my voice for that of my sister, she was gleeful for the call. "Hi Honey, how are you?"

Knowing she wouldn't think I was worthy of such a greeting, I clarified. "Umm Mom, it's me Veronica."

Immediately I heard a gasp on the other end and a quick change in tone. No longer jovial, her voice inflection turned to steel. "Oh my gosh, I didn't know it was you."

My tenor was one of cowardice and repentance. The act had begun. "Yes, I know. I wanted to tell you that I received your email, and I think you are right. I could tell that I upset you and I just think that this whole situation is completely out of control. You said that the next time we talk, it should be face to face. I am willing to do that, I mean if that is still what you want." I waited in fervent anticipation for her reply.

Still the controlled matriarch, she said, "Yes, we are willing to come down for a meeting."

"Oh thank you, Mom, that is so nice of you! You mentioned that it could be in the presence of a mediator, and, well, I'm sure you know I have been in counseling."

"Yes, I knew that."

"Uh, I asked my therapist if he would be willing to have the meeting take place in his office and he agreed to it. Would you be OK with that?"

Trying hard to control her enthusiasm, she said with delight, "Why yes, yes I would."

"Thank you so much for doing that for me, Mom. I was thinking that the sooner we do this the better. So, I know this is short notice, but would you both be willing to come down here on Thursday?"

"Thursday? You mean in three days?"

"Like I said, I know it is short notice, it's just that Dr. Storm has availability that day so I thought it would be good to take it."

Trying not to appear overly excited my mom agreed. "I think we could work it out. Let me ask your father." She muffled the phone so I couldn't hear her discourse with my dad. She failed. She was not really asking him as much as she was telling him that this was what they would do.

She returned to the line to let me know that they were willing to make the necessary sacrifices in their schedules to come down as a favor to me. I tried not to laugh. They were hardly ones with full calendars. My act continued. "I think it would be good to have the whole family there. It has affected all of them too. Would it be alright with you if I call them and invite them to the meeting?"

Now she was unable to mask her jubilation. Her son and other daughter were already in her camp. "Of course that would be alright. I think that would be great. Now let me get this straight. You are going to call them, not me."

Softly and with a humble tone, I stated, "Yes, I will handle it. One more thing. I know you said you wouldn't receive any more emails from me, but would you permit me to email you the details and directions to Dr. Storm's office? I want to respect your wishes so I didn't know if you would allow it."

Back to her solid tone she responded, "Yes, yes that would be fine. I will allow you to email those to me. Be sure and give me all the information on where his office is, the address, phone number, and directions." It felt as though icicles were forming on each word as she spoke it.

Contritely I replied, "I will."

"OK, so I guess I will see you Thursday?"

"Yes, you will."

"Thank you for calling and *I love you Honey.*"

Smirking on my end, I responded, "I love you too, Mom." I hung up.

One down, two to go. That took about three minutes. Let's see if I could get one more call in before Jerry got back. Next number to dial was my sister's. I knew my sister would go through hell and high water to get to Dr. Storm's office on Thursday. This was purely a formality. She responded exactly as I had predicted. I told her that I was taking her advice and would have a face-to-face with mom and dad. Without hesitation, she joyfully accepted the invitation to be there.

The plan was in motion; all the players were in their places. Only one more call to make, but I decided to wait until after dinner to call my brother. I watched as Jerry walked back to the car with the quarters in tow. I smiled and did a little victory dance as he approached. I jubilantly relayed to him my phone calls.

"Well, Mom and Dad are booking their flight even as we speak, and I'm sure my sister's phone line is on fire trying to get in touch with them. It worked Jerry! They are coming down."

"Are you kidding me? I have only been gone for five minutes. How did you pull that off in such a short amount of time?"

I filled him in on all the details as I about skipped down the sidewalk to the restaurant. That was all the confirmation I needed. I could see the plot coming together. No doubt in my mind the miraculous was taking place in my life; in three days, I knew I would be free!

****

We arrived home from dinner; it was time to call my brother. I hadn't talked to him since the meeting in Dr. Storm's office a week ago. The call was harder than I thought it would be. God had brought me this far; I was confident the rest would work out. Reluctantly I dialed his number, suspecting he would trip over himself to take the call. Within no time I heard, "Hi Ron, I'm glad you called."

Act three began. "Hi, how are you?" Talking to him was like vinegar on my tongue. It took effort not to have every word I spoke be dripping with disgust. I continued with my good little sister performance. "I know I said I needed a couple of weeks, but after I got your messages, I thought I should call you."

"I'm so glad you did."

"Yes, well you mentioned how concerned you were for me and that you thought it was in my best interest to begin communication with mom and dad, so I'm taking you up on it."

"You are? You are going to talk with Mom?"

"Yes actually, I already have. I called to see if they could come down on Thursday to Dr. Storm's office for a session. They agreed to the meeting. Our sister will be there too. I would love for you to come; after all, this was your idea."

"They are coming down this Thursday? I'm so happy for you! Yes, I can be there. So what do you think we will talk about in the meeting?"

I didn't see that coming! Quickly keeping my wits about me, I tried to manufacture an answer. I didn't want to lie, but, like Joseph, I'm hardly against it. An answer came to me and was actually a truthful one.

"I plan on talking about the state of the family and what the future will be."

"Oh, that would be good. I'm sure it will take more than just one get together to work everything out, but that is a good start. Do you think we can all go out to dinner after?"

Holy crud! This had proven to be the most outrageous of all my calls! Regrouping I said, "Why don't we just play that one by ear? We can decide if we are all up to it at the end of the session."

"That's a good idea. I hope it will work. I think it would be fun to all go out together."

"Yeah, right. Umm you are free to invite your wife to the meeting. I know you wanted her to come last time."

"Nah, she won't want to come. She will be taking the kids to swim lessons. Why, is Jerry going to be there?"

"Yes, he is."

"Oh, I don't know if I like that. I think this should just be for our family."

"It is; that's why he is coming. Jerry is part of the family."

"Hmm, I guess that would be OK with me."

I gave him the details for Thursday. "OK, so I will see you on Thursday in Dr. Storm's office."

In his droll way he replied, "I'll be there with rings on my fingers and bells on my toes, as the old saying goes."

About choking, I said, "Yeah, me too." Hanging up I could barely comprehend the call. I couldn't picture what imaginary world he lived in to not know what was coming down the pipe.

I felt as though Dr. Storm, Jerry, and I were part of a masterful performance created by God Himself. We all had been given our roles and scripts. However, in this production, no one knew what the other actors would be doing. We were to be independently obedient to our own portion and let God handle the rest. The theater was set; all the players were going to be there for the show. I was hoping my family didn't turn this into some kind of Greek tragedy. Very soon, those hopes would be obliterated. In less than seventy-two hours, the stage of my life would forever be changed.

CHAPTER TWENTY-FIVE:

All Hell

My alarm clock went off, and, in an instant, I had a smile on my face. It was the day! My whole family would be in Dr. Storm's office without a clue of what was in store. I was so steadfast with my decision to break free from the clutches of my family; I could hardly wait until the four o'clock hour. I had written some notes to refer to in case my mind went blank at the sight of them. I truly didn't think I would need them. What I would say would come from my heart.

It was early afternoon, about time to get ready for the drive down to the office. Jerry asked, "Are there any parameters you want me to abide by? Or am I free to say what I want to your family?"

"Yes, you have total freedom to handle them any way you choose. I know you have waited for close to twenty-five years to speak your peace. This is my only recommendation. As far as I'm concerned, I don't want to have any regrets when I leave Dr. Storm's office today. I don't want to regret not having the courage to say something I wished I would have, and I don't want to say something in anger that I wish I hadn't. I most certainly don't want to have to owe them an apology because I crossed the line."

Jerry agreed. "Yeah, that's pretty much how I plan on handling it."

"Do you already know what you are going to say?"

"I have a couple different scenarios planned. It really all depends on their reactions."

Enough was said. We decided we didn't want to rehearse our talks.

As I got dressed for the meeting, once again wardrobe was on top of my list. *I think I'll wear yellow!* This was such a happy day for me, I thought my outfit should reflect it. I chose a yellow spaghetti strap shirt, with plaid yellow, white and tan shorts. I was ready to be bright and comfortable.

While still getting ready, I entered my mental storage room. Once a place I was ashamed of, it had become a haven of comfort. The packages were so beautifully wrapped and the room was sterile, always ensuring that no cross-contamination took place. As I stood back to look, I thought it was a remarkable sight. Even with all of the evil contents in some of the packages, I had grown to love my storage closet. I recognized the room's importance in my life.

Looking to the top shelf, I saw the ominous box and was sure that God loved me enough to have that one remain untouched. Then I saw it once more, on one of the other shelves, the shadowy container that was coming into focus. Deep in the dark caverns of my soul, I knew all too well the gruesome contents of that box. The container was now totally recognizable to me. It was never to show itself out in the open like this. I was the storage keeper; I would leave it where it sat, unscathed and unopened. I exited my closet, carefully closing the door as I left.

The time had come; we headed out to the car and began our drive down to his office. I had nominal butterflies, nothing of real significance. I rehearsed what I would say in my mind the whole ride down. If I wasn't going over my speech, I was rolling scriptures around in my head to help maintain my peace. My favorite scriptures to help with the confrontation were Isaiah 54:14-15 (King James Version) *In righteousness shalt thou be established: thou shalt be far from oppression; for thou shalt not fear: and from terror; for it shall not come near thee. <u>Behold, they shall surely gather together, but not by me: whosoever shall gather together against thee shall fall for thy sake.</u>"*

Isaiah 51:12 (King James Version) *"I, even I, am he that comforteth you: who art thou, that thou shouldest be afraid of a man that shall die, and of the son of man which shall be made as grass."*

My mom tends to arrive at places ridiculously early, so, as soon as we pulled into our parking space, we quickly went up to Dr. Storm's office. As promised, when he heard us enter, immediately he escorted us back to his office. The air was tense waiting for the unknown.

Dr. Storm asked, "How are you both doing? Are you ready?"

I answered with a modest smile, "Yes, I think we are. We haven't told each other what we will be saying. We wanted to make sure it was genuine and in the moment."

I noticed that he seemed a little tense. He had sat and listened to me divulge cryptic tales regarding my family and now they would be in his office.

"Dr. Storm, how are you doing? Are you OK?"

"Yes, I'm a little nervous not knowing what will happen. After we get going, I'll be fine. Waiting is the hard part."

Jerry and I gave him instructions on how to escort my family into his office. If he stood by the door and pointed to the seats, they would inadvertently walk past us not noticing we were already sitting down. That was crucial. I didn't want to have to get up and greet them with a disingenuous hug. We went over the plan once more and then Dr. Storm asked if we could pray together. While praying, we heard the lobby door open as each family member began to arrive. After the "amen," we looked at each other in silence, listening to the sound of their voices.

Dr. Storm whispered, "Can you hear which ones are here yet Veronica?"

I gave close attention to each voice and said that I heard three of them. Within a minute, we heard the door open once more and the last one had arrived. It was 4:25 exactly.

Jerry said, "Let's make them wait until 4:30." Dr. Storm looked at me for approval.

Grinning I whispered, "Fine with me. The wait will do them good." I looked at Dr. Storm and sensed he was uneasy.

"You know what?" I said. "I know you want to get this thing going. I'm OK with starting now. Are you Jerry?"

Jerry nodded in approval.

The anticipation hovered over us like an unrelenting fog. Dr. Storm stood up, glanced at us, and then walked out to make his introduction. Jerry and I sat quietly hearing the polite banter between them. The sound of footsteps had me sit up straight; they were coming back to his office. He followed the plan to perfection. He blocked their view, as each one walked past me to take their places. When they turned, they saw that we were already there. They appeared somewhat surprised, even trepidatious, but resolved in their mission. They had come to bring this wayward, rebellious member of the pack back into the fold. I smiled and said "hello," knowing this was the last time I would ever see my family.

Dr. Storm began the session in the exact manner he had with my brother's. He laid down the ground rules for no interruptions, and each member agreed to the terms. He let them know that I would be the first to begin. My parents were sitting directly across from Jerry and me. My brother took the same place on the couch that he did last week; my sister was sitting to his right. Dr. Storm was in his usual spot, somewhat in the corner across from all of us. Jerry and I were on the smaller sofa, located next to the wall, to the right of my sister. Strategically, I was sitting closest to the door to ensure an unobstructed departure.

Help me God was the cry of my heart and then I spoke.

"Thank you all for coming. The past several weeks have been rough, but, thanks to you, I know it has gone on long enough." Looking at my brother I said, "Thank you for calling and leaving the voice mail about reconciling with Mom and Dad." Then, looking at my sister, I continued, "Thank you for coming to my house on Sunday saying practically the same thing our brother did." Then, turning my attention towards my mother: "But, most of all, thank you, Mom for sending me the email. It was then that I knew this was entirely out of control."

They appeared to like the way this was starting. After all, each one had the satisfaction of knowing he or she was the reason for the whole family being together. I thought probably that would quickly turn into a flaming accusation during future family gatherings. My mom was holding a pen and writing tablet, most likely to make sure she could chronicle this moment for future slayings. She was also carrying a folder of paperwork, no doubt my defiant emails. She needed her arsenal full of examples to show the doctor what kind of disloyal daughter I was. My dad sat next to her, leaning back, legs extended, crossed at the ankles with his arms crossed over and resting on his belly. My brother and sister were sitting upright looking mighty professional for the doctor to see. I inwardly chuckled at the fact I was the only one in shorts and bright colors. That should have been their omen.

While I was extremely careful with my tone and words during my brother's confrontation, that day I took an entirely different approach. No need to tippy-toe. In a few minutes I was sure I would be witnessing the pack rallying together for my emotional slaughter.

All anxiety had left me. I looked into their faces, having all four of them against one of me. With the knowledge that God was with me, partnering with me, I was ready to battle for my freedom. I began.

"Thank you for agreeing not to interrupt while I share. I give you my promise that I won't interrupt you when it's your turn. I assure you, after I am finished, you will all each have your own turn to speak." They all smiled and nodded demonstrating they were the perfect, polite Christian family. That exterior would soon disappear.

Going on with my speech, I said, "I am so happy that you all could come here today and see this office. I feel as though I have been blessed to have traveled to some beautiful places. I have seen the gorgeous Caribbean Ocean, traveled to Paris, Brussels and the Netherlands. I have seen the majestic mountains of Banff and Victoria Island in Vancouver. Nevertheless, in all that I have seen, none can compare to the beauty I see in this office. This is where I met Veronica for the first time. At times, the things that I needed to talk about in here were dark and ugly, but it was in the talking about them that I found true freedom."

My mom smiled. She was always smiling. She nodded her head in agreement so all could see her exuding warmth and support for her poor lost daughter. She undoubtedly knew I had talked about her to my doctor. She would be on her best behavior to prove that I was a liar. I took a breath and did what I had come to do. Expose the family secrets.

In almost a trite tone, so casually I said while looking at my brother. "As you know, he and I met here a week ago, and we went over several aspects of our childhood, didn't we?" My brother's face turned sheet white, and his eyes flashed to the door contemplating an emergency exit. Smirking, I continued. "For instance, when the babysitter sexually assaulted him and we were on the outside of the door, horrified at what we were hearing. We heard his cries and the babysitter telling him various things to do, all the while he was begging her to stop."

My mother was catching on. While still smiling, her eyes turned to a warning glare to signify I should stop. I returned with a smile, and she began to write on her tablet. I looked to see if my sister remembered the assault. She appeared confused, not knowing what this had to do with me coming back to the family. I continued with my focus in the direction of my parents. "We also discussed the fact that you never got him help after you found out. The police weren't called, no reports filed. All you said, Mom, was that you would handle it. Actually, none of us ever spoke of it after that."

My mom's stare was piercing as she looked at me making sure to make eye contact. When I mentioned they never called the police, she smiled and nodded her head in agreement. Still trying to appear relaxed and in control, she looked back down at her paper to take notes. Her conduct was one of a court reporter documenting a third party's account of a violent crime, not that of a mother hearing about her son's sadistic sexual assault and her daughter's trauma at having witnessed it.

Her nonverbal warning to shut me up, regrettably for her, had the opposite effect. At that moment, more charged than ever, sarcastically I said, "Now I don't want you to be worried. He did say it didn't affect him in the slightest." Looking back at my brother I said, "Isn't that what you said? It was no big deal at all. I did tell him that I thought it affected us all deeply, but he seemed to disagree. I then asked him, 'If it didn't affect you, then why did you begin molesting me when I was only eleven?'"

My mom's head snapped in the direction of my brother with a shooting look of rage across her face. My brother was slumped, looking down at his shoes, one arm holding onto the other, slouching in the corner of the sofa. He jerked his head up in the direction of the door, still contemplating running out. Not quite the relaxed, cocky demeanor he had the last time I brought this subject up. Believe it or not, my mother turned back to her paper and jotted down a few more notes. I couldn't help but wonder, *what does one write when given such a revelation concerning her son?* As I looked at my dad, he was still maintaining his reclined position, outstretched in his chair. It appeared as though he was watching a golf tournament, not hearing the fact that his son molested his daughter. My sister? She was looking at everyone, seeming slightly bewildered as to where this was leading. I must say, she didn't seem appalled by the subject matter.

Still talking as lightly as ever, I turned my gaze back to my parents. "I explained to him how hard it was to have a mom so cruel to me and a dad who knew, but did nothing to stop her. I explained to him that I can't quite figure out how it was all right for me, in my sophomore year of high school, to be allowed to date a sophomore in college. Not to mention when I was only sixteen, be allowed to date a twenty-five-year old man. What do you think those older men wanted with such a young teen girl? Well, that's exactly what they got. Now that I have teenage girls of my own, I can't fathom allowing them to go out with any man who would find such a young girl attractive." Smugly I said, "But I guess that's just me, and the rest of society."

Turning my attention towards my sister, who up until then had flown under the radar, I stated, "I told our brother last week how hard it was to have a sister who would throw me under the bus like you did. Whenever in need of a self-esteem pick up, you would set me up to have Mom slam me in order to give yourself a lift." I thought this would get her riled up, but she was still sitting there looking dazed. If anything, she was coming across as though she didn't know why she hadn't had her turn to talk. That figured! Honestly, there were so many of her boxes in my storage closet that I could have unpacked concerning her conduct in those years, but I never did. I didn't even reveal those contents to Dr. Storm. I would leave those boxes untouched as a good will offering not to humiliate her. Somehow, I knew I wouldn't get a thank you card.

With that last accusation, I could tell I was on borrowed time. My mom appeared to be getting agitated. So far, she had been able to be the picture of decorum. Maintaining the civil facade was imperative to her getting Dr. Storm on her side. She was, after all, the spiritual matriarch of the bunch. I'm not too sure how she thought the whole note pad thing was coming across.

Referring back to my brother's confrontation, I continued. "I told him last week, what he did to me affected me greatly. It led me down a very troubling and dangerous path. I began pulling my hair out until I had bald patches." Looking back at my mom, "That was about the time you went into your depression and started to take it out on me. Remember the time I almost overdosed on your prescription pills and you told me to make dinner?" My mom was unable to hide her contempt. She looked at me shaking her head in an attempt to silence me. I looked her dead in the eye, and she broke my gaze to make another note on her tablet. While she was still writing, I continued to unpack more boxes containing the details of my teen years—the unwarranted restrictions and how I was the one singled out and targeted which led to my drug use and drinking. I told them about my failed attempt at suicide, which made my mom grin in disgust. Obviously, she thought this was my ploy to gain sympathy. She was mistaken. This was not my attempt to get compassion. I was simply relaying the facts. I knew it was impossible for her to give what she didn't possess. She wrote down the little detail concerning my suicide on her paper as well. I finished with outlining my runaway plans when the suicide attempt failed. My mom was no longer looking at me; she was too busy writing in her notebook.

My mother's diabolical response to my unveilings was expected; my father's, on the other hand, was excruciating. At the revelation of his daughter wanting to take her life while under his care, he remained quietly still. He was looking at me, but, for the life of me, I couldn't figure out what was going on in the geographic regions of his heart and mind. The dad who I loved did nothing but sit and listen to my tales, outwardly unmoved or shaken. Resolved in the fact I had made the right decision to leave the evil mess that was before me, I persisted with my disclosures.

In a contemptuous tone, looking back to my brother, I added, "That takes me to age eighteen. That would be the last time he came into my room undressing me, groping me, not willing to stop when I begged him to. No worries though. He was kind enough to explain his actions to me, didn't you? It was just those pesky teen hormones of yours.

No one can blame a boy for that."

Now turning my attention back to my parents: "He tried to enlighten me that it was consensual, so that needs to be noted. I clued him in on the fact that an eleven-year-old girl couldn't possibly consent to such things. So I told him he could just wrestle with those demons in his night-time hours."

With great satisfaction, I thought to myself, *Now my dear brother - that is my version of a nod-nod, wink-wink moment!* Looking as though I was thoughtfully considering something, I continued to talk to my molester. "Then I got to thinking. Those stupid teen hormones might explain your behavior in the early years, but the last time you came into my room, you were about twenty to twenty-one years old. So, you see, you weren't a teenager at all. Since that is the case, it wouldn't mean it was teen hormones; it would mean you are actually a sexual predator!"

Well, that newsflash seemed to have gotten my brother's attention. The hillbilly bear burst out in the direction of Dr. Storm. "I have had enough! I know I said I wouldn't interrupt, but I'm not taking this anymore!" My mom glared in the direction of my brother, and my dad, on cue, followed her direction. He, too, gave an angry look towards his son. My mom, the record keeper, scribbled down some more notes. I couldn't help but wonder if she wrote the words "sexual predator" down on that little tablet of hers.

Before Dr. Storm could respond to my brother's outburst, immediately I spoke. "Oh, you will have a chance to speak, I promise. You can say whatever you want when I am finished. This won't take much longer."

Giving each of them a quick look, I picked up where I left off. "So after all of this, who do we have to thank for being here today? Is it you my sister for coming to my house and telling me how horrible you have it, having me as your sister? Telling me you feel threatened when we are out with our friends because you want to tell them about Mom's new puppy, but you don't, because you carry the heavy burden of not hurting my feelings? Or is it my brother, calling me the next day after we talk about incest, suicide, and your sexual assault. Did you talk about those things? Of course not! All you wanted to tell me was how important it would be for me, and in my best interest, to patch things up with the folks." Shaking my head while smiling, I remarked, "Nah, you two aren't the ones responsible for today."

As I looked at my mother, she seemed to know what was coming next.

"Mom, of course, it's you who gets the credit for all of this today. After I received your screaming email, telling me that the next time I speak to you, it had to be in person. Well, here I am, telling you in person that I will no longer be a part of this wicked family."

My mom cracked her surface appearance and slammed her hand down on her leg. Looking across to my sister with a maniacal smile, she burst. "I knew it! Didn't I tell you this was all a set up! I talked to six different psychologists and my pastor; they all told me this is what you were up to! I knew this was going to be a bushwhack! I can't believe I bought two plane tickets and wasted my money on this!"

My sister shot a look in my direction to see if I was serious. My brother shook his head in unbelief, not knowing how this all unfolded. Much to my surprise, my dad took control over his wife, placing his hand on her thigh as an act of authority to silence her. She instantly turned to him and shut up. My dad, looking across the room at me, nodded for me to continue.

I got in my oversized purse, pulled out an 8 x 11 picture frame and showed it to my mother.

"Look Mom, I framed it! Mind you, I did change the color in your email to red, it just seemed more appropriate. I will proudly display this in my house for my children to see what I have rescued them from. All they will ever have to do is read the email you sent me and they will know why all ties were broken. I will tell them how the Lord has blessed us with a new heritage and legacy."

My mom's eyes were like sharp daggers, shooting me with her wrath in an effort to communicate her loathing. Remarkably enough, she managed to keep the smile on her face as she glared at me. Never had anyone crossed her like this before, but, alas, I was still not finished. Bringing up an event that my brother had no knowledge of, I tell of what took place while his kids were under my mother's care.

Looking in the direction of my mother, I continued. "As much as I don't like labels, it seems to fit the way this family operates. When you were watching your grandchildren about three years ago, I couldn't believe what you did to them. While they were all sitting around your dinner table, unprovoked, you took turns degrading them. In what you classify as your duty, you began telling each one of them what you thought of them. One was an underhanded sneak, one was a tattle-teller, one a manipulator, and the other boy you emasculated by telling him he was the baby whiner of the family. Sneering, you actually called my sister and me bragging at how you put all of them in their place. Then, of all things, you proudly told us that the kids all turned on each other and began to call each other names and agreed with the labels you placed on them. They all got such a kick out of watching their siblings get an unwarranted verbal annihilation from their grandmother. Their attack on each other brought you such pleasure. What kind of grandmother does something like that and then brags about it? If you noticed, you were never allowed to be alone with my kids after such horrible conduct."

It was my brother's turn to look angrily in my mother's direction. My mom had not broken her fierce stare at me. She was chomping at the bit to begin her verbal massacre. Continuing to shake her head at me, she was seething that I exposed that little secret to her son.

There only remained one more item on my list that needed to be covered. Refusing to cower in her presence, I avowed, "You fancy yourself the spiritual matriarch of this family. Well, I believe you are carrying a mantle all right; it is the one grandma passed down to you."

Looking now at my sister, I warned, "Make no mistake, it will be passed down again to someone, but not to me or my children! I will have nothing to do with this family."

To my utter surprise, my mom again smiled and nodded her head in agreement that the mantle was not only passed down to her from her wicked mother, but would, in turn, be passed down again to one of her daughters. Out of all her reactions during the meeting, this was the only one that shocked me. I expected her to deny such a mantle existed, not acknowledge it, and nod in agreement that she will pass it down.

Now for the final crescendo to the performance, I executed the grand finale. "As promised, you will all have the opportunity to speak, but I won't be here to listen. There is absolutely nothing you can say to me that I would consider listening to."

With that said, I jumped up, grabbed my purse and headed for the door. Before leaving, I looked at my father for a last farewell. The other members of the family unleashed their rage as the room ignited in an all-out verbal explosion! My dad and I met eyes and I mouthed to him. "This is because of you. Why didn't you just leave me alone when I asked you to?" With a look that he appeared to understand, he nodded once more. That would be the last time I would ever see my father.

While rushing for the door, I heard their riotous proclamations. "That's not fair! You get back here! You can't leave; we're not done with you yet!"

I heard Jerry instantaneously beginning his counterstrike. In an angry firm tone, he shouted over their voices. "When she says she doesn't want anymore contact, she means it! No phone calls, text messages, emails, visitations, nothing! You leave her alone!"

In what I herald as "stupid on steroids" my brother retorted back. "Oh no, we don't have to listen to you. You stay out of it!" OK, now what kind of imbecile tells the husband of the woman he molested that he doesn't have a right to speak? Yep, that would be my brother!

The screeching yell of their voices made its way out to the elevator lobby. I could hear the heated volcanic ramblings while I waited for the elevator to reach the tenth floor. Finally, the door opened; I rushed in, quickly tapping repeatedly the "first floor" button. I anxiously kept pushing the button until the door closed. There was an insurmountable quantity of adrenaline rushing through my veins. I had an unmistakable sense of exhilaration as I recapped in my mind what had just taken place. Holy crud, I did it! I said everything I wanted to say! I thanked the Lord for giving me the strength and courage to go through with it.

I dashed across the street to my friend Stacey who wanted to be there for support. She gave me a quick hug, and we both got in her car waiting for Jerry to arrive. My body was trembling from the adrenaline rush as I began to fill Stacey in on the details. In less than five minutes, we both saw Jerry walking fast in our direction. I gave Stacey another hug, thanked her profusely, and then jumped out of her car and into my own. Jerry was visibly agitated with what had happened after I left. In an expected twist, without me even being there, God was still working on my behalf. And, come to find out, He had saved His best for last!

CHAPTER TWENTY-SIX

Unconditional Love

Jerry seemed to be on an adrenaline rush of his own. In swift execution, our car went in reverse, making our escape out of the parking lot. Turning with a smile, he said, "Well, I don't think you'll hear from them again."

I wanted the details so bad, I could scream. Laughing I said, "Why, what did you do?"

"After you left, your brother actually had the audacity to tell me I wasn't allowed to speak. When he said that, I jumped to my feet, pointed my finger at him and began shouting, '*Well then let's hear from you! Why don't you answer Veronica's question from last week. If your son did to your daughter the very same things that you did to Veronica, what would you think about that?*'"

"The question took him completely off guard. He began stammering, looking at Dr. Storm. He knew he couldn't deny what he did to you, after admitting he molested you last week in front of Dr. Storm. He just looked down at his feet. While he was trying to figure out what to say, I blasted, '*If your son said to your daughter, "This is how I go down on you, would that be OK with you?*"' He still didn't answer me, so I screamed, '*If he said, "This is the missionary position," would <u>that</u> be OK with you?*'"

"Oh my heavens Jerry, did you really say that in front of my parents? What in the world did they do?"

"Your brother was completely shaken, still stuttering. Your parents finally stopped yelling, then looked at your brother for an answer. So I continued demanding a response. I blared, *'Answer Veronica's question. If your son told your daughter, "This is called 69."* I waited, still no response. Then I yelled, *"What if you son told your daughter, "This is anal sex?" What would you say if you found out he did that?'* He still wouldn't respond. His eyes remained firmly fixated on the floor. He wouldn't even look up. So then I yelled, *'If your son did the unthinkable to your daughter, hour after hour, day after day, having her never know when he would stop, would that be fine with you?'"*

I sat listening in disbelief as Jerry itemized each grotesque violation my brother had done to me. I could hardly believe he had said those things in front of my family. Still amped up, I asked, "What did my brother say?"

"Nothing, so I kept demanding he answer your question."

"You actually said those things? I mean, literally explicitly detailed them?"

"Yes. Remember, before the meeting I asked if there were any parameters that you wanted me to stay within, and you said no. As far as I am concerned, I think he needs to answer for what he did to you. All you ever say is 'molested.' That is such a broad term. I wanted him to know that I knew exactly what he did to you and for the rest of your family to know too. I wanted to make sure they know who it is that will be passing the mashed potatoes at Thanksgiving!"

Now I was the one visibly shaken. I could hardly comprehend my husband being so explicit and, of all things, in front of my parents! Still laughing I asked, "What did my parents do? What was my sister doing while all of this was going on?"

"At first they were too stunned to speak. Your mom was glaring at your brother in disbelief. Then she demanded, *'Is that true? Did you do that to her?'* Your brother didn't say a word. He didn't deny having done any of it to you. He simply wouldn't answer them. Your dad was your dad. He didn't say anything. Your sister still looked confused but not horrified. Anyway, I kept insisting he answer your question, but all he could do was stumble over words. He looked like a little kid getting into trouble as I named a sexual position or act.

But, this is where it gets unbelievable. Your brother, unwilling to respond, looked at Dr. Storm, pointed his finger and yelled, 'You! What kind of doctor are you? You have no right setting me up like this!' Then, just as you predicted, it was complete mayhem. They all turned on Dr. Storm and began yelling at him at the top of their lungs. 'You should be ashamed of yourself! What right do you have being part of something like this?'"

Horrified for Dr. Storm, I squealed, "Oh my gosh! What did Dr. Storm do? That poor man, I knew they would turn on him."

"Don't worry; I didn't even give Dr. Storm a chance to reply. I just started yelling at them, *'Leave him alone; he didn't know anything about this! He didn't set this up! We did!'* That had absolutely no impact on them. They continued to rant and move towards the door with your mother in the lead."

Connecting some mental dots, I asked, "Let me get this straight. You had just told them exactly what their son did to me. Their son doesn't deny it. They know he was in that office only last week, so if you were making it up, Dr. Storm would have defended him. Even with all of that, they aren't mad at him? They are only mad at Dr. Storm? That's crazy! What on earth are they going to do with that information anyway? After everything they heard, they think their son is the one violated here and Dr. Storm is the one who should be ashamed, really? Then what happened?"

"After I told them to back off, your mom looked at your dad and told him they were leaving. I stepped up and said, 'No, I'm leaving, and I am not to see you in the lobby!' Surprisingly, she stepped back and told me to leave and that they would wait. So I took off."

"You left them with Dr. Storm? That's hilarious! I wonder what happened after you were out of the office."

"I don't know; I'm sure he can handle them"

"Oh, really? I wouldn't be too sure. No one can handle my family!"

We drove home to pick up our unsuspecting children for a weekend getaway. When we had scheduled the session with my family, we were concerned that they might show up on our doorstep wanting to continue the insane dialogue. To protect our kids from this potential visit, we took them out of state for a few days to let the dust settle down. Jerry had to be there on business anyway, so we went along for the ride. On the drive to our destination, we began the excruciating task of filling them in on the last several months of my counseling. It was one of the most heartbreaking moments in my life. To tell my children about my past, my family and all the sick inner dealings was chilling.

For my children to realize that they really didn't know their mom's history was painful for both sides. It went as well as could be expected. I began by telling them that we had just been with Grandma and Papa and their aunt and uncle. Right when I said that, one of my daughter's faces turned to shock. Noticing her immediate reaction, I asked her what was wrong. She wanted to know if I had reconciled, which meant she was going to have to be with her grandmother. It was an unforeseeable confirmation that I had made the right choice for severing ties. I looked at her and said, "No, Honey, it was the opposite. We told them that they were never to bother us again. I said my goodbyes to my family."

She threw her head back on her seat with a sigh of relief. It was a sad, telling moment.

We drove for close to five hours, and Michele was anxiously awaiting my phone call to fill her in on the session. We finally arrived to our hotel at midnight, but I decided not to call her. She was away on business in another time zone, with a three-hour time difference. It was 3:00 am where she was. My phone rang, and, of course, it was Michele.

"I'll fill you in tomorrow, you need to sleep."

"I can't possibly sleep Veronica! I have been waiting for six hours for you to be able to talk. I'm not hanging up until you tell me what happened."

In our usual way, we talked, laughed and cried all in the same conversation.

She was thrilled I had been brave enough to go through with it. After telling her all the graphic details that Jerry exposed, she was horrified at my parent's reaction, or lack thereof. She inquired, "Jerry actually detailed what your brother did and they don't yell at him, they yell at Dr. Storm? What kind of freaks are they?"

"I know, but I feel guilty for leaving Dr. Storm with them. I don't think he fully appreciated what they were capable of."

"Oh, Dr. Storm is a big boy; he can take care of himself. You don't need to worry about him. I'm glad you won't ever have to see your family again. Do you think they will actually not contact you?"

"They have to live the lie, Michele. They will never get back in touch with me. I will be a reminder of what kind of family they really are. Nope, I am dead to them." We talked for close to one-and-a-half hours. Exhausted from the day's events, I thanked her for loving and supporting me the way she does. We said our goodnights, and I went fast to sleep.

The morning arrived, and my body actually hurt from what went on the day before. Regrettably, sleep had not given my body the repair I so desperately desired. I had lain in bed reviewing my performance in Dr. Storm's office. Everything went as planned; I was free from my family. This realization resonated into the reality of what was now my life. Contemplating what Jerry had said to my brother, I inwardly chuckled at how it all came together. Then like a flash of lightening whose charge electrified me, I sat straight up in my bed and burst, "Wait a minute! How did Jerry know what my brother did to me?" I told Dr. Storm in that early session, I would never let those words leave my mouth. I would take what he did to me to my grave and I meant it! It was frustrating to me that Jerry was in meetings all day. I would have to wait until late that night to talk with him.

Trying not to dwell on it, I got up and told my kids to get ready for the pool. While basking in the sun, I watched them have fun cooling off in the river pool. Being alone for the first time, my heart began to sink. It was so necessary for me to be on an emotional high for the confrontation. The adrenaline served as a heavy dose of empowerment. It was equally as necessary to have it wear off and face the truth— my parents defended my brother. They heard me outline in clear detail the events of my childhood and all my mom did was scribble on the ridiculous notepad of hers. I never saw sorrow or compassion from her. I only felt distain. You would have thought my dad was watching some boring program on TV with the lack of expression he had on his face during my disclosures. Why didn't any one of them instinctively smack my brother in disgust? How could they be so controlled and unwilling to come to my defense?

To assume you have little value in a family is one thing; to have it confirmed is something else entirely. Then sudden fear gripped me with the knowledge they were left alone with Dr. Storm. I have always kept them safely tucked away from any other contacts in my life. They destroy whatever they touch in my life. I knew, at the very least, my mom would have tried to spin a web of deception, and rewrite the past events for Dr. Storm. They would have re-buttals to my claims knowing I was not there to defeat them. They were always so convincing and alluring in their tales of perfection. Would he see through their lies, or would he be like the rest of the unsuspecting listeners and believe in their spiritual superiority? If that was the case, they would advise him on how to correct my ways and send me back in repentance. This method of operation had been successful many times before. These thoughts tormented me, and I was unable to move past them.

Finally, at around eleven, Jerry returned to our room for the night. While lying in bed, we both discussed the clamorous behavior of my family from the night before. Jerry, still elated on how it went, said, "I would love to have been a fly in your parent's car for that drive back to the hotel. How do you go back to business as usual after that? And what in the world is your brother going to tell his wife about what happened? Somehow, he will have to explain to his children why we are no longer in their lives. How can he possibly spin this one?"

Somewhat changing the subject, with deep seeded curiosity, I had to ask Jerry how he knew what my brother did to me the summer I was eleven. A bit apprehensively, I said, "I don't understand how you knew what to describe to my brother. All of sexual positions and acts—I have never told anyone. Last night I was on such a rush; it didn't have a chance to sink in. The fact that I never told you what he did didn't hit me until today. How did you know?"

Jerry's tone changed dramatically. No longer elation, he then conveyed a more serious manner. "I prayed."

Those two words floated in the air, circling above my intellect. Trying hard to grasp the revelation, I pleaded, "What? You prayed?"

"Yeah, after you confronted your brother, and he was so cavalier about the subject, I just couldn't let it go. You were so unwilling to be graphic in your depiction of what he did to you. You would only use words like 'molest' and 'violate.' Those are so vague and can be easily misconstrued for smaller acts like '*you show me yours and I'll show you mine.*' I have seen your night tremors and I have been a firsthand witness to the after-effects of what he did to you. I knew it was so much more then that. I couldn't stand the fact that he thought he got away with it. You weren't going to tell anyone the violations that happened to you in that home. You wouldn't even tell Dr. Storm."

With determination in his voice, he continued. "So, I prayed. I asked God to allow me to be your voice. If you weren't able to speak for yourself, then I wanted to have the privilege of speaking for you. In an instant, it came to me what he did to you. Veronica, someone had to hold him accountable, and as your husband, it was my honor to do so."

With the gross feeling of abandonment that I had experienced poolside, at that moment I was engulfed in pure love and protection. I had never been as deeply connected with my husband as I was in that moment. But, with as much comfort I felt from him, I couldn't help but feel betrayed by God. No one was to know what happened to me. That was my story to tell, and I had decided not to tell it. The unpacking of those details made me feel dirty and blemished for the world to see. I know "molest' and "violate" are indistinct terms—I chose them because they were. Because God took it upon Himself to tell my secret, my husband, Dr. Storm, and the entire family knew the details. On the surface, this seemed like such a betrayal. Why would He do such a thing? Just when I had concluded God loved me and was trustworthy, He talks behind my back. In my deepest conviction, I was thoroughly convinced God loved me, so what am I missing?

My next appointment with Dr. Storm was not for another four days. They would prove to be the longest four days in my life. I desperately wanted to know what happened after Jerry left his office. Did my family woo him to their camp? Hearing what happened to me when I was eleven, would he be able to look me in the eye? I was only able to go into his office week after week because he didn't know the details. Now that he knew, I was so ashamed. Despair gripped me in the awful way that only despair can do.

Eventually, the day had arrived for the follow-up session with Dr. Storm. I informed Jerry that I needed to go alone. As I sat in his waiting room, my heart had a flurry of butterflies once more. I envisioned him coming out with my file, telling me it was great to have worked with me and then escort me out the door. I was sure he wouldn't want to have any more sessions with me after my family got through with him. All hell broke loose in his office, and I was the reason it did. He probably thought enough was enough. Fearing rejection and disapproval, I continued to wait.

Hearing footsteps, I looked up to see him approach. With an expansive smile, he greeted me.

"Hi Veronica! I've got one question for you: *Are you adopted?*"

Laughing in complete relief, I gushed, "No, I'm not adopted."

A little more serious, he asked, "Are you sure? Have you ever seen your birth records or had a DNA test?"

Knowing that he was serious, I said, "Oh my gosh, that is the nicest thing anyone has ever said to me! I can assure you, I'm not adopted. I really am a part of that family."

"Well, I have been going over this in my mind all weekend. It just doesn't make sense to me. You don't look like them, and you most certainly don't act like them. The only logical conclusion that I could come up with was you must be adopted."

We entered his office and took our seats. The fear that he thought I was one of them had quickly evaporated into thin air. Not wanting to wait one second longer to know what took place after we left, I asked him to spill. He gladly obliged.

"I'm sure Jerry filled you in on how explosive it got in here. It was like being in the midst of a pack of angry jackals. They looked like a bunch of wild animals circling their prey. You had warned me about them, but you almost have to see it to believe it. They were furious!"

"I really am sorry for leaving you like that. I have been worried all weekend how it ended up."

"Oh, I was fine. After Jerry left, they had calmed down a little, so I told them I would be happy to help them sort out some of the issues. Your mom barked, 'You are the last one we want to talk to.' Your dad was funny to watch. He really only does what he sees his wife do. He followed her lead and angrily said, 'Yeah, that's right. We don't want to listen to you.' Your sister was a sight to see. She looked completely baffled. She just kept staring at everyone. I kept waiting for her to dial in, but she never did. She let your mom do all the talking. They all filed out of my office after that. Jerry had told them not to follow him to the elevators, so they just lingered in my waiting room for some time to pass. I was going to go talk to them, I turned for the door, and lo and behold, your mom had come into my office. All I could think was, 'Veronica said her mom would get me alone, and she did.'"

"Oh gosh, what did she do?"

"She thrust her hand into the air and bellowed, 'Validate these!' She was holding all three of their parking tickets in her hand. You are right; she didn't want to spend a dime on this thing. Anyway, I took the tickets, turned to reach into my desk for the validation stamps, and when I turned back, she began her rant. She was completely furious. She pointed her index finger at me and began wagging it in my face. Her eyes narrowed, her nose crinkled and she said in a scowling tone, 'I want you to know my daughter is evil. She lied about us letting her have older boyfriends when she was a young teen. She was a sneak then, and she is a sneak to this day.' When she said that, I burst out in laughter. I couldn't believe she was doing exactly what you said she would do. You nailed it! I continued laughing and said, 'Veronica said you would say that!' That really sent your mom over the edge. She grunted and looked at me totally enraged"

Continuing, Dr. Storm said, with a smirk on his face, "I said to her, 'So now let me get this straight. Your daughter knows you better than you know yourself, and I know your daughter better than you do.' It was great! She grunted again and reached up for the parking tickets. I held my hand over my head and said I would be happy to deliver them myself. You're right, she's small, but she is mighty."

A little repentant, he continued. "I think I owe you an apology for what I did next. I went out to the other three standing there and handed over the parking passes. Then I told them, 'You all have some decisions to make. You no longer have Veronica as your sacrificial lamb in this family. She is dead to you. You are to leave her alone forever. However, without her, which one of you will take her place? You will have to choose another person to blame and that must scare you, since you all know what you are capable of. I would encourage you to choose wisely. The label seems to stick for a very long time.' After I said that, they all left the waiting room in a huff. I really am sorry if I crossed the line. I was just so angry after what they did to you."

"Are you kidding me? You don't owe me an apology; you're my freaking hero! Jerry defends me to my brother and you defend me against my mother. That is amazing! Thank you so much for standing up for me."

"All I can say Veronica: your mom is one scary woman! You predicted it exactly right. They did everything you said they would do. Never in a million years could I come up with how your mom would get me alone, but she did."

"Yeah, the part I like best is, she landed on the thing that can easily be proved. Everyone knew my parents were aware of my boyfriends. For my sixteenth birthday party, they were the ones who contacted my college-age boyfriend to get me out of the house for the surprise. Of all the things she could have tried to dispute, she chose the worst one!"

Dr. Storm then asked, "How are you doing? Aren't you proud of yourself for confronting each of them? You were magnificent. When you pulled out your framed email, it was hard not to laugh. I thought, 'she actually brought a prop!' That was great."

Laughing, I said, "That was Jerry's favorite part too. He had no idea I had framed it and packed it in my purse."

Changing direction slightly, I inquired, "What do you think my brother is doing about all of this? Now that it's out in the open, how can he possibly explain his behavior to them?"

"Actually, when I was waiting for them to leave, I over-heard him talking to the other members of your family. He told them that after he came here last week, he contacted someone from his church to talk about it. They both decided it wasn't a big deal. It was common for brothers to be curious and cross the line. It was no different than playing 'post office.'"

I didn't see that one coming. Too astounded to speak, I sat looking puzzled in Dr. Storm's direction. Gathering my thoughts, I said, "He said that to them? That it was no big deal? Apparently, he didn't clue the person into everything he did. How could someone in the church have the nerve to tell him it was nothing to feel bad about? Obviously, my brother left out the parts about him being a pervert through my entire teen years. I guess he inadvertently didn't mention coming into my room when he was an adult! I swear, some people are so messed up! I guarantee the only thing my brother will bring away from this experience is, not what I said—or what Jerry said, but what that mindless idiot told him when he didn't bother to get all of the details."

"Well, Jerry did a great job letting them know it was a big deal and not just some childish sexual curiosity."

"Yeah, about that...," Now a little awkward and embarrassed I asked, "Why do you think God would tell Jerry what happened between my brother and me ?"

Dr. Storm was noticeably confused. Trying to understand, he asked, "What do you mean?"

Looking down, I continued, "Jerry told me everything he said to my brother, and then later I asked him how he knew."

"Wait, are you telling me you didn't tell Jerry what your brother did?"

"Of course I didn't tell him. I told you from the start that I would never allow those words to come out of my mouth."

"Then I don't understand: how did Jerry know?"

With as much astonishment as the first time I heard it, I answered. "He said he prayed."

Dropping his pen and my file on the floor, Dr. Storm's expression changed from inquisitive to shock. As if in slow motion, I watched the pen bounce across the office floor. Getting my attention, he said, "He prayed? That's how he knew?"

403

"Yeah, I would have NEVER told him. I meant it when I said I would take it to my grave. You said that it was my story to tell. I didn't want anyone to know. Now both you and Jerry know. Why do you think God did that?"

Dr. Storm couldn't quite seem to get words out of his mouth. He still appeared puzzled trying to compute what he just heard. Composing himself he finally said, "I don't really know for sure. Perhaps He was trying to get your brother's attention. None of us knew the extent he took the molestation. When Jerry was listing the positions, you should have seen your brother's face. He was aghast at what Jerry had the nerve to say in front of everyone. Clearly, Jerry wasn't off base. I would imagine if he didn't do any of the things Jerry accused him of, he would have blown his top! He wouldn't have been silently looking down at his feet.

God was probably trying to wake him up."

"So you're telling me I needed to take one for the team? God would go against my wishes and humiliate me for the sake of my brother? That doesn't make sense to me. I have been taking one for the team for years. I trusted God with my secret. I just can't imagine why He told Jerry."

"I don't really know, but you know there has to be a reason, Veronica. Let me ask you something. Why didn't you want it to come out? Your brother should have to answer for what he did."

With my head down and my eyes burning with tears, I whispered, "You and Jerry were never to know. Don't you see? I can't stand the two of you knowing what he did." Looking back up, I said, "It's all so humiliating."

I wish Dr. Storm's facial expression could be frozen in time. With eyes full of compassion and an appearance of kindness I had never seen before, he implored, "Oh Veronica, don't you know that made me love you even more? My heart literally broke as I heard the horrible things your brother did to you. You did nothing to deserve that. Jerry and I were honored to have defended you. There is absolutely no reason for you to be ashamed."

With tears still streaming down my cheeks, I looked at him wondering if it could be true. Then, in that moment, I was able to understand why God exposed the secret of that summer so long ago. Not only did He think I, His daughter, was worth avenging, He wanted to show unconditional love through the only two men I trusted: my husband and my psychologist. For the first time in my life, one of my secrets was wholly known, and, to my utter surprise, I wasn't rejected. Then the thought hit me, *you can never be fully loved until you are fully known.*

I would have lived my life with the wrong notion that the only reason my husband stayed with me was that he didn't know what actually took place in my home. I would have also concluded that Dr. Storm's motive for defending me, or being willing to be in my presence at all, was because he also had no mental picture of those events. Now, with both of them knowing, he tells me that it only made them love me more.

God's love about knocked me off my seat! Over the years, in my efforts to protect myself, I had guarded myself from not only not allowing people to hurt me, but also never allowing people to know me. I realized I was my own worst enemy. For the first time in my life, I grasped what real love was.

Yes, eighteen months ago, I had asked God to partner with me for the miraculous. I had no clue what I was in for. I can honestly say, there is nothing more miraculous than discovering God's unconditional love. There is no chasm too wide or too deep that God's love cannot fill. Now that's what I call redemption!

CHAPTER TWENTY-SEVEN

Box on the Top Shelf

Several days had passed since my last session with Dr. Storm. He had mentioned as I left his office that his job was almost complete. Now that I had confronted my family, he felt the counseling sessions were nearing an end. I smiled and told him how greatly I appreciated all he had done for me. He reiterated that he had not done much. He felt God was the One charting the path. He was just thrilled to have come along for the ride.

He still had no knowledge of the rest of my inventory. I knew I must go back to my storage room once more. The ominous, beautifully wrapped container was calling out to me. I wanted to mask the inner voices by diving back into a busy schedule to quiet its summoning. Silently begging God to let it remain, I walked in and looked up to my top shelf. There it sat, so striking in appearance and yet so evil in content. I knew what I must do; I had come too far to turn back. The four-step process needed to be carried out on this package, as it was with the rest.

In extreme distress, heart pounding, palms sweaty, I stood on my tippy-toes reaching for the container. Dreadfully, with tremendous caution, I lifted up the lid, carefully placing it on the table before me. My hands were shaking as I reached in to remove each artifact with watchful precision. As I peered down at the table, my heart broke recalling that frightful day. Each article was as I had remembered it to be. They were dark, evil relics that no child should have had to place in her inventory.

Unlike before, I was not angry with God for having to review the contents of this box. I had come to understand and even appreciate the process. I knew the revealing portion would be to my benefit. I picked up the phone to make an appointment with Dr. Storm. I would have Jerry join me in the session. He had every right to be there.

The next day, with great consternation, I walked into Dr. Storm's office with Jerry by my side. Although we began our session in the usual manner, instead of Dr. Storm continuing, survival kicked in and I took control. I informed both Dr. Storm and Jerry that I had another container that I needed to unpack. I had rehearsed in my mind the contents of the box, and I knew how to present them without crumbling.

"OK, I have another box that I need to unpack. But, before we begin, I need to give you both directions on how this needs to be done. I also need you to agree to some terms, or I will not be able to go through with it."

Looking at Jerry, who was sitting on my left, I began, "What I am going to tell you will be very painful to hear. It is about something that happened to me when I was around five years old. I don't care how emotional I get; I don't want you to reach out to comfort me. What I am going to talk about is evil, and I don't want your touch associated with it, OK?" Jerry looked anxious but nodded his head in agreement.

"Now, Dr. Storm, I will unpack the box and be very detailed about what happened. I don't want you to ask me many questions at the end. If you think there is something that I still need to address, you can ask me. If at any time I wish for you to stop, I must insist that you do. Do you agree with those conditions?"

Dr. Storm was looking at me with concern. "Yes, I will respect your conditions."

In an unwavering tone, I began. "OK, now this last one is really important. I will talk about this today, but I do not intend to discuss this after our session. As far as I am concerned, I will reveal what is in the box, go through the necessary dealing step of the process and then I will be through. It will be for me to handle. I need you both to promise that you will not ask me questions after today. Will you two promise me that?"

Jerry, unable to speak, nodded his head. Dr. Storm intently looked at me with his eyes slightly narrowed , tilted his head a bit, and then reluctantly agreed. "Yes Veronica, if that is how you want to handle it. I won't mention it after today."

Nervously, I began the unpacking process. "When I was around five years old, my parents moved us to Missouri." Chuckling I said, "You will have to see the irony in this, they were going to help start a church. Anyway, we lived in a house that was near a construction site. They were building homes and all the kids on the street use to play there when the workers weren't there. The dirt is different in Missouri than it is in California. After the rains, the ground would dry and then it would begin to lift and crack. It somewhat resembles puzzle pieces. As children, we would love to try to pick up the pieces without having them break in our hands. It was a mindless game that would kill several hours in an afternoon. I was too young to go there by myself; I was only allowed to go if my brother or sister went with me."

Slowing in my presentation, I looked down at my hands that were clasped together as if holding onto life itself. My knuckles were white, while, subconsciously, my hands were wringing back and forth in some form of a twisted dance. Breathing had become an act of labor, as I began to unpack the gruesome part of the contents. What words was I to use to describe such an event? How was I to relay the evil thrust onto me without warning? Trying to formulate my next sentence, I looked up to see them both staring attentively in my direction. Assuring myself that it would be over soon, I continued in my controlled state.

"So, one day, my friend and I joined the other kids on the street to go play at the housing site. It was a rather large area, with houses that only had their foundations and framework completed. Every street was in various stages of construction. It was fun to play in the houses, but we had to be careful of the building materials, especially the nails. My friend and I separated ourselves out and ran off to another part of the construction site. We found a house that had its framework complete and began to frolic around inside. There were sacks of concrete lining the streets with the white powder residue filling the air. We danced and laughed while playing in one of the rooms."

"While dancing, I looked out and saw a group of

teenage boys on their bikes riding towards us. We weren't supposed to have been by ourselves. I quickly glanced around to see if any of the other kids we were playing with were anywhere around. Frantically I was looking down the street, knowing no one knew where we were. My friend and I stood perfectly still as we watched the boys approach. One by one, they got off their bikes, throwing them down in the dirt beside the house. At first, they were just talking to us, teasing us at having seen us dance. I remember being very afraid in that moment; I just wanted to go home. My friend and I began to jump down off the foundation of the home, but a few of the boys blocked us. I guess that's when I knew."

Stopping to catch my breath, I refused to look at either of the men in the room. My hands were still wringing, my knuckles were still white, and my mind was taking control over my heart. In a very logical manner, I refused to give in to the inner pleading of my heart to make this all stop. Only looking at my hands, intertwined in some artful contortion, they appeared as an outward display of an inward condition. The evil mental images were rallying together, vying to be heard.

"My friend began to cry when they wouldn't let us leave; I didn't. They somewhat corralled us to the center of the house, standing in a circle around us. They demanded both of us undress in front of them, and, all I could think of was, I don't want to step on a nail. My friend was hysterical, but, for some reason, I wasn't. I guess you know what happened next. However, let me be clear, none of them actually raped us."

411

Then like a newscaster reporting on a felony that took place so long ago, I began to describe in systematic detail the unthinkable acts that each one of the teen boys performed on us. With each word and every sentence that came out of my mouth, I grew increasingly unattached to the events of that horrendous day.

My neck was aching from the stress of the moment. It was in a locked position looking down at my hands, still contorted in their dance. Continuing, I reported, "A mob mentality kicked in, and they began goading each other to take it to the next level. While one was assaulting us, the other boys actually laughed while waiting for their turn." Unlocking my head from its fixed position, I looked up and asked in a factual way, "I can't imagine laughing while a child is being attacked, can you?" It wasn't as much a question as it was a comment. Not waiting for a response and returning my eyes back down to my lap, I continued.

"When they were done, they told us to get dressed. My poor friend was at her end. I, on the other hand, just bent down, picked up my clothes and got dressed standing up. I was literally hopping around trying to get my pants on. I refused to sit down; I was terrified of the nails. Then, what to me at the time was one of the worst offenses, they laughed, watching me get dressed. They thought it was hysterical to see me hopping around, unwilling to sit."

"After we got dressed, they told us to go home and never tell anyone what happened. We both swore we wouldn't, so they stepped back from the circle and that gave us an opening to escape. We both ran as if our lives depended on it towards our homes. She lived right next door to me. As promised, neither one of us told our parents."

In kind of an afterthought, I said, "Do you know what? I still hate the smell of powder-dry cement. The scent always takes me back to that day."

I sat breathless, feeling as though there was a heavy fog in the room. My mind was roaming aimlessly. It kept trying to find a mentally safe place to land. Instead, it was stuck in the crowded maze of my memories, wanting desperately to get back to my storage room. In there, it was safe and sterile with every event housed in its own container. All of the beautiful packaging allowed me to enter without dread. I had to return this awful container. It needed to be placed up on the top shelf where it could do no harm. In my quest for freedom, I thought I had made a crucial mistake. I shouldn't have unpacked that box. The collateral damage was significant. I was psychologically and emotionally unable to carry its weight. My survival instincts were in a hyper-state, with the "fight/flight" inclination in high gear.

I returned the package to the top shelf, and I once more was in control. This event needed to be contained; I would not give it the power to break me. Regrettably, that meant I had to diminish the true caliber of pain it inflicted on me. If I placed it in a "manageable" category on my inventory control sheet, than perhaps that would convince me it actually was manageable. Back in complete charge of my emotions and mental state for the first time, I looked at Jerry and Dr. Storm to examine their reactions. I had to insist that they stick to my terms.

They were both adhering to my conditions precisely. Jerry was sitting motionless, afraid to move. I looked in his direction, maintaining a controlled exterior and relented. "That's it. That's all I have to say, I'm finished."

Jerry asked permission to reach out to me; I told him it would be OK. I untangled my fingers and reached across to take Jerry's hand. I can tell this package and its contents were more than he could bear as well. Carefully choosing his words, he said, in a sorrowful inflection, "That's awful. I'm so sorry that happened to you. That must have been horrifying."

I offered a slight smile in an effort to let him know I was alright.

Dr. Storm asked permission to ask me some questions.

I answered, "Yes, but you have to stop when I tell you to, OK?"

His questions probed into the events of that day. Mostly he inquired about the lack of emotions that I professed having at the time of the violation. "Are you sure you weren't crying? Why do you think you didn't cry? Did your parents ever find out? Did you ever see those boys again? Were you still friends with your neighbor after that day? Did the two of you ever discuss what happened?"

I answered each one concisely not leaving any of his questions unanswered. He appeared unsatisfied with my lack of emotion. He knew my masterful ability to emotionally disconnect. With that in mind, he went deeper, in what I assume was his attempt to have me come to terms with what happened. I refused to go there emotionally, but I could mentally engage in conversation. Many of the other questions were concerning my friend: did I know her name, did we keep in contact, and so on. While scribbling in my file, he began to ask one more time about the fact that I did-n't cry that day, but I stopped him before he could finish. At that point, I was tired of answering the same question.

Fatigued, I told him, "I don't know why I didn't cry, I really don't. I do remember thinking that I wouldn't give them the satisfaction of seeing me cry. For some reason, I thought at the time it would have been embarrassing. They were all laughing at my friend and me. I tried to show them I wasn't scared. I really can't explain it."

I felt beaten and exhausted. I refused to give any more time to this demoralizing container. I asserted, "OK, I'm through. I don't want to talk about this anymore. You both need to keep your promise at not mentioning this ever again. You'll do that, right?"

They caught the eye of each other, then looked my way and gave me their assurances. We continued the session, keeping a discreet distance from that subject matter. Honestly, my mind was gone. I had no recollection of what we talked about after that. We set another appointment on the calendar. As I got up to leave, it felt as though there were three hundred pound weights on each one of my legs. The box might have been placed back on the shelf, but it was hardly finished with me yet.

After several days, I could still see the assault playing out on the TV screen of my mind. It was as though I was looking down on the framed house, hovering over it, wit-nessing it repeatedly. I would think, *Those poor girls. Why won't anyone help them? Why didn't at least one of those boys come to their defense?* I was disgusted with humanity's ca-pacity to commit evil.

Although I hadn't thought about the assault in years, I remembered it with such clarity. But, even with the vivid recollection, I still felt no emotional attachment to it. About a week had passed since the unveiling and something seemed terribly wrong. I went from *Conceal* to *Reveal*: why was I not in the *Dealing* portion yet? I had been down this road before, and it wasn't supposed to be this calm. I should have been in the thick of it emotionally by then.

When it came to my healing, I had an insatiable appetite. I would not be denied my freedom. Concerned that the package still had some hold on me, I began the mental task of retracing my steps to see where I had gotten off course. Due to the late hour, my family had long since gone to bed. I did mental gymnastics, endeavoring to have my lack of emotion make sense to me. After several unfruitful hours, I had the brainstorm to pray. I had to place that into the "better late than never" column. Pleading with the Lord as to why it wasn't working this time, I got a revelation. I found myself concluding, "God can't take something from me that I don't own." It occurred to me, unlike when I had seen my other flashbacks, with this event, I saw the two girls as just that: two girls. I wouldn't allow myself to own the harsh reality that one of the girls was me.

The epiphany left me breathless. Not only had I been able to emotionally disconnect from this container, I had somehow managed to have it be in some sort of "third person" format. With the speed of lightening and its shocking force, the flashbacks returned. This time, I no longer saw them detached and from above, I looked at them at ground level, through the terrified eyes of a little girl. The attack was barbaric in nature, and it sent me curling into a fetal position on the sofa in my home. Great sobs rose from within me; I cried the tears that hadn't been cried so many years ago. I found myself rocking back and forth pleading, "No, no, please stop" as I begged for mercy from my invisible assailants. The *Dealing* step had begun.

Daylight sprung forth and a new day began. With heaviness of heart, I picked up the phone to call Dr. Storm for an appointment. As always, he adjusted his schedule to make room for me. Jerry returned with me for the session. He could tell that I was in no mood for small talk. We both sat in silence waiting for Dr. Storm to greet us. His approach was pleasant but not at all jovial. He assumed this emergency session was going to be hard for me. We strolled past the water cooler, down the short hallway to his office. I had walked this hallway many times over the past five months.

I have found there to be a certain ebb and flow that comes with counseling. It is best equivalent to being in a river. Sometimes the current is flowing at a slow peaceful pace. Other times it has a tumultuous pull, with white water rapids and sharp rocks that seemingly can cause harm. That is the importance of having the expert on this journey. Dr. Storm had traveled down this river before. I trusted that he would navigate me through the rough waters and get me to the desired destination. That was why I had returned. I feared that I did not have the expertise to unpack this box on my own. I tried it by myself in the last session, but to no avail. That time, although terrified, I would allow him to guide me on the emotional river I had to travel. It would be the only way for me to arrive safely on the other side.

Without engaging in pleasantries, we dove right into the session. This time, I only had one request. I gave Jerry the same instruction that I did last go around. I told him that I did not want his touch to be linked to what I would be talking about. When ready, I would reach out for his physical support. That being the only ground rule to follow, Dr. Storm began the painstaking process of helping me unpack my box. He knew the contents, so he began to coax me into giving the details of that horrifying day. Unlike before, I was not only there physically, but emotionally as well. The images flashed before me, and, in an exercise of futility, I thrust my hands over my eyes as a way of escape. I began to cry uncontrollably and turned my body away from Jerry. I placed my elbows on the arm of the sofa with my neck craned down. I wrapped my arms around my head in an attempt to cover my ears. The internal sounds of laughter from the boys plagued me as I shook my head back and forth in an effort to distract my mind from the assault. It was useless. My eyes were tightly closed, trying to blind myself from the flashbacks of the teenage boys' aggression. I felt the attack with every fiber of my being. I was not going back in time; on the contrary, the past was being brought to the present.

With all of my adult faculties functioning, I cried for the loss of my innocence that took place at a dirty construction site, so close to my home. Cowering on the corner of the sofa, I didn't want to do this alone any longer. I turned my body towards Jerry, and I collapsed into his waiting arms.

With my body trembling and cries coming from the depths of my soul, Jerry wrapped his arms around me trying to give solace. Dr. Storm's words went from inquisition, to words of comfort; we were through the rough waters.

After two long hours, the session was over, and I felt depleted. In the void, an undeniable cleansing had taken place. The ominous box that had been the cause of so much fear had been examined in its entirety. It would take some time, but I knew the vast space that fear once occupied would soon be replaced with peace. I returned the box back to my storage room, complete with its gorgeous wrapping. I paid particular careful attention to its bow, shaping it into an item of beauty. Smiling, I knew it was now ready to be displayed amongst the other packages in my closet. The top shelf that once represented terror was now only a shelf to hold one of my many containers.

With great relief, I knew my counseling sessions were nearing their end. We had scheduled one more appointment; it would be a good-bye of sorts. All the hard work had paid off, I knew I was free. So much had been accomplished in such a short period of time. In less than five months, the landscape of my life had forever been altered. I was cut off from an extended family that caused me much pain. I was cherishing my relationships with my husband and children.

My fragmented personality was continuing to integrate. And, although emotional health was something I desired, I did not think all the pieces had to be back together for that to take place. I was not convinced full integration was possible and, for me, not even preferred. I thought it could possibly be counterproductive. This was the only way I knew how to operate. As for my storage closet, it would remain with me forever. It housed all the artifacts of what makes me who I am. Some good, some bad, they all are welcome and have their place.

A week had passed since my last session. It was the day I visited Dr. Storm for the last time. There weren't many issues to discuss, just tying up some loose ends. Mostly it would be reminiscing about everything that had taken place. I would also take the opportunity to pick his brain on where I go from here. I felt like I was standing in an airport, bags packed, elated to be off on a new adventure. The only thing was, I didn't know where I was supposed to be going. I was eager to start finding a way to help others with what I had learned.

With a bounce in my step, I greeted the security guard standing at his station and entered the elevator. A smile was splashed across my face as I made the climb up to the tenth floor. Dr. Storm came walking out of his office, beaming.

"Veronica! Welcome back. How are you doing?"

Exchanging a quick hug, I gushed, "Great, thanks. How are you?" We engaged in familiar banter, catching each other up on events of the past week.

There was one huge issue I wished to have his help with, so I inquired, "OK, now I'm ready to start rebuilding my life. However, I feel somewhat ill-equipped on the subject of trust. I still have great misgivings when it comes to Christian men in authority. I really do love the church and people in it. But I'm not going to say that they haven't been the cause of some of my pain. I know how to determine whether any other person on the planet is trustworthy, but, when it comes to some of the leaders in church, eesh, they can scare the snot out of me!"

Chuckling at my forthrightness, he advised, "You have been hurt by men in authority. You have every right to be careful. Unfortunately, you are correct about some men in the church. They can misuse their authority and be, as you say, 'bullies with bibles.'"

That was all I needed to hear. My soapbox was out and ready for use. I went full throttle with my complaint. "OK, this has always bugged me. I don't understand the leadership mentality in some churches. My tail feathers get ruffled on what I think is a male-dominated view on women's roles in life and church. It seems to me that many men in the church view women as second-class citizens birthed to be their caretakers."

"Of course, this is only a belief that factors into a church meeting, especially a weekend service. They seem to acknowledge that women can teach men in a secular classroom. It also isn't frowned on if a male has a female boss. But God forbid she have a high position in the church. To have bigotry not only tolerated, but also celebrated seems ridiculous to me. If a female college professor were to give her instruction in class, then when she was finished, go volunteer at church, her options become greatly limited. She may teach children or run a women's meeting. Never should she think she is capable to go to the pulpit where men would have to receive instruction from her. If this type of prejudice were given towards a person because of the color of their skin or ethnic background, the church would be furious! Because it is towards a gender and a few misinterpreted scriptures, they feel totally justified."

Dr. Storm patiently listened to my ramblings. He jumped in when he saw I was finished pleading my case.

"Some churches are the last of the 'Good ol' Boy Clubs.' Don't let that stop you. Many don't feel that way. You can proceed with trusting men, with caution, and follow your instincts. I presume you have an accurate radar when it comes to assessing people. In fact, I bet you can enter a room and within five minutes, you know who is genuine and who you need to stay away from. Am I right?"

"Yep!"

"I thought so; you've needed great instincts to survive. Honestly, Veronica, I would trust your instincts over mine actually. You'll begin to slowly add people to the list of individuals you can trust. I do want you to be careful though. Your list does not need to be long."

Dr. Storm was a leader in his church, and he was one of the safest men I knew. I had to acknowledge that I, too, have prejudices. My assumption that all Christian men can be authoritative bullies was not acceptable, no matter what my background was. It wasn't the slightest bit fair or accurate to have me improperly define most Christian men as male chauvinists. There were many who didn't ascribe to the demeaning views of women. Many Christian men had a healthy view of marriage and the husband's and wife's separate roles. I know that there are a lot of churches which embraced women in their gift of teaching and acknowledged them to be equally anointed to teach the gospel as any man could, to either male or female listeners. So why did I land on the ones which didn't? I still had much work to do in my own heart. When I only looked through the eyes of pain, my vision was blurred at best. It would behoove me to make the changes in my life that I desired in the lives of others.

We had gone on about various subjects for close to one-and-a-half hours. The session had reached its end. Standing up, with a quick hug, we said our heartfelt goodbyes.

"Take care Veronica, and be in touch. I want updates on how you're doing!"

"Thanks, I will, and you do the same!" With that said, I left his office for what I wrongly presumed would be my last visit.

The shadowy box would demand its turn. The worst had yet to come…

CHAPTER TWENTY-EIGHT

Just One More

Four months had passed since my last session with Dr. Storm. In my heart, I knew this moment would come; I just thought I would have had a longer reprieve. I had not wanted to give the shadowy container its rightful due. However, the contents were unwilling to wait. It was with great trepidation that I made my appointment with Dr. Storm. I knew the artifacts in the ghastly package, and I dreaded their exposure.

I entered Dr. Storm's office like so many times before; however, this time was so different. I no longer saw him as my counselor, friend, or even teacher, for that session he was my enemy. Usually relieved to be there, that day, I loathed having made the appointment. I knew what was going to happen in the 1½ hour session, and I found myself hating Dr. Storm for it. How easy it was to want to "kill the messenger." I realized my anger was displaced, but I found myself not caring. I didn't choose him logically; it was simply a matter of convenience.

Although he was not the originator of my pain, he would escort me to address it, and, for that, I found him equally culpable. Simply to ignore the package was totally impossible. The articles that were once silent were now screaming at me and they demanded my full attention.

Dr. Storm seemed to sense my complete apprehension. The tone at the beginning of our old sessions was always so light, not at all that time. I walked over to the large picture window and looked outside across the landscape. Dr. Storm followed me to the window and stood beside me as I silently looked down on the rooftops below. Oh, how I wanted to become vapor, to seep through the pane of the window, and evaporate into the heavens above. Refusing to make eye contact, I told him I loved his view and always have. I wanted to stand there killing time not yet ready to start the unveiling.

I continued to look at the outdoor shopping mall, which was adorned in massive holiday decorations. Christmas was only a few days away, which made this appointment particularly difficult. I could see the majestic holiday displays, twinkling white lights and carols playing over the speakers that invited all who listened to celebrate that time of year. Holiday shoppers were busy rushing from store to store looking for the perfect gift that would add to the excitement of Christmas morning. How I wished I were one of them, but, instead, I was in my counselor's office, unwrapping another kind of package. The box that I created was also wrapped in beautiful paper; however, it was not a gift; it was a nightmare that I couldn't wake up from.

Dr. Storm sat in his usual chair, and I knew that was my cue that our session needed to begin. Slowly I walked over to my spot on the couch grabbing the decorative pillow as I sat down. It was my turn to speak, but I couldn't find the words. I looked across the room to the doctor. There was absolutely no idle banter between us, not that time. The mood was sobering, and the air was still as he waited for me to begin. With great dread, I carefully and methodically unpacked the contents of my box as salty tears streamed down my cheeks. Describing each article mentally set before me, I told him about the most grotesque of all my violations.

Dr. Storm's expression was one I had never seen on his face before. With all my packages and all the contents, nothing compared to these. His eyes were sad, appearing to fight back tears. His mouth was tight holding back any urge to speak, shaking his head to comprehend evil so unimaginable. He sat as one who had been selected for jury duty, and his task was to listen to the gruesome details of a crime done so long ago. His face held the pained expression of one who was witnessing an unthinkable act on such a young child.

Dr. Storm did what he had to do. He took me to the beginning of that evil night. Speaking softly, he slowly and steadily asked the questions to help make the memory complete. The questions were deep, and they punched with each word sent my way. I despised him for being so meticulous. He took my answers to formulate his next question, so the entire event would have been unpacked before I left. He was my guide who walked me into darkness asking for details that must come out of me. Still avoiding eye contact, with my head down, I answered each and every question with such recollection one would think it happened only yesterday.

I sat there with my anger still misdirected, resenting Dr. Storm's line of questioning. I came to him for help. Then I abhorred him for giving it. He continued to talk, but my mind was a flurry of images and self-loathing, so all I heard was his voice; however, I couldn't make out the words.

I wanted to scream until there was no breath left in me. To have all the anger, rage and betrayal merely escape through my vocal cords. Instead, I remained silent, immobilized, fearing this event; the contents of my box had marked me as used and damaged goods. Was I someone who should be discarded and was beyond repair?

After some time, my horrific container was empty. All articles had been examined. I felt as though all the life had been drained out of me, or wishing that it had. Weeping uncontrollably, I continued to avoid eye contact, not wanting him to see into the darkness of my soul. Dr. Storm knew the box was empty; there was no more to tell. Collecting his thoughts, he said something that I was shocked that he had the nerve to say.

"I bet you think he would have done you a favor if he had just killed you when he was through, don't you?"

With intense emotion, I rebuffed, "I don't *think* it would have been a favor; I *know* it would have been. No one should have to live with barbaric contents like these. Don't you see? This explains everything. I have always had the grand illusion that I am in control. I am the decision maker. Protecting myself from what I fear might be a hurtful relationship, which has only resulted in having me live in emotional isolation. The reality is, I have never been in control. Everything in my life was linked to this!"

Dr. Storm remained calm and tried to bring relief. "No one is in complete control of their life, Veronica. In some ways that can be the most freeing revelation for you to walk in. All any of us can do is trust God with the ultimate outcome knowing that He is faithful to keep us in His plan. He doesn't orchestrate the madness or evil, but He can bring good out of it."

"I know, but do you know what this feels like to me? Having this happen at such a young age, it defined my whole outlook on life and people. The only way I can explain it is like this: It's as if when he was finished attacking me, he threw me in a boat that he created and handed me two oars. I took those oars and started rowing with every fiber of my being. I never seem to land where I think I should. But I look down at my oars, and I am exhausted with my rowing efforts, so I assume I was the one charting my course. Now, I look at the back of the boat to see a rudder come up to the surface. That night, that event was the rudder. It has always been there just below the water level, safe where I couldn't see it. That idiotic rudder has been charting my course the whole time; it was the navigator. The oars were only a grand ruse to keep me busy and thinking I was the captain!"

"And do you know what the worst part is? The filthy coward is dead! I can't even confront him. Now what do I do, huh? I hate this; I hate all of this! My life is half over and I am just now finding out why I do, what I do. I loved and trusted him, and he gruesomely raped me."

Catching my breath and changing my tone, I whispered, "Did you know you could have flashbacks with your eyes wide open? Well, you can. There is no escaping this. It's like having dual vision all of the time. As I sit here looking at you, I can see that night in my mind's eye. I view the terrible images playing out in my mind constantly. Sometimes it surprises me, and I actually flinch because it came so unexpectedly."

Dr. Storm quickly caught up with my mood swing and encouraged my emotion. "What would you say to him if you could? Go ahead: pretend I'm him and what would you say?"

"First thing, yuck, you are not him! I would never transfer such crimes to you. Second thing, if he were alive, I would march up to the door of his house, bang on it and demand he open the door. When he did, I would shove him and shout loudly so even his neighbors could hear, 'You rotten, filthy son of a bitch, I remember! Do you hear me, I remember! You thought you got away with it, but you didn't!' Then I would walk away not allowing him to respond. He doesn't deserve the right to take any of my time. He already took enough of me."

"Then what would you do?"

"I would hop back into my car and catch the first flight back home. It would have been great to look the devil in the eye and call him out. But I'll never have that opportunity. Here's the real kick in the butt: what if he accepted Christ before he died? That would mean that not only did he not have to answer to what he did to me in this life, but he also wouldn't have to answer to it in the afterlife either."

Dr. Storm was shocked at my reasoning. "What do you mean he didn't have to answer to God for it?"

"Well, the Bible clearly tells us that if you accept Christ as your personal Savior and ask Him to forgive you of all your sins, He is faithful to do it. It also tells us that He casts our sins as far as the east is from the west. He no longer remembers them. He might never have to pay for what he did to me. If I cannot confront him, who will? I feel like no one had my back then, and no one has my back now."

"You can't be serious, Veronica. You don't think God was angry with him and held him accountable on his judgment day? I can assure you God's fury was unleashed in the Throne Room that day. I imagine even the angels left the room in fear while God was dealing with him. God never looks the other way when a child has been so violently assaulted."

"You don't know that for sure. What if God looked at him and had compassion on him? What if God said that he was a victim too, so He totally understands why he lashed out? He is a God of mercy, but, to be perfectly honest with you, this is a deal killer for me. I don't know how to serve a God who could pardon my attacker simply because he said the sinner's prayer. I imagine him standing in the presence of God and God looking down at him saying that what he did was so terribly wrong. Then God says that it pains Him to cast a verdict, but He has to. With great love and compassion, He tells him his sentence and how greatly disappointed He is that He has to do it. I see them both standing there crying for what should have been, but was never realized. If that's what happened, I'm telling you right now, that would be totally screwed up!"

"Wow, you have thought this through. Please take my word for it, that's not how it played out at all. God is a God of mercy; He is also a God of judgment. His wrath was in full swing while dealing with him. You have to believe me on this one, OK?"

Something had happened to me. Whatever Dr. Storm had said in the past, I had always taken it as gospel. That time was different. I didn't know if what he was saying was true or not. I knew he believed it in his heart of hearts, but that wasn't good enough this go around. I needed more. I wanted more. I told Dr. Storm that I was hardly convinced.

"OK then, I'll tell you what. My prayer for you is that God will reveal it to you in such a clear way that you will never doubt that He was your advocate. Maybe He will give you a glimpse into what went down on his day of reckoning."

My attitude had turned cold and indifferent. God was not going to show me what happened that day; He never does. When the disciples asked Jesus what happened to Judas - if he went to heaven or to hell, Jesus told them that wasn't for them to know. The only thing the scriptures show us is what deeds separate us from Him, not actual personal examples. In addition, if you ask for forgiveness if you committed those deeds, He forgives you.

The session was over, and I knew I would never return. We already had another date on the calendar, but I would call to cancel it as the time approached. I didn't want to face him to say goodbye; that would be too painful.

Dr. Storm had done all he could do. There was no need for further appointments.

I wanted this to end so differently. He had worked so hard; he deserved to see me happy and whole. I felt like I had failed God, Dr. Storm, and myself. He had been such a wonderful guide on this journey to freedom, but this was greater than the two of us. I was no longer in need of an earthly counselor. I needed a Redeemer.

Before leaving, I had to ask him one more thing. "Can I ask you a question?"

"Sure, what is it?"

"How do you do it? How can you listen to my horrible stories with all the graphic details and still be willing to have me come back? Does it affect you at all?"

"It does affect me, sometimes deeply. First, I grieve. I grieve for you and then for the evil that could cause someone to do something so horrible. After that, I do what you do; I give it to the Lord. I have to; that's the only way I can handle it."

"Oh, OK. I get concerned for you sometimes. You know I feel responsible for your well-being, I always have. I have never wanted you to have to deal with the images I have to."

"Yes, I know you feel responsible for me. I don't want either of us to have to deal with those images."

"Yeah, if only it were a perfect world, eh?"

The mood at the end of each session was always so cleansing, even if it was a tough one. There was usually laughter and a true sense that progress was made toward my freedom. At the end of this session, the mood was heavy like there had been a death. Mustering a smile, I left his office wishing him and his wife a Happy New Year.

My anger with the doctor had dissipated; I knew I would miss him greatly. He had been such an important part of my life these past six months; I wasn't too sure what my life would look like without him. He had gone from stranger to counselor, to father, then teacher, and, on occasion, even my enemy. Ultimately, his real role was my psychologist who shone a light on the path we were walking on. His words of comfort and wisdom were the morsels I fed on to keep me going as we traveled. While on the path, he would pick up little nuggets of truth that he found lying on the surface of the trail we were traveling. With these discoveries, he would help lead me to the meaning of what we just found, trusting God for insight along the way.

I had asked Dr. Storm early on to promise me that he would never give up on me, and he kept his word. He went far above the call of duty on so many occasions, and I love him for it. That part of my recovery was finished. Now it was time for me to go back to my beginning, I had to go back to the Word. This was between God and me. I had questions to ask Him that only He could answer. I felt that this was personal. I was either His daughter worth fighting for or I was just as insignificant as my earthly dad thought I was. I had to know and the answer could only come from Him.

God surely knew my heart. I didn't want retaliation for my attacker; I wanted justice. To avenge him would mean I wanted the same thing or something even worse to happen to him. I absolutely did not want that to happen. What he did to me was so incredibly inhumane, I wouldn't wish it on a junk yard dog. However, I did want to know I was worth getting angry over, that God actually held him accountable.

Getting over my traumas had been work, but I was able to labor through it pretty quickly. The anger and sorrow would consume me, and then, almost magically, I would feel God's healing power in exchange for my pain. It was not working this time. I wanted to get past it, but it felt as though the scope of what my attacker did to me was unquantifiable. It went to every level of my awareness and emotions. How does one get past such an act of violence when one can't confront their attacker? Worse yet, know that their attacker might have been pardoned because he said a prayer.

I strolled to my car feeling the brisk cool air on my skin. I began to shiver, not only due to the low temperature but also because of my emotional state. I wrapped my arms across my chest with my hands stroking my arms in an effort to warm me. Christmas was almost here; it was overwhelming to me. Always one to enjoy the holiday season, all I wanted was for it to pass quickly.

In an ironic twist of fate, some of the coping mechanisms that had always worked to help me endure tough times were compromised through counseling. By getting help, I then felt helpless to deal with that container. I longed to be able to splinter off, as I once did, and simply become someone who was happy without a care in this world. I didn't know if I should allow myself that luxury anymore.

I found that I spontaneously cried at the drop of the hat. When the images of that night randomly appeared, tears welled up in my eyes uncontrollably. Normally one to surround myself with friends during the holiday season, I chose to withdrawal from them. I didn't want to explain my downcast mood or sudden tears. Laughter had left me; the light was gone. I feared I would never be who I once was.

Bible study was the next day, but there was no way I was going. To be with my friends and have them find out that I was in counseling again was something I didn't want to do. I felt as though this event disqualified me as a sane person. No one comes through something like that and not be tainted or scathed.

That night I told Jerry bits and pieces of my session with Dr. Storm. I couldn't bring myself to tell him the graphic details; it was for no one's ears to hear. He had carried enough of my images from all the other packages I had un-packed. That time I told him only enough for him to know the depth of my pain. I also told him that I could hardly stand that my attacker might not have been held account-able. Jerry shared Dr. Storm's sentiments regarding the issue.

"OK Veronica, what do you do with the scripture that says 'If you offend a child, it would be better for you to have a millstone wrapped around your neck and thrown into the sea?' God does not take it lightly."

"Alright, then what do you do with the scripture that says if you ask God to forgive you, He will not only forgive you but He will no longer remember it? Or, what about the scripture that says if you believe in Christ old things are passed away and everything becomes new. God would, in His divine mercy, shower him with love and welcome him into His kingdom. He would be His son and He loves him just as much as He supposedly loves me. That doesn't seem like love to me."

"I don't know how to answer that. All I know is, I don't believe he got away with it even if he did become a believer.

I'm pissed off at what was done to you and I don't have the capacity to love as deep as God does."

Jerry and I talked for hours wrestling this tough theological question. The sadness remained like a dark force separating me from my Maker. How could He have offered clemency to someone who knowingly tried to destroy me? My attacker wasn't after my body; he was after my soul. The little girl who went to bed that night trusting she would be safe and instead was so violently attacked: who is the one God cries over?

Those thoughts plagued me as I tried to sleep. Tossing and turning, I wondered if I would ever have the answers to my questions. The morning came, and my emotional darkness did not find its way out through my dreams. It felt as though my body and soul had been put through a wood chipper and only the bloody pieces remained on the floor. I rolled out of bed ready to face one more day. As I walked downstairs in my house robe and slippers to start a pot of coffee, the Lord spoke.

"Go to Bible study today, you will find your answer."

I continued making my coffee not acknowledging His direction. Unable to shake it, I went back upstairs and threw on some clothes. I didn't know what He had in store, but I'd do anything to get my answers. I assumed He planned on me finding comfort in my friends and the company of women. I hadn't shared any of this with my friends in my small group. I was sure He wanted me to remember to be authentic and find comfort in their compassion. Whatever; I really didn't care. I grabbed my Bible and my lesson book and headed out the door.

On the drive over, I started to think of the attack once more. The flashbacks and images were the same as the day before, and tears began to well up once more. I began my conversation with my Counselor.

"Were You angry at him? Did You care? I can't handle knowing that You chose not to remember what he did to me simply because he said a prayer."

I began to sob as I drove down the highway. I just wanted to know that He got angry and that He held him accountable no matter if he was a believer or not.

Then it happened. My Counselor spoke.

"What would you do if you had to witness your daughter being so violently sexually assaulted and your hands were constrained from helping her? You had to stand only inches away hearing her cries and seeing the look of devastation on her face and you have to stand powerless to help her. Would you be angry Veronica? Would you feel the pain? If he apologized for his actions and you forgave him, would that excuse him from liability?"

"In rage I wouldn't be able to constrain myself. I would buckle under the weight of such a sight."

"Don't you know? I was there; I saw it all. I was devastated when I saw such evil being thrust onto you as an innocent child. I saw your face, I heard your cries of pain, and, make no mistake: I was enraged with an anger you have never known. I made a vow to you that night that I would make it up to you and then a vow to him. I would take care of him in due time. My judgment was known. It always is. I AM not only a God of grace; I AM a God of justice. I Am the same yesterday, today and forever; read My Book. As I told you when you started the healing process, it

437

would be for your benefit and My glory. You are my daughter, and, yes, I was angry on your behalf. I love you more than you will ever know."

His words struck me with a commanding, healing force. In an instant, I gained understanding: I was OK. I only wanted to know if He got angry, if He was willing to hold my attacker accountable, and He did. That was all I cared about. The rest of my pain would be handled in time.

My mother and father didn't seem angry on my behalf in Dr. Storm's office when they found out about my brother. My worth and value as a human being was called into question, so much so that I didn't even know if anyone cared about what happened so long ago.

I found out that my mom wrote a Christmas letter and sent it to her friends and family stating that God had blessed them with another wonderful year. She gushed at how splendid life had been, seemingly an uneventful year. She even sent the card and letter to my in-laws. She also stated in the letter that they enjoyed a great Thanksgiving with my brother and his family. She bemoaned that she missed having my sister and her husband join them. My mom wrote that my sister was unable to come because she was at home healing from some injury. It appeared official; My mom only had two children.

I may have been non-existent to my earthly family, but I am alive and have relationship with One who is so much grander. Having fully realized that my Heavenly Father not only got angry but also would take care of my abusers, I was free to release them. I understood that He loved me and cried for me and was even enraged on my behalf. His love encompassed me in my car; I had found the answers to my probing questions.

Remarkably, I made it to Bible study not having crashed my car. To my astonishment, My Counselor had not finished His session with me—there was still more He wanted to tell me. He had proven to be my advocate; now He would show Himself as my Redeemer.

CHAPTER TWENTY-NINE:

Free At Last

I freshened my face before walking into the house where
my Bible study met. A small group of friends had already
arrived with much chatting and laughter in progress. I had
come to love these women more than I thought I ever
would. They had laughed with me, cried with me, and held
me up in prayer. Although I had not told them about my
latest memory, it was not because they couldn't be trusted
with the information; I simply didn't want to be exposed
once more. I had told a few—that was all that was necessary for the healing process to begin. Some things in life are
meant only to be carried by a few, not the multitude.

I walked in, still basking in the healing presence I had
felt in the car. We were studying a curriculum about the
book of Esther from one of my favorite Bible teachers. We
each enjoyed our cups of coffee while grabbing our lesson
books and Bibles to begin. Jennifer plugged in the teaching
DVD, and we sat silent to watch.

To my surprise, the lesson that day seemed totally out
of the ordinary for a study on Esther. The instructor started
to outline the pain and abandonment Esther must have felt
when she lost her parents as a child. She went into great
detail about how the loss of one parent significantly affects

the life of a child; however, Esther lost both her mother and father. One funeral was bad enough, but, with two funerals, the affects are incalculable on a child. She used personal illustrations to drive the point home about how a girl back in Bible times might have been treated as an orphan.

She continued to expound on Esther's loss of not only losing her parents, but also of that loss being under the care of a male cousin. There was no nurturing female figure in the home to help her through puberty and to be there to answer all of the typical questions teen girls have. After the Bible teacher finished transferring all the information on her notes into our hearts, she said something I would never forget.

She explained how Esther must have thought she was disqualified from ever being chosen by the king to be his queen because of her past. Her childhood was something a girl in that day and age would have been ashamed of. What Esther didn't know was, God didn't have the king choose her to be queen *in spite* of her past; He chose her *because* of it. Due to her painful childhood, she had gained the integrity and fortitude to stand before her husband, the king, and be able to save her people from certain death.

She then went on to say that some of us have such painful past experiences we want God to amputate them from our lives; then and only then, we think we would be qualified to serve Him. However, if that were the case, we wouldn't need a Redeemer. We are never to forget where we came from or what we have survived. Our very existence shouts that we serve a God who can heal and restore. How will the world know Him if we don't declare what He has done for us and where we have come from? In almost a pleading tone, she begged her listeners to allow God to remove the pain but not the memory; it is what will save another.

I couldn't believe my ears. I wanted to cry, and not just the normal cry—I wanted the ugly cry. You know the one where you sob hysterically with shoulders shaking unable to regain your composure? Yeah, that one. That dreadful evil night, the night where it all began didn't disqualify me. The fact that I was sitting there, with all my faculties functioning, was a miracle and not one that should be taken lightly. I had a Redeemer who had orchestrated from the beginning of time for me to be sitting there, hearing His voice through the teaching of another. He planned this; He is the best Counselor ever!

After Bible study, we usually went out to lunch as a group. That day, in God's divine plan, Kathi who is a friend had asked if I wanted to have lunch, just the two of us. It was a sweet gesture, and I quickly took her up on the offer. She asked how things were going and said that she could tell something was up. I trusted her enough to tell her in small detail about the latest contents of my package. She shared some about her past and how the Lord had helped her to make it through her pain. Our stories weren't even remotely similar, but pain is pain no matter who the offender or what the offence is. It is always so therapeutic to openly share in the safety of one who loves you.

Lunch was lovely but it was time to pick up my daughter from elementary school. Kathi and I shared a hug as I raced out the door for the school run. As I mentally reviewed what God had done for me that morning, I recalled the scripture about not offending one of His little ones. When I went over that scripture in my mind, He told me, *"There is no qualifier in that scripture."* Wait, what? What did He mean that there was no qualifier? Apparently, God wasn't finished with it yet.

I picked up my daughter and the other girls in the carpool, dropping each of them off at their homes. Before the girls got out of the car, giggling, they made plans for endless hours of playtime that afternoon. My daughter and I continued the conversation about her school day. She filled me in on all the antics the boys were playing against the girls and what their counterstrike would be. She was gleefully happy at their scheme and couldn't wait to launch it into action the next day. Pulling into the garage, she quickly jumped out of the car and ran into the kitchen for her afternoon snack.

I was anxious to get my Bible out and research the scripture I was thinking about. earlier.

Matthew 18:6-7 (The Message) *But if you give them a hard time, bullying or taking advantage of their simple trust, you'll soon wish you hadn't. You'd be better off dropped in the middle of the lake with a millstone around your neck. Doom to the world for giving these God-believing children a hard time! Hard times are inevitable, but you don't have to make it worse—and it's doomsday to you if you do.*

I read this repeatedly. He was right; there was no qualifier there. The scripture wasn't distinguishing between believers and non-believers. It covers the general population.

It wasn't talking about whether the offender would spend eternity in heaven or hell; that had nothing to do with it. This wasn't a salvation scripture—it was a warning to *anyone* who harmed one of His precious little children. God is always true to His Word and keeps His promises.

As I continued to contemplate this new revelation, another scripture came to me.

Luke 11:13 (King James Version) *If ye then, being evil, know how to give good gifts unto your children: how much more shall your heavenly Father give the Holy Spirit to them that ask him?*

So if I, who am an imperfect parent, know how to love and give things to my children, how much more does my Heavenly Father want to give me things for my well-being? I am so incredibly flawed, and, even in my broken state, I would hold a person accountable who did wrong to one of my children. God is perfect and is a righteous judge; He truly did take care of it. God absolutely loves the offender; however, His love is never absent of justice or accountability.

My vision of what happened to my attacker on his day of judgment had dramatically changed. I saw the wrath of God and justice being served in a way that was terrifying. With this new illumination, a strangely unexpected thing occurred within me. I found myself unable to be angry any longer. I actually found myself having compassion for him.

I mentally envisioned a man trembling while his merciless executioner was wrapping a rope around his neck with a large weight tied on the end. I felt his fear and torment knowing that there was no escape. He saw the cold dark ocean and knew he was about to take his last breath before being ruthlessly shoved into

444

the perilous sea. Then I saw my attacker, standing in the Throne Room of the Most High God. He too saw the man helplessly standing next to his executioner. My assailant watched him quake, knowing he was going to die a painful torturous death. Remarkably, my assaulter, who saw the man and knew his fate, would give anything to trade places with him. He stood perfectly quiet, to afraid to speak as he began to hear the rush of a Mighty Wind. His heart was pounding and adrenaline was making its way through his body; he would give anything to escape this moment. Instead, he was required to stand in the presence of a God who was ready to cast judgment for the evil he did on a little girl so long ago. God Almighty needed to hold him accountable for victimizing and brutalizing His daughter. Then the Righteous Judge took His place at the bench; court was now in session. The accused was powerless in the presence of such a commanding force...

My heart ached that I doubted justice would be apportioned, and I experience sorrow for the reality that it did. I could hardly comprehend his terror as he stood in the Throne Room of his Creator who in His sovereignty demanded justice. I didn't have to hold him accountable, and my little confrontation would have been no match for what ultimately took place. I had no anger or un-forgiveness; God took care of it. Instead, I was painfully aware of my own shortcomings and in need of my own mercy and forgiveness. I had sinned so many times; I am not one who should ever think that I could stand in the place of judge and jury.

That mental vision removed any doubt I might have had as to what took place that day. In that quick instant, I had my answers. Pain was still present, but freedom was mine. Then the harsh reality struck me that it wasn't at that moment that I had been freed; it was just then that I realized it. These truths had been present all along; I didn't have the presence of mind to receive them.

I had heard long ago that elephant trainers would chain up their animals starting when they were young. They would use a large and heavy chain that was connected to a peg dug deep into to the ground. The young elephant would pull and try to break free but soon found his efforts were useless. As the elephant matured, the trainers would keep the shackle around the leg of the elephant but they would replace the heavy chain with a smaller lighter one. The peg was no longer in a deep hole but rather a shallow one. Although the animal weighed around 9000 pounds, he still thought a chain that he could have easily broken restrained him. How easy it would be for the elephant to have simply walked away from his captivity; however, he remained bound due to the memory of his past when he couldn't break free.

I had always been free. I just didn't know it. The chains of my family and childhood that used to constrain me were abolished long before I was ever created. The price was paid on a bloodied cross with my Savior taking my place. I hadn't understood that I was never to be bound by the painful contents of my packages and the need for retribution for my abusers. Nevertheless, freedom isn't truly freedom until it is known. I had found the key to my prison cell, which I unknowingly had in my possession all along, and I used it to open the door.

With this part of my journey completed, it occurred to

me how my whole life had changed. It's truly an odd thing to have happen to you. I had gone from completely unknown to outright exposed to my close friends, husband, and children. From trying to get God to approve of me, to relaxing in the realization He always did.

Although much of Dr. Storm's work was complete, mine was only beginning. I still needed to grow in the knowledge of "trust" and "normal." This would take some time. Learning to live with the contents of my packages in plain sight was also a challenge set before me. Still the master of inventory control, I no longer locked the storage room of my mind when I exited. It was to remain open and available, exposed for my healing.

I still share the same DNA as the ones who hurt me, but I would have no part of their legacy. I started new, fresh with my redefined family circle of husband and children. This was what I desired from my counseling journey, to have endured the pain of the process for the sake of my liberty. I went from *Conceal*, to *Reveal*, to *Deal*, and then to *Heal*. It was a hard four-step process but definitely worth the effort.

CHAPTER THIRTY

Only the Beginning

With the inventory accounted for and all my packages stacked neatly on the shelves of my mind, I stepped back to view all of them with vivid clarity. It excites me to know that I can share the boxes with my children. It's important that they understand: these are not heirlooms to be passed down; quite the contrary, they will remain with me. I desire for my children to know me and the events in my life that helped, in part, to shape me.

Although they are never to take ownership of my boxes, the contents are not to be disposed of or burned either; they are the sum of who I am and where I come from. They no longer have the authority to define me; I define them as tools that were used to help shape me. Once ashamed, I now proudly display them for all to see. To deny or shun my past is to deny me of who I am. All the tragedies and triumphs now live together in complete harmony, safely stored in their beautifully wrapped containers, housed on the shelves of my mind forever.

The power that the articles of my packages once had over me, they no longer do. That is not to say that I have power over them; I, in no way, think I have that ability. Nevertheless, I have come into an intimate relationship with the One who dwells within, who possesses enough energy and might to overpower all that threatens my peace. In my weakness, He shows up strong. It is a blast having affinity with One who loves to "show up" and "show off"! He does all things well.

Having met myself for the first time this past year, I am still discovering who I am. I have come to love the realization that I am a living and breathing contradiction. I am a timid powerhouse, a cowardly tenacious warrior, secure in my insecurity, simplistically complex, tumultuously peaceful, rebelliously obedient, utterly secret and fully exposed, wholly broken, both young and old, and so easily discarded by some loved ones yet claimed as valuable by the One who matters most.

It occurs to me that not only am I a walking contradiction, but humanity is as well. Good people can do dire and evil deeds, and bad people are capable of good and decent acts. So here is the question: is it possible for a person to not only perform evil but also to be evil incarnate? Only God knows for sure. However, if the answer to that question is "yes," I don't think that mortals have been given the authority to decide when that line is crossed. Nevertheless, because we are all capable of performing evil, we must admit that the human condition is inherently flawed at best. That being the case, whether we consider ourselves good or evil, we all need a Redeemer.

At times, I feel as though I am a mere fraction of who I was originally created to be. Bits and pieces of my body and soul have been stolen from me by those who had no right to it. Therein lies the miraculous as well. For just as in the miracle with the five loaves and two fish, that was more than enough to feed the multitude, God has also done that miracle in me. From coward to courageous, devastation to destiny, He will make all of His children more than conquerors if we dare to believe in Him. What pieces remain are more than enough for Him to create a beautiful mosaic, fit for the Master's use.

Through the betrayal of my brother, God, in His strategic sovereignty, would introduce me to a love I had never known. While looking out at the vast ocean, that He alone created, I was struck with the notion if He could care for the smallest of fishes, He could care for me. For Him to have been able to use such a toxic situation to be the vehicle in which He would drive home His perfect love, proves nothing is too difficult for Him. Only God can have all things work together for good in even the most evil of circumstances.

After having tasted the sweetness of God's amazing unconditional love, how could I ever return to the artificial high the world has to offer? There is simply no substitute or equivalent for a love like His. In a world where most people only look at the exterior of the person to determine their worth and value, this is nonexistent to Him. We create cultures where billions of dollars are made from industries that exalt such artificial beauty as the norm; we have so much to learn. Faces are lifted, fat is suctioned, and wrinkles can magically disappear with the stroke of a knife, in our endless pursuit of our outward perfection.

In contrast, God delivers beauty from the inside out. He brings His scalpel to our hurt and wounded hearts to help complete His work of perfection to our damaged souls. He loves to mend things He did not break, restore what He did not take, and bring healing where He did no harm. God's love does not require performance or splendor for one to qualify; it is given without measure to all who want to receive. I am learning to focus, and even crave, the Beauty of Holiness as opposed to the holiness of beauty. His love demands no less.

Although I wouldn't wish the contents of my boxes on anyone, I also know I wouldn't exchange them for all the money in the world. In them, I found that there is no pain so deep that God's love cannot heal. The artifacts point to the revelation that evil is not such a mighty force that my God is not able easily to overcome it. They continuously remind me that there is a Power so much grander than I am, and He alone will judge and cast the final sentences. I don't presume to know the outcome; I have trusted Him to have the last word.

I have come to embrace what I once despised. The delicate articles that caused such fear are now used proudly to declare that my Redeemer lives. He promised me that this journey would ultimately be used for my benefit and His glory; I now know this to be true. The emotional scars will remind me that, although healing has come, it does not eliminate the contents of my packages or erase my painful memories. The possession of such containers gives me the awesome privilege of needing to tap into God's limitless supply of grace each and every day. I can share with my children what I have learned about grace and our Creator, what an amazing truth to be able to pass down. They will know they are worth fighting for and a new generation has begun.

I don't believe what I have learned is only applicable for me: it is universal. The afflicted and injured live among us. They are our neighbors, co-workers, friends, family, and in-laws. With the bright smiles plastered on their faces, we never know the secrets that lie just beneath the surface. Everyone has within them the ability to compartmentalize. If emotional damage is incurred, we can create our own unique system of visualizing a physical storage unit where our most painful memories are housed. Some choose to store the contents of their lives in mental antique trunks that are lined with beautiful ornate lace and trim. Others hide their secrets behind mental closed doors or perhaps closets for which they alone posses the key. Still, there are many who have their precious articles safely behind closed curtains that only they can open.

What is birthed in secret will one day be exposed. It is imperative to acknowledge the contents of our lives, especially if stored in darkness, so they won't be destined to be repeated in future generations. Lids need to be opened, doors unlocked and drapes pulled back so the contents can be examined. Knowing this, our hope is in the fact that there is nothing and no one so big that can stand between our destiny and us. Our past and our future are one—they work together to help us achieve what it is we were placed here to do.

To choose to walk in the light of the truth can be blinding at times, and liberty has its price tag. There was a high fee associated with my freedom. It has cost me greatly but not as dearly as my Savior who paid the price for my redemption over 2000 years ago. He thought I was worth fighting for, and even dying for—this revelation brings me great joy. With His help, the help of a counselor, a husband, and of so many loved ones around me, I can honestly say with all of my heart, to God be the glory, I AM FREE!

Epilogue

Almost a year had passed since my last counseling session. Dr. Storm and I had kept in touch. I had been given some opportunities to share my story, both to audiences and in writing. I found the process of writing my book to be excruciating and cathartic all at the same time. While writing about my story, there were certain questions that remained unanswered, such as, when does childish sexual curiosity turn into criminal activity? Or, what is the difference between playing the childhood game "post office" and determining that someone has crossed the line into being a perpetrator? For my own soundness of mind, I needed to distinguish between the two. After talking to Rob, an attorney, who had worked for a time in the sex crimes unit of the District Attorney's office, I was convinced to go deeper on the subject. I had to admit that, after having talked to some people about their experiences with childhood molestation, it was all too clear that most were confused.

When I first decided that I would write a book, I asked Dr. Storm if he would be available to help me if I needed to interview him. Although he retired from private practice, he was gracious and helped me whenever I needed his input. I asked him to clarify when childhood sexual curiosity turns into criminal activity. We used the events in my past to help clarify the difference.

Children can sometimes find themselves in games like "post office" or "truth or dare." When young children play these games with peers, they can find themselves in compromising situations. However, when an older person, usually in authority, sets up a situation for a sexual event to occur it is no longer a childish act or game.

When my brother planned and then sought me out for his own sexual pleasure, a dangerous line was crossed. "Grooming" is a term used when describing a perpetrator preparing his target for molestation. My brother waited for me to come back to the bathroom and then dropped his towel upon my arrival as a test to see what my response would be. He continued this behavior for close to a month, exposing himself to me on several occasions. When I was shocked, but didn't tell on him, he took it as his cue to continue the grooming. I was thinking it was an accident, so why would I tell on him. Perpetrators are often under the delusion that their victims think as they do. If the victim doesn't fight back or tell another authority figure, it gives them the false "green light" to continue with their actions. It is all a part of the grooming process.

Another red flag was when my brother, after the molestation, told me to keep it secret. The very act of secrecy demonstrates he knew his actions were wrong. As the person in charge while my parents were at work, he used his position of authority to gain control and convince me his sexual advances were a natural part of a sibling relationship. That is what sexual predators do. A very subtle act of manipulation happened when he told me if we were caught, we would both get into trouble. Perpetrators make the victim feel equally as culpable, thereby insuring loyalty and ultimately silence.

Dr. Storm pointed out that because my brother used games to introduce sex to me, it was part of the grooming process. Sexual predators often use situations that are familiar with their victims to help lure them. This act should also be considered criminal. Dr. Storm was emphatic that sexual misconduct isn't limited to touching the victim. A crime also occurred when my brother continued his sexual deviance throughout my teen years by exposing himself to me on many occasions. However, my brother coming into my room and undressing me when he was twenty to twenty-one years old definitely constitutes a crime.

For some reason, even after all of the counseling, I had never seen what my brother did to me as criminal. After I had confronted my brother, I couldn't make out where his mind was; back then or in the moment of the confrontations. Dr. Storm's clarification of the subject matter made me see his conduct in a whole new light. I have to admit, identifying a family member, whether past or present, as a sexual predator, is no easy task.

****

Many people have asked me if anyone in my family has tried to contact me since the confrontation. No, they have not. When I am asked such a question, I realize how difficult it is for outsiders to understand a family like mine. Right after the family confrontation, a long-time family friend called to tell me my sister had told her what happened. My friend wanted to let me know that she loved me and would not turn her back on me. She was the only person I knew who was in contact with both my family and me.

We got together the next week and talked about what happened. To my shock, she had no idea what actually took place in Dr. Storm's office. Apparently, my sister only told her I had decided to walk away from the family and the decision had hurt her deeply. My sister told our friend that she didn't want to go into details, but that it got pretty ugly. She said my sister relayed how injured she felt and how unfair I had been not to allow her to see my children. She continued to lament about Christmas and how horrible it would be for her from here on out. She made no mention of the molestation from my brother or any of the other details concerning my treatment from the family.

After my friend found out what the confrontation was really about, she was horrified that my sister didn't say she was furious with our brother. The fact that my sister left out all details about me ever being hurt by my family defied her comprehension. She said she was appalled that my sister did not sever ties with my brother, knowing that he so callously disregarded the molestation. She couldn't imagine feeling sorry for herself, only feeling complete sorrow for her sister if she found herself in the same situation.

For the first time, my friend expressed how she had always noticed that my mom, through the years, had treated me differently from my sister. She was particularly critical of how I was treated in my teenage years. My friend said she had noticed that, while only being sixteen, I had to be financially responsible for more than any other teenager she knew. Furthermore, she was horrified that my parents didn't come to my defense, but rather chose to ignore what their son did and remain in relationship with him as though nothing had ever happened.

My friend asked if my sister or parents had sent me a card, telling me they were sorry. I told her they had not. Again, she reiterated that she felt my sister should have at least sent a note expressing sadness for me, and understanding for my need to walk away from the family. We talked for close to four hours as she tried to grasp the history of a family she thought she knew, but found out she didn't know at all. I only saw that friend a couple more times.

I have concluded that exposing some of the family secrets not only affected the family, but many others as well. It has cost me several relationships, even outside my family relationships. However, I have no regrets for shining a light into the darkness of my past. After all is said and done, I could finally say I unpacked every box that had to do with the things that happened to me.

I am enjoying living free from the chains of my past and the family who hurt me. For the first time ever, I have no dread for the future. As for the rest of my family's secrets, they are carefully placed in their boxes, sitting on my imaginary shelves safely guarded from the outside world. I have chosen never to speak of them. Some things will never change. I will admit that I have always been and will always be my family's self-appointed *secret keeper.*

Veronica Wright currently works with International Crisis Aid in helping them implement their "Safe Campaign" to rescue girls from sex trafficking. She encourages her readers to step out in faith to help others. "We have been healed so that we might be instruments of God's healing in others. We have been freed to fight for those yet in bondage—those who are still prisoners of their own '*Boxes of Secrets*.'"

If this book has inspired you to reach out to help in the relief efforts of abused women and children, you are invited to contact
International Crisis Aid

To help in the rescuing of girls who have been forcibly sold into the sex trafficking industry both in America and worldwide.

<u>www.crisisaid.org</u>
For more information

You may contact us at
<u>veronicakwright.com</u>
for more information regarding Veronica's ministry and her speaking availability